Patent Policy and Innovation

Patent Policy and Innovation

Do Legal Rules Deliver Effective Economic Outcomes?

Hazel V.J. Moir

Centre for Policy Innovation, Research School of Social Sciences, ANU College of Arts and Social Sciences, Australian National University

Edward Elgar

Cheltenham, UK • Northampton, MA, USA

Published by
Edward Elgar Publishing Limited
The Lypiatts
15 Lansdown Road
Cheltenham
Glos GL50 2JA
UK

Edward Elgar Publishing, Inc.
William Pratt House
9 Dewey Court
Northampton
Massachusetts 01060
USA

A catalogue record for this book
is available from the British Library

Library of Congress Control Number: 2012949448

This book is available electronically in the ElgarOnline.com
Law Subject Collection E-ISBN 978 0 85793 279 2

MIX
Paper from
responsible sources
FSC® C018575
FSC
www.fsc.org

ISBN 978 0 85793 278 5

Typeset by Servis Filmsetting Ltd, Stockport, Cheshire
Printed and bound by MPG Books Group, UK

Contents

Preface

I did not pay much attention to the 1994 Uruguay Round of trade negotiations. I assumed I didn't need to – that they were standard trade negotiations. They were not. I was very taken aback to find that under the auspices of the term free trade all nations who wished to stay (or become) members of the General Agreement on Tariffs and Trade (GATT) now had to introduce legislation to provide monopolies for inventions and creations. Quite apart from the dishonesty of slipping these monopoly systems in under the rubric of free trade, I was shocked that low income countries would not be allowed to use the strategies that high income countries used at a similar stage in their economic development – imitation and copying. Nor could I understand why the citizens of Laos and the Central African Republic, for example, should add to the already very high profits of international pharmaceutical companies.

I was not alone in being taken by surprise. In discussions with a wide range of people since 1994 I have found that very few understand what the package approach of the Uruguay Round has done. Most had simply thought that the new name for GATT was the World Trade Organization (WTO). Nor are most people aware of the content of the Trade Related Aspects of Intellectual Property Rights (TRIPS) Agreement. It has been a real surprise to Australian legislators that their desire to promote the health of their citizens by limiting tobacco advertising may run foul of the WTO package of treaties.

When I had the good fortune to leave the paid workforce at an early age, I turned my attention to what I might contribute in this area. As I investigated copyright and patents I was surprised to find that most academic writing on these issues was based on argument (the lawyers) or theory (the economists). In particular I found that much contained a large subjective element – arguments were framed and words chosen to support a particular view. Those with a pro-intervention bent chose words such as 'protection' for a patent, 'free-riding' for using public knowledge and 'pirate' for someone using material without paying copyright royalties – even in a country which does not provide copyright monopolies. Those who prefer competition as a driver of innovation tend to refer to patents as 'patent monopolies', language that deeply offends the pro-intervention group.

Yet the privileges granted by patents allow the patent owner to prevent others from working in that specific field – a clear and strong monopoly right. The term 'intellectual property' – covering a wide range of disparate government interventions to provide monopolies – is a modern invention. It came into use about 1980 (http://books.google.com/ngrams/).

This constant spin makes working on the patent system a minefield. There are continual language traps that can tempt one away from the empirical evidence. For there is substantial empirical evidence – it is just that much of it lies outside the academic literature on patents. In particular there is now a great deal of empirical evidence about how firms achieve a return to their investment in new products and processes. And, with the exception of the pharmaceutical industry, firms generally report that the patent system is the least effective mechanism. These data question whether patents are in fact necessary (or indeed even effective) as an element of innovation policy.

As I dug further into the system I started to read some patents. It is surprisingly rare for academics working on patent policy to read patents – they are tedious and incomprehensible in the extreme. But I persevered and found that in case after case, once I had translated the claims from 'patentese' into English, it emerged that the alleged invention was non-existent. There was no inventiveness. So I started asking why. I found that the answer lay in the "plethora of presumptions and procedures [which] tip the scales in favor of the ultimate issuance of a patent, once an application has been filed" as the US Federal Trade Commission (2003: 8) found in its enquiry into the patent system.

This study takes an economic perspective on patent systems, digging into the details of the legal rules used to determine if a patent monopoly should be granted or not. By exploring in detail a set of patents, the study shows how the current rules have shaped a system which now has almost no threshold for grant of a patent. It breaks new ground by using the actual claims in the patent specification as the basis for a qualitative assessment against the yardstick of whether there is any new contribution to knowledge. This yardstick is used because the key social benefit from innovation is spillovers from new knowledge. If there is no new knowledge or know-how a patent can contribute only a private benefit. If there is no benefit to society, there is no basis for the government to grant a 20-year monopoly.

The patent contract is simple. Society agrees to intervene to regulate the market and provide a monopoly. This interference with competition is expected to lead to a higher level of innovation and the community will benefit from spillovers from the new knowledge and know-how embodied in these induced innovations.

A small universe of 72 Australian business method patents is tracked through 54 parallel applications in the USA, 38 at the European Patent Office and 13 in the UK. None contributes any new knowledge or know-how, though two may be new ideas. The possible new ideas have no associated new knowledge. These data suggest that the large majority of currently granted patents produce no benefit to society, and do not meet the normal definition of the concept of 'invention'.

I was able to investigate such patents because I have had a wide and varied career. My first job was in the flat glass industry and in fact I have worked in that industry both in the UK and the USA. My time in market research was in a company that worked closely with its advertising parent. I spent time in health insurance, overseas development assistance, the university sector, private consulting and government. I have lived in nine different countries and observed a range of business processes such as travel, retail and banking across these different systems. During my time in government I spent four years working in what is now IP Australia. My role there gave me responsibilities for a new building, financial reports to government, delivering the mail, providing information to the public, introducing continual improvement processes throughout the organisation, identifying and providing staff development opportunities and so on. All these roles involve business processes. Since 'retirement' I have managed a superannuation fund, run the international secretariat of a professional body and provided travel advice. It was the rare patent in the dataset that addressed a topic I did not have any familiarity with. Colleagues and friends educated me in these few areas.

The dataset analysed shows that it is the legal rules, often developed through case law, that are responsible for the grant of these uninventive patents. In particular, limits to allowable knowledge and prescriptive rules about how to judge inventiveness have resulted in a test for trivial difference – a very poor yardstick for inventiveness. The narrow legal doctrines result in the computerisation of well-known methods being judged both novel and inventive. They allow obvious combinations of old ideas and trivial variations of existing processes to be granted patent monopolies. Patents are regularly granted for the application of known methods to new areas for which they are well suited.

As the TRIPS Agreement mandates no discrimination between fields of technology, the results of this investigation are generalisable to genuine technology fields. They add to the already overwhelming evidence that the patent system is overdue for reform. The major focus for reform should be re-writing the novelty and inventiveness requirements as a requirement for a genuine contribution to knowledge or know-how. This would radically reduce the volume of patents granted without in any way removing the possibility of a patent where there is a genuine invention. Because the historical record shows how easily the patent system has been undermined by those who benefit from it, this reform should be strengthened using lessons learned from tax policy reform. Clear objectives need to be written into patent acts, principles must trump detailed rules where there is a conflict and there must be penalties for trying to undermine the economic goals of the patent system. Such an improved patent system, with a genuine inventive step, would benefit innovative firms in all countries and would also substantially mitigate the impost of TRIPS on lower income countries.

To prevent falling into traps where language is a poor reflection of the underlying concept I use quotation marks to identify a questionable use of a word. For example I use 'invention' to refer to inventions which are uninventive; 'problem' to refer to the trivial issues identified in patent specifications as problems; 'protection' to indicate that patent 'protection' is actually the prevention of competition, more accurately referred to as regulation or monopoly. Double quotation marks are used for actual quotations.

I have personal experience of the way in which patent system complexity is designed to exclude outsiders. Nonetheless it is quite possible to work one's way through these exclusionary barriers. I have learned much about patent systems, though am aware there are many areas I have hardly touched. My learning was assisted by many people. In no particular order of importance or chronology I would like to thank Don Lamberton, Glenn Withers, Peter Drahos, Stuart Macdonald, Luigi Palombi, Wanda Gunawardana, Pam Sharpe, William van Caenegem, Bill Kingston, Natalie Stoianoff, Paul Jensen, Elizabeth Webster, Chris Arup, Kay Collins, Neil Porter, Reg Gibson, Danny Kingsley, Kevin Scally, Elzbieta Wieniawa-Narkiewicz, John Kerin, Anna George, Geoff Burton, Margaret Fanning, Sean Applegate, Shiva Thambisetty, Bruce Murray, Dave Herald, Tony Varty and many others whom I have met at conferences and seminars over the past eight years. Needless to say any errors or omissions are my own responsibility.

List of abbreviations

ACIP	Australian Council on Intellectual Property
AIPLA	American Intellectual Property Law Association
ANZAAS	(The) Australian and New Zealand Association for the Advancement of Science
BIE	Bureau of Industry Economics (Australia) (became part of the Productivity Commission)
BPAI	Board of Patent Appeals and Interferences (internal USPTO Board)
CAFC	Court of Appeals for the Federal Circuit (the US court which hears all patent appeal cases)
CBO	Congressional Budget Office (US)
CMS	Carnegie Mellon Survey (1994, US)
DIISRT	Department of Industry, Innovation, Science, Research and Tertiary Education (part of the Australian Commonwealth government)
EPC	European Patent Convention
EPLA	European Patent Lawyers Association
EPO	European Patent Office
EC	European Commission
FTC	Federal Trade Commission (US)
G7	The seven industrialised nations of Canada, France, Germany, Italy, Japan, the United Kingdom and the United States
GAO	Government Accountability Office (US)
GATT	General Agreement on Tariffs and Trade
GL	General Ledger
IBM	International Business Machines Pty Ltd
ID	identification
IIPI	International Intellectual Property Institute
INPADOC	International Patent Documentation Center (EPO database)
IPAC	Industrial Property Advisory Committee (Australia) (replaced by ACIP)
IP Australia	Intellectual Property Australia (government body within DIISRT responsible for patents, trade marks, plant breeders' rights and designs, including the Australian Patent Office)

IPC	International Patent Classification (system)
IPCRC	Intellectual Property and Competition Review Committee (Australia)
IPER	International Preliminary Examination Report (issued under PCT arrangements)
IPSR	International Preliminary Search Report (issued under PCT arrangements)
IPTA	Institute of Patent and Trade Mark Attorneys of Australia
IRS	Internal Revenue Service (US)
ISBN	International Standard Book Number
JSTOR	Journal Storage: an online archive of academic journals (www.jstor.org)
NAFTA	North American Free Trade Agreement
NBER	National Bureau of Economic Research (US)
NOIE	National Office for the Information Economy (Australia)
PAIR	Patent Application Information Retrieval (a USPTO database)
PCT	Patent Cooperation Treaty
PHOSITA	person having ordinary skills in the 'art' (US version of PSA)
POS	point of sales
PhRMA	Pharmaceutical Research and Manufacturers of America
PSA	person skilled in the 'art'
R&D	Research and development
RFID	Radio-frequency identification
SMS	short message service (text message, usually sent by mobile phone)
TRIPS	(Agreement on) Trade Related Aspects of Intellectual Property Rights
USPTO	United States Patent and Trademark Office
VAT	value added tax
WIPO	World Intellectual Property Organization
WTO	World Trade Organization

PATENT COUNTRY CODES

Country codes indicate the country or organisation where the patent application was filed or granted. Standard patent codes used here are:

AU	Australia
EP	European Patent Office

GB	United Kingdom
US	United States of America
WO	World Intellectual Property Organization (WIPO)

OTHER SPECIFIC TERMINOLOGY

art	technology
citations	the specific pieces of pre-existing knowledge provided in a patent application or identified by the examiner in examining the application
citations, forward	the extent to which a patent is cited as 'art' by later patent applications
claim(s)	that part of a patent specification which sets out the area claimed as the invention, and thus claimed as a monopoly
esp@cenet	EPO database particularly useful for tracing parallel applications
expedited examination	fast-track examination
family	a group of patents which are related to each other by way of the priority or priorities of a particular patent document
filing	application
integer	element
manner of manufacture	defines a patentable invention in Australia, and is defined in Section 6 of the 1623 *Statute of Monopolies*
modified examination	exempted from examination in the country as already examined in an approved overseas country
pdf	Adobe's portable document format (for electronic documents)
prior art	existing knowledge; exactly what existing knowledge can be used is defined in statute and case law and differs between the novelty and inventiveness tests
priority date	the date which defines existing knowledge against which claims are tested
prosecution	the process of applying for a patent, including examination
Yale survey	Yale University Survey of firms (1984, US)

Cited cases

AUSTRALIA

3M	*Minnesota Mining and Manufacturing v. Beiersdorf (Australia)* (1980) 144 CLR 253
Aktiebolaget	*Aktiebolaget Hässle v. Alphapharm Pty Ltd* (2002) 212 CLR 411
CCOMa	*Ccom Pty Ltd v. Jiejing Pty Ltd* [1994] FCA 902 (10 February 1994)
CCOMb	*Ccom Pty Ltd v. Jiejing Pty Ltd* [1994] FCA 1168 (22 June 1994)
Grant 2005	*Grant v. Commissioner of Patents* (2005) FCA 1100
Grant 2006	*Grant v. Commissioner of Patents* [2006] FCAFC 120 (18 July 2006)
IBM	*Re International Business Machines Corporation v. Patrick Anselm Smith, Commissioner of Patents* [1991] FCA 625 (13 December 1991)
Lockwood	*Lockwood Security v. Doric Products* [2004] HCA 58 (18 November 2004)
Microcell	*Commissioner of Patents v. Microcell,* (1959) 102 CLR 232
Mirabella	*NV. Philips Gloeilampenfabrieken and Philips Lighting Pty Limited v. Mirabella International Pty Limited* [1993] FCA 404 (26 August 1993)
NRDC	*National Research Development Corp. v. Commissioner of Patents* (1959) 102 CLR. 252
Szabo	*Re Peter Szabo and Associates Pty Ltd* (2005) 66 IPR 370
Welcome	*Welcome Real-Time SA v. Catuity Inc,* [2001] FCA 445 (17 May 2001)

Unheard

Cancer Voices	Cancer Voices Australia v. Myriad Genetics. NSD643/2010

UK

Aerotel	*Aerotel Ltd v. Telco Holdings Ltd (and others) and Macrossan's Application* [2006] EWCA Civ. 1371
Astron	*Astron Clinica Limited and others v. The Comptroller General of Patents, Designs and Trade Marks* [2008] EWHC 85 (Pat)
CFPH	*In the matter of Patent Applications GB 0226884.3 and 0419317.3 by CFPH L.L.C.* [2005] EWHC 1589 (Pat)
Crane	*Crane v. Price* 1 W.P.C. 393
Hamilton	*Hamilton E. Harwood and Another v. The Directors, etc of the*

	Great Northern Railway Company, (1865) 11 HLC 654, 11 ER 1488
IBM Corp	*IBM Corp's Application* [1980] FSR 564.
Liardet	*Liardet v. Johnson* (Hulme, 18 L.Q.R at 287)
Losh	*Losh v. Hague*, 3 Hayward's Patent Cases 125
Macrossan	*Macrossan's Application* [2006] EWCA Civ. 1371
Symbian	*Symbian Ltd v. Comptroller-General of Patents* [2008] EWCA Civ. 1066 [UK Supreme Court of Appeal]
Von Heyden	*Von Heyden v. Neustadt* (1880) 50 L.J.Ch. 126
White	*White v. Toms*, (1969) 37 LJ Ch 204

USA

ACS	*ACS Hospital Sys, Inc*, 732 F2d at 1577
AMP 2010	*Association for Molecular Pathology v. U.S. Patent and Trademark Office*, No. 09-cv-4515, 94 USPQ2d 1683 (S.D.N.Y. March 29, 2010)
AMP 2011	*AMP v. USPTO, CAFC,* (http://www.cafc.uscourts.gov/images/stories/opinions-orders/10-1406.pdf)
Benson	*Gottschalk v. Benson* 409 U.S. 63 (1972)
Bilski	*Bilski v. Kappos*, 130 S. Ct. 3218, 561 US __, 177 L. Ed. 2d 792 (2010)
Diehr	*Diamond v. Diehr*, 450 U.S. 175 (1981)
Flook	*Parker v. Flook*, 437 U.S. 584 (1978)
Graham	*Graham v. John Deere Co. of Kat. City*, 383 U.S. 1 (1966)
Hotchkiss	*Hotchkiss et al. v. Greenwood et al.*, 11 Howard 248 (1850); 52 U.S. 261
In re Appalat	*In re Appalat* case (33 Fed 1526 (1994)
In re Bilski	*In re Bilski*, 545 F.3d 943, (Fed.Cir. 2008) (en banc)
KSR	*KSR v. Teleflex* 127 S.Ct. 1727 (2007)
Lundgren	*Ex parte Lundgren* 76 USPQ 2d 1385 (BPAI 2005)
Mayo	*Mayo v. Prometheus Laboratories* 566 U.S _ (2012)
Prometheus	*Prometheus Labs., Inc. v. Mayo Collaborative Services*, 581 F.3d 1336, 1345–49 (Fed. Cir. 2009)
Research Corporation	*Research Corporation Technologies, Inc. v. Microsoft Corporation*, F.3d (No. 2010-1037, Fed. Cir. 2010)
State Street	*State Street Bank & Trust Co. v. Signature Financial Group, Inc.*, 149 F. 3d (1998)

NEW ZEALAND

Wellcome	*Wellcome Foundation Ltd v. Commissioner of Patents* [1983] NZLR 385 (CA)

EPO APPEAL DECISIONS

Vicom Systems Inc. T 0208/84 15 July 1985 available at http://legal.european-patent-office.org/dg3/biblio/t840208ep1.htm [*Vicom*]
Duns Licensing Associates T 0154/04, 15 November 2006
File search method/Fujitsu T1351/04, 18 April 2007
Gameaccount Ltd T 1543/06, 29 June 2007

1. Introduction

1.1 PUBLIC INTEREST IN PATENT LAWS

Patents are a fascinating example of how well-meaning economic policy can go wrong. This book adds to the evidence about the major difficulties with current patent policy.[1] It does this through an in-depth exploration of how inventive something needs to be to gain a patent. The data presented in this book show that no inventiveness is needed for a patent, if inventiveness takes either its normal meaning or the meaning of contributing new knowledge or know-how.

Patent policy is economic policy. Its essence is a very simple bargain. Society accepts the harmful effects of patent monopolies in exchange for a higher level of invention, and thus a higher level of economic growth. This simplicity of principle has been extremely hard to put into practice – just how inventive should something be to obtain a patent? Where is the point at which the monopoly and transaction costs of patent systems are fully offset by the benefits of inducing innovation that would not otherwise have occurred? If induced innovations generate new knowledge and know-how this provides benefits that spill over to the community to offset the costs of the granted monopolies. But how much new knowledge is enough?

It is challenging to evaluate patent policy. How do the costs imposed by preventing innovation in rival firms and raising prices to consumers compare with the benefits of induced new knowledge that flows to other firms?

Although patent offices hand out many thousands of patents each year, they do not collect any information on how these monopolies are used, making direct evaluation of patent policy an impossibility. Indeed Machlup's 1958 report to the US Senate, based on an analysis of principles and a breadth of knowledge about industry and innovation, remains perhaps the best overall practical evaluation of the economic impact of patent systems. Machlup concluded that at that time the costs and benefits of US patent policy were finely balanced; he certainly considered that any increase in the strength or ambit of the patent system would tip the balance to a negative economic impact. He also implied that for countries with a smaller industrial base and lower technology exports the balance of evidence would be in favour of a reduced level of patent 'protection' (Machlup 1958: 80).

Despite this conclusion, and without any supporting empirical evidence, over recent years patent systems have become stronger and more widespread. One key driver has been a small number of major global companies operating through their influence on international 'trade' negotiations (Drahos 2002; Sell 2003). Another has been a series of judicial decisions that have broadened the subject matter reach of the patent system and reduced the quantum of inventiveness required to obtain a patent.

Almost simultaneously survey data on innovating firms and the means they use to protect their innovations have become available. These address the question of how much innovation is induced by patent systems and how much would occur anyway – the central concept of induced innovation. The most important of these are two US surveys: the 1984 Yale survey of large R&D performing firms and the 1994 Carnegie-Mellon survey (CMS) of large and small firms (Levin et al 1987; Cohen et al 2000). Replicated in a large variety of surveys outside the USA, these data consistently call into question whether patent 'protection' has any major positive effect on industrial innovation outside of the pharmaceutical industry. The more recent of these studies show an increasing use of patents for strategic purposes (Blind et al 2006; Encaoua et al 2006). This dissonance between the trend in patent policy and the increasing body of evidence questioning the effectiveness of patents has been noted by such renowned authorities on industrial innovation as Nelson (Mazzoleni and Nelson 1998a), Cohen (Cohen 2005) and Scherer (Scherer 2006). Why this dissonance between policy and evidence?

Where regulatory interventions create the possibility for some parties to reap substantial benefits, they have a strong incentive to help set up complex and arcane rules that hide such benefits from general view (Braithwaite 2005). Where those who foot the bill for such regimes are widely dispersed, there is little chance of effective lobbying to offset this – their sole hope is that their interests will be protected by their elected representatives. These features underlie the development of the theories of public choice and regulatory capture (Olson 1971). Landes and Posner conclude that the strengthening of the patent system at precisely the time other markets were being extensively deregulated rested in public choice theory – the small number of entities reaping significant benefits from stronger patents have been successful in their lobbying efforts (Landes and Posner 2004). Democratic protection of the public interest has so far failed.

The complexity of the patent system is well known, and there is a strong degree of animosity by the patent community to those from outside taking any interest in it. The American patent bar lobbied successfully to prevent the US Government Accountability Office – a highly respected research body – from undertaking a study into business method patenting. Such a study had been part of the penultimate draft of the *American Inventors Protection Act 1999* but was removed in the final statute. This and other derailed efforts to collect and analyse data on how the patent system operates are documented by Kahin (2003a).

The market for innovation has perhaps the greatest degree of government intervention of any market. Yet as Yale Professor John Beggs remarked in the context of an economic review of patents:

> There are general principles which are of the highest importance, that markets should be left to operate freely whenever possible, that one must look further afield than those involved in and regulating an industry when canvassing opinions regarding changes in public policy, and finally, if a market environment is created which can be abused or manipulated then such a market will be abused and manipulated. (Beggs 1981: 44)

This salutary warning about patent policy remains pertinent today.

While some economists have not hesitated to undertake econometric analyses using patent data, this is not always informed by an in-depth understanding of patent systems as they actually operate. The time required to develop an understanding of these complex systems can be off-putting. One purpose of this book is to provide a clear and non-legalistic insight into the actual workings of the patent system for economic researchers and industry and innovation policy makers. At present economic research on the patent system has little if any impact on policy makers as much focuses on abstract concepts unrelated to patent practice (van Pottelsberghe 2011). A better understanding of the realities of patent policy might assist in developing more policy relevant research. This book exposes some of the key operating rules affecting the quantum of inventiveness required for a patent grant.

A second purpose is to present the results of an empirical investigation into the actual height of the inventive step. As a concept inventiveness is clearly a continuum; some things are marvellously inventive and others are only a little different from what already exists. The challenge in patent policy is to determine where the boundary lies between quite obvious inventions – mere workshop improvements as it were – and those inventions that genuinely contribute new knowledge and know-how thus providing spillover benefits to offset their costs. This is an essentially subjective judgement, involving as it does guesstimates of future benefits and costs. The proxy variable to short-cut this arduous process has been the concept of inventiveness.

Initially spelled out in section 6 of the *Statute of Monopolies 1623*, the definition of a patentable invention invoked concepts such as "not . . . mischievous to the state, by raising prices of commodities at home, or hurt of trade, or generally inconvenient". This complexity is well summarised in the 1641 Massachusetts code of laws: "There shall be no monopolies granted or allowed among us, but of such new inventions as *are profitable to the country*, and that for a short time" (Article 9, emphasis added).

A third contribution this book makes is its economic perspective on the legal doctrines that constitute patent policy. While there are some exceptions, much legal analysis of the patent system fails to focus on the fact that the policy objectives are economic. This economic perspective on detailed rules may be of some value to those who usually only consider such rules from a legal perspective. A focus on the impact of the rules on innovation investment and national benefit is quite different from the 'property' perspective some others take. 'Property' derived from government intervention and regulation in the market is quite a different thing from the normal concept of physical property acquired in relatively competitive markets.

This book follows the philosophical view of the 1641 Massachusetts code: monopolies should only be granted when they provide a net benefit to the nation, as opposed to a specific benefit to the monopolist. It takes as a foundation principle that the most important policy for a healthy economy is sound and effective competition. It assumes that policy makers intend that patent systems should have a positive economic impact on their nation. It takes the economic perspective that the benefits of a patent system are the knowledge and know-how spillovers from those innovations induced by the patent system. Costs flow from all granted patents, not just those induced by the patent system. They are the higher prices paid where a genuine monopoly can be exercised, the transaction costs in obtaining and enforcing patents and higher search costs where there are large volumes of patents. A further cost is the development of a rent-seeking attitude in business. Where costs are more than offset by the spillover benefits from induced innovation a patent system will be economically beneficial to a country.

1.2 THE CENTRALITY OF INVENTIVENESS

Measuring spillovers is extremely difficult (Griliches 1990), but the underlying assumption – that it is new knowledge which creates the need for and return from the patent system – may be broadly related to the degree of inventiveness. Of course some kinds of new knowledge may generate greater spillover benefits than others, so one cannot expect a clear and direct association between inventiveness and net benefit to the nation. Nevertheless, the concept of inventiveness has become the principal criterion operating today as a gatekeeper to patent grant. The quantum of inventiveness required for grant – the so-called inventive step – is thus of critical policy interest. Yet because of its very subjectivity there is little independent evidence on its height.

Once inventions moved from the mechanical realm to chemicals and electronics, inventiveness became an increasingly difficult decision. Judges developed various rules of thumb – legal doctrines – which became codified in common law countries as policy rules. Often these were imported from case law into statute law without any evaluation of their economic effects.

The net impact of these rules on the quantum of inventiveness required for a patent grant has led many patent system scholars to comment critically on the very low threshold required. British and then Australian law came to require a mere "scintilla" of inventiveness. The US standard has also fallen to a very low level and there is a large critical literature on the non-obviousness criterion in the US system (e.g. Harris 1989; Hunt 1999; Barton 2000; Lunney 2001; Jaffe and Lerner 2004; Lunney 2004).

Because of its subjectivity, objective proxies for measuring inventiveness have been elusive. Dahlin and Behrens (2005) have developed a proxy for identifying radical inventions. This indicator identified six out of 581 tennis racquet patents as radical, and this definition appears robust on the basis of complementary evidence. While "about 1 per cent" might feel right in terms of the proportion of patented inventions which are truly radical, the other 99 per cent includes at least a proportion of 'inventions' which are reasonably inventive, if not radically so. The challenge is to define clearly what is sufficiently inventive to merit a monopoly. Certainly it is more than a scintilla. But it is not possible to simply invert Dahlin and Behrens' approach – the issue of identifying uninventive inventions is asymmetrical and developing a standardised measure of *lack* of inventiveness is challenging.

Qualitative studies are not generally preferred in economic analysis as small sample sizes make robust statistical analysis inappropriate. Nonetheless a case study approach seems the most appropriate means to investigate the actual height of the inventive step. The data presented in this book are the results of an analysis of the new knowledge or know-how contained in a set of granted patents. This is the reverse question of that asked during the process of obtaining a patent. In several major jurisdictions there is a reverse onus of proof policy – it is the patent office which has to demonstrate that an application is uninventive rather than the monopoly applicant who has to demonstrate inventiveness. The question the examiner addresses is whether there is sufficient documented evidence to deem the 'invention' obvious. So asking what is the knowledge or know-how contributed uses a radically different yardstick to measure the impact of the legal doctrines which constitute patent policy.

Presenting the results of such a study requires laying out the evidence so others can judge for themselves whether the subjective judgements made are valid. Much of this book is concerned with this issue, presenting details of the core 'inventive' contribution of each patent and assessing their contribution to new knowledge or know-how. In case after case a complete lack of new knowledge is demonstrated. There are two cases where there is a *possible* new idea. But these possible new ideas do not contribute new knowledge or know-how, either in the idea or in the implementation. In both cases the claims seem to fully pre-empt other uses of the idea. This is generally seen as undesirable – ideas should remain for all to use. Only specific applications of ideas are patentable.

Investigating cases in this detail also allows the identification of the specific legal doctrines giving rise to the grant of so many patents that appear totally devoid of any contribution to new knowledge. While reading the rules set out in patent examiner manuals would also suggest that the quantum of inventiveness is highly constrained, these cases show just what a challenge it is for patent examiners to reject uninventive applications. Particularly in the USA and Australia examiners are tied by the plethora of rules that the Federal Trade Commission (FTC) identified as favouring patent grant once an application is lodged (FTC 2003: 8). The patents in the dataset are traced through parallel applications at IP Australia,[2] the United States Patent and Trademark Office (USPTO) and at the European Patent Office (EPO). This allows a consideration of whether there are rule differences affecting the height of the inventive step. The correspondence between examiners and applicants shows just how difficult it is for patent examiners to protect the public interest.[3]

Because of my specific expertise, the cases selected all fall into a new and controversial area of patenting – business methods. But business method cases have the advantage of allowing a wide range of readers to judge for themselves the quantum of new knowledge involved. This 'technology field' is relatively accessible to many analysts, covering as it does financial, trade, logistics, marketing, business performance, human resources, purchasing and other closely related business systems. The nature of the 'inventions' can be described in accessible language and the reader will often be in a position to make an independent judgement about any knowledge contribution. This contrasts with leading edge research in genuine technology areas, where such an assessment would be limited to a small number of experts. It is possible that this new field is unrepresentative; but all signatories to TRIPS must treat all fields of technology identically, applying the same decision-making rules. If a consistent application of the standard rules generates a vast majority of patents with no new knowledge in this field, then it would be worth investing the specialist resources needed to make a similar assessment in genuine fields of technology.

In a sense this study does nothing more than confirm what is already known: the quantum of inventiveness required for a patent is abysmally low. Indeed in some jurisdictions is appears non-existent. In attending patent conferences and meetings over many years, it became clear that members of the patent community are well aware of this. Indeed members of this community refer to the 5-10-85 rule – that some 5 per cent of patents are truly inventive, another 10 per cent are reasonably inventive and the remainder are simply "rubbish". Barton (2000) confirms these estimates in noting that less than 25 per cent of US patents survive re-examination without change. Quillen (2006) notes that before the establishment of the Court of Appeals for the Federal Circuit (CAFC) in 1982 two-thirds of litigated patents were found to be invalid. Three decades ago Griliches noted that the standard for a patent grant was "not very high" (Griliches 1990: 1663). The low standards were noted even earlier by Edwards, who commented that "[a]s it reaches the patent office the application combines technological and legal invention, and the latter, if of superior quality, may do much to offset deficiencies in the former" (Edwards 1949: 218).

Despite the substantial evidence that the inventiveness standard is extremely low, the rules used to define the inventive step have been impervious to reform. Existing evidence, strong as it is, has not yet been sufficient to offset the influence of lobbyists. Further empirical analysis of this key policy variable is clearly required if patent policy is to be set on an evidence base and reshaped to deliver a net national benefit. This book is a contribution to that process.

1.3 HOW THIS STUDY IS STRUCTURED

Patents have rarely held a central position as a subject of interest in the economics profession. Indeed some 60 years ago it was suggested that following the near-abolition of the patent system in the UK in the late nineteenth century economists largely abandoned the field to lawyers (Machlup and Penrose 1950). Nonetheless patent policy is quintessentially economic policy, and economic rationales are regularly presented by bureaucrats and lobbyists to support its ever-widening reach. Some discussion of both the economics of patent policy and the development of legal doctrine is therefore needed to interpret the policy impacts demonstrated by the case studies.

Background on the economic arguments used in discussing patent policy is presented in Chapter 2. This focuses on the key *assumptions* in competing theories about the generation and dissemination of new knowledge. Assumptions about how economic agents behave are central to most economic theories, so their validity is critical to accepting or rejecting a hypothesis. The assumptions underlying theories about patents can be assessed against the increasing empirical evidence now available. This is a very useful step forward. It is possible because of major US innovation studies from the early 1980s and 1990s later confirmed through National Innovation Surveys (NISs) in many other countries. This assessment of the empirical evidence leads to some interesting conclusions about the economics of patent policy.

Attention is then turned in Chapter 3 to how patent law has developed, first with respect to subject matter scope and then with respect to inventiveness. The expansion in the coverage of the patent system to new 'technology' fields has culminated in the grant of patents to business methods, often requiring no technological application. This massive change in scope occurred largely through case law: "the greatest changes in the legal system made by judges, without legislative review or approval, have occurred in the area of patent law" (Boldrin and Levine 2008: 63). The changing doctrines on novelty and inventiveness are reviewed in Section 3.4 as an introduction to the empirical analysis in later chapters. These concepts developed from the mid nineteenth century and patent law inventiveness is now determined by a series of prescriptive rules around an artificially constructed representational skilled worker.

There have been some significant changes in inventiveness rules in recent decades in the USA and Australia, often in cases where private parties are in dispute and the public interest is not represented. The CAFC has developed quite different obviousness standards than those used by the Supreme Court (Harris 1986) allowing a far larger number of granted patents to be deemed valid (Quillen 2006). The Supreme Court has partially addressed the CAFC's elevation of secondary considerations above the statutory obviousness tests. In the *KSR* case it also determined that the skilled worker should be deemed to have normal rather than no imagination. In Australia imagination is still not permitted and severe constraints on the knowledge this person can use were only lifted in 2012.

Chapter 4 draws this economic and legal background together in a consideration of what tests would best ensure that patentable inventions are those which deliver a benefit to the nation. Challenges in developing effective proxies mean that first-best solutions are not feasible. However a focus on the new knowledge or know-how contributed by an invention offers a useful second-best option. This approach aligns with the question posed by the UK Appeal Court in 2006 (*Aerotel*) when it summarised a key part of the examination process as being designed to answer the question: "What has the inventor really added to human knowledge?" This is in fact quite different from the approach usually taken during examination or in litigation about inventiveness. In developing an alternative approach to determining patent eligibility a number of related issues are canvassed. Should a technology basis be required for a patent to be granted? Should mathematical algorithms be patentable in any form? Is more than pure logic needed for an 'invention' to be patentable? What is the appropriate distinction between an unpatentable idea and a patentable implementation? Does the problem/solution approach assist in identifying knowledge contributions?

Chapter 4 also discusses the selection of a representative set of cases and the methodology used in this study. In summary the inventiveness of the selected 72 patents is assessed on the basis of their claims, which are "construed" to determine the essence of the 'invention'. The core inventive element is then compared to existing knowledge and know-how at the priority date for the patent. The chapter concludes with a discussion of the characteristics of the selected cases. This includes the first presentation of some case material. The 10 cases presented in Section 4.4 are selected to provide a flavour of the range of patented business methods across industries. No new knowledge or know-how contributions are found.

Chapters 5, 6 and 7 present the detailed assessment of the inventiveness of the remaining cases. The inventiveness story is told in terms of the contribution to new knowledge or know-how. It is interwoven with the story of the specific doctrinal rules which appear to determine the grant of a patent even where there is no new knowledge or know-how. While the initially selected set of cases was based on Australian patent grants, 64 have parallel applications overseas. Altogether 190 separate overseas applications were identified with 54 at the USPTO and 38 at the EPO. The cases are traced through the Australian, US and European patent systems comparing outcomes and differences in the rules that led to the grant of obvious patents.

Existing studies of business method patents suggest that a major reason for the grant of so many obvious patents is the difficulty in documenting existing processes in a field where these are rarely written down. This hypothesis is tested in Chapter 5 where the first issue addressed is whether there are difficulties in tracing pre-existing knowledge ('prior art'). For almost all cases existing documented knowledge was found. Once examiners identify existing knowledge applicants regularly redraft their specifications to ensure that this knowledge does not defeat their application. So the other issues addressed in Chapter 5 are whether existing knowledge can be evaded though amendment (Section 5.3) or the reverse onus of proof policy (Section 5.4). The fact that it is patent offices which have to disprove inventiveness, rather than applicants who have to prove it, creates a lower threshold for the inventiveness test. No new knowledge or know-how is found in any of the 24 cases discussed in this chapter.

In Chapter 6 attention is turned to the vexed question of combination patents. These are 'inventions' that take known elements or processes and combine these in new ways. At their simplest this involves the mere computerisation of known business processes, and there are 22 such cases. There are a further 20 cases where two or more known processes are combined, usually in computerised form, and often using modern electronic networks. There has been a shift in legal doctrine in the USA and Australia lowering the inventiveness standard for combination inventions. The 15 cases discussed identify no contributions to knowledge or know-how.

The cases presented in Chapter 7 cover a more diverse range of issues. The chapter starts by looking at cases where there has been a grant at the EPO or by the UK Intellectual Property Office (UKIPO). The European Patent Convention (EPC) specifically excludes software and business methods from patentability. Some also argue that the EPC has a relatively high inventive step. For both these reasons there is an expectation that outcomes from parallel applications at the EPO and UKIPO would be different from those in the USA or Australia. While there are more cases of clear refusal from these offices, there are also a surprising number of grants. Particularly astonishing are the three cases where the EPO rejected 'inventions' as neither technical nor inventive, but then granted a patent after a few words were moved from dependent to independent claims. The nine cases granted by either the EPO or the UKIPO seem no different in inventiveness from the cases refused by these offices.[4] There are no contributions to knowledge or know-how.

Other issues illustrated by the cases presented in Chapter 7 are the analogous use doctrine – which seems not to be used even where it is clearly warranted – and workshop variations, again an issue raised but clearly not effective in refusing grants (Section 7.3). These legal doctrines were developed to set a floor to the inventiveness standard for patentability but they are now noticeable by their absence. A variety of other patent doctrines – the problem/solution approach; the issue of tangible output; the patenting of ideas; and the use of patents in one country to obtain patents in another – are illustrated through the six cases presented in Section 7.4.

The results are assessed and policy conclusions drawn in Chapter 8. Problems in identifying existing knowledge are not the principal reason for the grant of obvious business patents. For the majority of cases relevant written knowledge was identified – indeed the amazing finding was the extent to which patents have already been granted for a range of very ordinary business processes. The data in this study show that uninventive patents are granted because of the specific doctrinal rules set up to objectify the concept of inventiveness. Rules about what knowledge can be used, the breadth of the relevant technology, very narrow readings of specific words, the ability to continually amend claims and the reverse onus of proof have all been critical in allowing these grants. This suggests that a radical overhaul of how the key concept of inventiveness is defined and implemented in patent law would assist in returning balance to patent systems. A more balanced patent system would contribute to, rather than detract from, national economic welfare.

The lack of inventiveness in recently granted business method patents also raises questions as to the degree of inventiveness in genuine fields of technology. The evidence presented here strongly indicates that it is *the doctrinal rules* applied in all technology fields which lead to an almost non-existent inventive step. Other technologies are subject to the same rules, and this does much to explain, for example, the European Commission finding of that "*individual medicines* are protected by up to nearly 100 product-specific patent families, which can lead to up to 1,300 patents and/or pending patent applications across the Member States" (European Commission 2009: 10, emphasis added). A pharmaceutical product is a chemical compound, clearly definable. If new knowledge or know-how were required for grant of a patent it would simply not be possible to acquire so many patents for one chemical compound.

An 'invention' which contains no new knowledge or know-how cannot contribute spillover benefits, though it imposes deadweight losses (Jensen and Webster 2004). While it might be argued that such patents will have limited power in the market place, this cannot be assumed. Allowing a company a patent on a known process gives it the power to approach other companies asking for royalties or to cease certain activities. Signature Financial Group's US 5193056 patent computerised government guidelines for minimising tax on certain investment products, foreclosing all other options (Stern 1999: 132). It had significant market power despite being mere computerisation of tax office rules. The case that led to the view that business methods were patentable in Australia imposed costs on Catuity, which was found to have infringed a well-known use of dynamic storage (*Welcome*).

There is little incentive to challenge an uninventive patent unless there is an infringement suit. This is because the litigating company bears the full legal costs and business risks, while the benefits of a successful outcome are shared with all competitors. Given the high cost and considerable uncertainty of patent litigation, there is substantial evidence that many companies take the path of least resistance and comply. We are all worse off for this entirely understandable response. Indeed in the USA, the fact that one company has paid a licensing fee is now used as indirect evidence that a patent is valid, though it has nothing to do with inventiveness (Jaffe and Lerner 2004). There are other kinds of perverse outcomes evident when one takes a closer look at the actual operations of patent systems (see, for example, Thambisetty 2009). Using litigation to correct deficiencies in patent administration places an unfair burden on innovating companies. The problems of asymmetry and cost also mean it is ineffective as a means of ensuring robust patent policy. Further, many of the rules which create very obvious patents have been introduced by courts.

The only effective means of reforming the system and bringing it back into balance will be action by executive governments and parliaments. A careful consideration of the substantial evidence – as opposed to the self-interested views of interested parties – would make it clear that thorough reform of patent systems is long overdue. The evidence presented in this book shows that a good starting point would be to introduce a requirement for a contribution of knowledge or know-how thus substantially raising the height of the inventive step. Such reform would have a strong positive effect on innovation. As Quillen (2008) has pointed out, it is not the patents you own that promote innovation and commercialisation – it is the patents which *others* own which prevent it.

2. The economics of patent policy: assumptions, paradoxes and evidence

2.1 INTRODUCTION

The principal economic argument supporting patent policy is founded on the assumption that copying knowledge is virtually free. Once an innovator has developed a new artefact or process, competitors are able to replicate this at very low cost, undercutting the original innovator in the market. They can price close to marginal cost as they do not have to recoup the overhead costs of developing the new knowledge. This argument also implies that very little time is needed to copy the new knowledge to the point of having a fully developed competing product in the market, so that the original innovator has little if any period of market exclusivity.[1]

An alternative view, derived from the information economics school of thought, considers that it takes both time and money to learn and use new knowledge. Indeed the cost of acquiring new knowledge is sufficiently high that it is a barrier to the diffusion of new technology. This alternative perspective draws the conclusion that many new industrial artefacts and processes will have a period of exclusivity in the market when there are no competing products. During this time the product can be priced above marginal cost so ensuring a return to its R&D investment. An exception may be where initial development costs are very large (e.g. aircraft, submarines, clinical trials). Here the initial period of market exclusivity may be insufficient to allow full recoupment of the R&D investment.

These two opposing perspectives have co-existed for many decades, with virtually no cross-over between the largely theoretical literature supporting the view that patents address a market failure and the quite separate literature on the challenges of technology diffusion. But empirical data are now available to test the assumptions on which these conflicting theories rest. These data provide insights into how industrial innovation works in practice and are reviewed in Section 2.2. If copying is fast and cheap innovation markets may frequently fail, except for very trivial innovations. But if copying is expensive and/or slow, then markets may fail only for the very largest and most expensive projects.

If innovation markets fail regularly then there will be less investment in innovation. Why is this a problem? Investors could simply put their money elsewhere. The reason a lower level of investment in innovation is assumed to be a problem for society is the view that the social returns to industrial innovation exceed the private returns. Thus if an innovation succeeds the innovator will profit, but so will society as there are net positive externalities from the innovation. If the investment does not take place, society is the poorer for the lack of these benefits.

The net positive externalities are the sum of all the impacts of the innovation on other parties. Thus if the consumer surplus from the new product exceeds the consumer surplus from any displaced products, there will be a benefit. Further if the new knowledge embodied in the innovation provides other producers with ideas which in turn lead to further new products or processes, there will be further benefits through faster innovation and so stronger economic growth. Section 2.3 considers the empirical evidence on net externalities from innovation.

From a policy perspective there is another important issue beyond determining whether these two critical assumptions are supported by the evidence. That is, are patents effective in inducing *additional* investment in innovation? Do patents *induce* innovation investment that would not otherwise occur? This question is partly related to the cost and speed of copying, but it provides an alternative approach to assessing the evidence on whether the first mover period of exclusivity is sufficient. The issue of the extent to which patents induce innovation – as opposed to providing a windfall transfer from consumers for innovation that would take place anyway – is addressed in Section 2.4.

If the above questions are all answered such that a patent system provides positive benefits, then the next important policy issue is: at what cost? There is surprisingly little empirical evidence on the cost of patent systems, and what there is tends to focus on the private costs to users of the system rather than the policy question of the net cost to society. But there are a range of social costs, particularly higher prices during the period of patent exclusivity and additional costs imposed on innovators from having to invent around if they are not first to the patent office. The privileges awarded by a patent centre on exclusion and prevention of unauthorised use. This is a very strong form of monopoly – it goes beyond preventing copying. It allows the patent holder to prevent independently invented innovations from being sold in the marketplace. The available evidence on patent system costs is discussed in Section 2.5.

The chapter concludes by considering the evidence about the net economic balance from patent systems. Are there net benefits or net losses? Economists' answers to this question traditionally tended to be theoretical. As Cheung characterises the classical economists, Bentham considered patents provided something for nothing, Taussig that they provided nothing for nothing, Plant that they provided nothing for something, and Arrow that they are inferior to direct subsidies for research and development (R&D) (Cheung 1986). Now, however, there are a range of useful empirical studies of industrial innovation. These data allow the choice between competing economic theories to be based on evidence: a great step forward from the earlier era when "[c]onviction was pitted against conviction, argument against argument, assumption against assumption" (Machlup and Penrose 1950: 28).

Unfortunately, it is no longer possible to conduct natural experiments about the impact of patent systems as the TRIPS Agreement requires a minimum standard system in exchange for World Trade Organization (WTO) membership. However in earlier times there was more variety particularly in respect of chemicals and pharmaceuticals. Historical evidence from nineteenth-century trade fairs suggests that the existence of a patent system changes the focus of innovation but does not increase the level of innovative effort (Moser 2005). Italy provides empirical evidence that allowing patenting of chemical compositions does nothing to promote the chemical industry (Scherer and Weisburst 1995). There are also several heroic studies which attempt to isolate the impact of patent regimes on economic growth from all the other relevant variables.[2]

One major conclusion from the available evidence is that balance is critical if patent systems are to deliver net economic benefits. The threshold for grant of a patent must be such that there is genuine new knowledge contributed so that there is at least some chance of a sufficient quantum of spillover benefits to offset the costs of allowing monopolies. The quantum of inventiveness required for a patent is therefore critical in determining net balance in patent system outcomes.

As social benefits flow only from induced innovation, a critical question is whether inventiveness works as a proxy for induced innovation. The answer of course is that it is very imperfect on this account as it is the absolute size, or lumpiness, of the innovation investment compared to the period of natural exclusivity that is important here. But benefits are also related to whether there are net externalities from the induced innovations, and in this regard there is a closer relationship with inventiveness. If inventiveness works as an effective proxy for the contribution of new knowledge or know-how and is set at a level where a reasonable quantum is required, then granted patents are more likely to confer net external benefits through knowledge spillovers and the patent system overall is more likely to confer net economic benefits. If, however, the inventiveness standard is very low, then many granted patents will confer no external benefits and patent systems are more likely to confer net economic losses.

2.2 COPYING: IS IT FREE AND FAST?

2.2.1 Direct Evidence on Copying

The earliest of the empirical studies on industrial imitation was of manufacturing firms in the north-eastern part of the USA. Mansfield and colleagues found that on average imitating an industrial artefact cost 65 per cent of the original innovation cost, and took 70 per cent of the original time (Mansfield et al 1981). For one in seven innovations, imitation costs were as high as the original innovation costs, largely due to the innovator's greater technological capacity. There was considerable variation around the reported averages. High relative imitation costs were associated with high relative time costs (and vice versa).

These results provide very striking evidence that in general copying takes time and money and that the more complex and expensive the innovation the more money and time is needed for copying. Thus it is likely that more expensive innovations will have a longer period of market exclusivity. While minor innovations may have only a very short period of first-mover advantage, it may well be possible to recoup their development costs during this time. This would, of course, need to include the relevant risk-adjusted profit margin.

The Mansfield study also investigated whether patenting made a difference to imitation, and found that about 60 per cent of patented products were imitated within four years. Patenting increased both the time and the cost of successful imitation: the median increase in cost was 11 per cent, but for pharmaceuticals was 30 per cent.

Further data on imitation were provided in the 1983 Yale Survey, covering 650 large US firms in 130 industries. This again found substantial variability in time and cost of imitation, but variations in the imitation cost ratio were greater within than between industries. In general, imitation saved around 50 per cent of the cost of the original R&D. Major innovations were more expensive to replicate, and replication took longer – sometimes over three years; most often at least six to 12 months (Levin et al 1987). These results are significantly different from the assumption that copying is fast and free.

Surprisingly there have been few further studies about the cost of copying industrial innovations. A search of all citations for Mansfield's original study yielded no further empirical work.[3] Attention in the field turned to another aspect of the Yale survey – data on the role of alternative mechanisms to appropriate returns to innovation. These data are explored in Section 2.2.2. But first it is useful to consider why copying new knowledge should take time and effort. This is important given the contrast with the dominant view that, despite the evidence, copying is virtually free and instantaneous.

Knowledge is a prime input into inventive activity and builds over time. Its use in industrial innovation involves a complex chain of feedbacks and interdependencies: "a collective, social, learning, evolutionary process" (Mandeville 1998: 49). Because new knowledge is not yet codified – not yet reduced to a clear written description – it is costly to acquire. At this stage it resides in the minds of researchers and inventors. It is expensive to turn tacit into codified knowledge, but only the latter can be exchanged easily in the market and relatively cheaply absorbed. But both language and learning are needed to absorb, interpret and use codified knowledge: one cannot readily absorb codified knowledge unless one has the requisite language and sufficient learning (Saviotti 1998). As a result the number of people who can appropriate new knowledge can be quite small. Those who can readily access such new knowledge can do so because of earlier expensive investments in their own learning.

But even for such knowledgeable researchers it is not always easy to extract the relevant knowledge from innovations and use this to generate a competing product. A new product embodying new knowledge does not necessarily disclose the underlying technology (Monk 1992). It takes time and resources to move from the artefact to understanding the technology, to being able to use it to replicate the artefact, let alone to improving it. Of course, the relative ease or difficulty of accessing such underlying technology will vary along a number of dimensions. Students of innovation have developed classifications of industries and technologies to understand better different patterns in the creation and diffusion of innovation (for example Pavitt 1984; Merges and Nelson 1990).

Imitation is an important element of learning but requires investment (Cohen and Levinthal 1989). Indeed imitation and adaptation (further incremental innovation) are essential parts of the process of building the stock of knowledge, and Mandeville (1996) suggests that there is no clear distinction between innovation and imitation. Radical breakthroughs can occur on the back of a process of incremental innovation (Magee 2002). Knowledge grows through use, and there is a multiplicative effect when new knowledge is added to old knowledge as different users take different perspectives, so adding to the body of underlying knowledge (Mandeville 1996). Most innovation takes place in the realm of uncodified knowledge, and mechanisms for the diffusion of uncodified knowledge – such as well-functioning labour markets – are critical to an effective innovation system.[4]

Once attention is turned to the inventor as a recipient as well as a creator of new knowledge, issues around the diversity of local knowledge emerge. Differences in local knowledge or mind-sets underlie the high value placed on team-work in many areas. Individual and firm differences in local knowledge mean that imitation will often lead to a range of re-interpretations and improvements (Ricketson 1992).

Because the cost of developing new knowledge is independent of the scale on which it is later used, there can be considerable economic advantages in sharing knowledge widely.[5]

This depth of perspective about knowledge flows derived from the information economics school of thought (Lamberton 1999) contrasts sharply with a small number of assumptions about knowledge flows made in neo-classical economics. The theoretical economics literature on patents generally assumes that any innovation can be discretely identified and is independent of and unrelated to most other innovations. The substantial mathematical literature on 'first' and subsequent innovations, takes the initial innovation to have no intellectual history, though the subsequent innovation derives from the earlier one. The analysis then focuses on appropriate incentives to ensure the right returns at each stage (see, for example, Scotchmer 1991, 1996; Gallini and Scotchmer 2002). Such analyses fall far short of the real-world complexity of how knowledge is used in industrial innovation.

They also contrast sharply with the information economics focus on the role of market mechanisms in providing a return to R&D investment. Now that it is widely accepted that most markets are imperfect, the existence of temporary rents and excess profits (first mover advantages) is the accepted paradigm.[6] Other natural protections of new technology, such as knowledge imperfections, transaction costs and the need for complementary assets (Teece 1986), create at least temporary barriers to entry, and therefore opportunities for returns to innovation. Where the tacit component of knowledge is high, the cost of learning to use new products is also high. Such barriers apply to consumers as well as rival producers. Consumers who have incurred high learning costs, for example with computer software, are reluctant to switch between products, so there are great advantages to early market entrants. It is now also recognised that in markets with such network effects, early movers and dominant players have considerable market advantages. The first party to bring an innovation to market may thus reap a considerable on-going reward through this mechanism.

2.2.2 Indirect Evidence on Copying

Given the centrality of the free and costless copying assumption to the rationale for the patent intervention, it is somewhat astonishing that after the two early studies there has been no further empirical work directly addressing the subject. This is particularly surprising given that there is some anecdotal evidence suggesting that copying may have become faster and possibly cheaper in recent decades. Reasons for this include new technologies such as computer aided design and manufacture as well as the rise of firms specialising in the production of cheaper alternatives to high-priced products.

One reason for this gap is that academic attention has been diverted to the related question of what mechanisms firms use to appropriate a return to innovation. The 1983 Yale survey not only provided direct evidence on copying, it also asked firms to assess a range of mechanisms for their effectiveness in ensuring profitable investment in innovation. Lead time (first in market), learning and sales/marketing were all seen as more important than patents to obtain a return from new products. For new processes, lead time, learning curves, sales/service, and secrecy were all reported as more important than patents (Levin et al 1987). There were a small number of exceptions: those industries where new products are highly codified, principally fine chemicals and pharmaceuticals, relied more heavily on patents. While the Yale survey focused on larger firms the 1994 Carnegie-Mellon survey (CMS) covered 1,478 firms, including smaller firms, and confirmed the findings of the Yale survey (Cohen et al 2000). Both surveys presented strong evidence that, in general, patents are *one of the least effective mechanisms* for obtaining a return to investment in R&D. The high importance assigned to lead time provides indirect evidence that innovating firms rely on a period of market exclusivity to obtain a return on their fixed investment.

The combined analytical power of the Yale and Carnegie-Mellon surveys is enhanced by their relative timing. The Yale survey occurred before the 'strengthening' of the US patent system, generally dated from the creation of the CAFC in 1982, and the latter after this 'strengthening' had begun.[7] Cohen et al (2000) conclude that the major change in mechanisms to ensure profitable innovation is a considerable increase in the importance of secrecy.[8] They also suggest that patents may be more central for larger firms and that there may be a larger minority of industries where patents are counted as a major mechanism of appropriation (Cohen et al 2000: 13). Given the significant increase in the value of patents as a result of decisions by the CAFC, such an increase is not surprising. It does, however, need to be interpreted in the light of the reasons given for patenting, which are discussed in Section 2.4. Overall, however, the data from the CMS confirm the findings of the earlier studies: except in a narrow range of industries patents are far less important than market mechanisms in ensuring a profitable return to R&D expenditure. That is, with a few exceptions, there is no market failure in innovation.

While these data do not directly address the question of copying, they provide complementary evidence that copying takes time. Firms in most industries confirm that being first in the market (lead time) is a critical mechanism for ensuring their innovation investments are profitable. These findings have been replicated in Japan, Canada, Switzerland, and in many European Union countries.[9] The overwhelming evidence from this wide range of empirical studies is well reviewed in López (2009).[10] The policy implications are significant.

The findings also raise the question of the so-called "patenting paradox". If patents are largely ineffective, why do firms take them out? The answer lies in the strength of the monopoly provided by patents – the ability to prevent use of independently invented innovations. Substantial data are available on reasons for patenting, and these clearly indicate that a very large majority of patents are taken out as insurance against infringement suits or to participate in cross-licensing regimes. The evidence on reasons for patenting is considered further in Section 2.4 when attention is turned to the proportion of innovations induced by the patent system.

Overall these empirical studies show little evidence of market failure because of costless copying. The market for innovation only fails in very particular circumstances – where knowledge is highly codified and there are relatively large numbers of firms with the requisite knowledge. These features characterise the pharmaceutical industry but few others.

2.3 NET EXTERNALITIES

New technologies drive economic growth through the diffusion of new knowledge, which spills over to parties not involved in its production. Such spillovers are a very important factor in productivity growth. They are also frequently invoked by industry lobbyists as a reason for 'strong' patent 'protection' (e.g. Maddock 2002). The exclusion (monopoly) mechanism of patent policy is designed to reduce these spillovers and thus directly impedes economic growth. At the same time, if more investment in new technology is encouraged, this can drive a higher rate of economic growth.

Most theoretical expositions on knowledge spillovers are for closed economies. As spillover benefits (positive externalities) need paths to flow through, and can flow overseas, this is a major limit to their value to a nation. A number of analysts have noted that optimal patent policy in a technology-importing nation may well be very different from that in a technology-exporting nation (Penrose 1951; BIE 1994; Gruen et al 1996). In smaller countries, or countries with little depth in their industrial base, the domestic social rate of return may not be much above the private return to R&D, due to cross-border spillovers (NOIE 2004). Very few countries are net exporters of technology. But even in a technology-exporting nation, the flow of spillover benefits to other countries may affect the net benefits of a patent system.

The social return to innovation includes the private return and any externalities. The externalities take two principal forms: increases in consumer surplus, and knowledge flows.[11] To the extent that an innovator can exercise monopoly power, consumer surplus benefits will be lower. To the extent that patents are effective in preventing imitation and adaptation, knowledge flows (spillovers) may be lower. The net positive externalities flowing from industrial innovation are thus likely to be higher when a patent regime has high inventiveness standards.

There are two types of empirical studies on the externalities from industrial innovation. Econometric studies generally used highly aggregated data, for example national accounts data, stock market data, or linked company and patent databases. Case studies use more finely granulated data but are limited in their sample size. Both are plagued by measurement problems. There are massive problems in adequately measuring knowledge, changes in knowledge, own knowledge, public domain knowledge and knowledge appropriated from private owners. Nor is it easy to separate knowledge from capital – indeed there are arguments as to whether *disembodied* knowledge can have any direct impact on economic output.

The seminal case study used as evidence of high social returns from industrial innovation is the 1977 study by Mansfield and colleagues which estimated the median social return to R&D at 56 per cent. This study is repeatedly cited to indicate that industrial innovation generates a high social return, though the authors themselves emphasised the care that was needed in interpreting their results, given the limitations created by the assumptions in their model (Mansfield et al 1977). What is rarely reported is that this study is based on only 17 innovations (13 products and four processes). Nor is it always noted that the methodology is based on estimated consumer surplus, and does not attempt to measure knowledge spillovers. The estimates are gross consumer surplus not net surplus after taking account of products displaced by the innovations. The estimates therefore need to be reduced by such offsets if they are to be used to estimate *net* consumer surplus benefits from innovation.

A further finding of the study that is rarely referred to is that six of the 17 innovations had both high private and high social returns so may well have occurred without the patent incentive. Another five had low or negative social returns so it would not be rational to encourage these. Only six of the 17 had both a high social return and a low private return (Mansfield et al 1977: 233). That is, only about one-third fell into the category that would be targeted by rational patent policy: innovations with high gross social returns but where the private return might be too low for the investment to take place. A core policy question is whether today's pervasive R&D support programs would, alone, be sufficient to induce such innovations.

Also available, but less widely quoted, is the Bureau of Industry Economics (BIE) study of spillovers, which usefully considers both consumer surplus and knowledge spillovers (BIE 1994). Benefits frequently flow along the value chain, i.e. between parties in a market relationship with each other: suppliers and customers. Where there is such a relationship benefits are measured as a change in consumer or producer surplus, rather than as spillover benefits. The study also emphasises two factors that are critical for benefits to eventuate: in regard to knowledge spillovers, *market depth*, i.e. a sufficiency of other firms, is necessary for there to be high social returns. In regard to firms in market relationships, *competition* is essential if the innovator is to pass benefits to users of the innovation.

Turning now to the econometric studies, two review articles reach somewhat different conclusions, but are useful in marshalling the available evidence. Sena (2004) reviews four types of econometric studies and concludes that sizeable intra- and inter-industry spillovers exist. In contrast the US Congressional Budget Office (CBO) considers the evidence from three different types of studies is relatively speculative, largely because of severe measurement difficulties. The large econometric studies give very divergent estimates of the value of social returns to industrial innovation. In particular, estimated spillovers are much lower from time-series than cross-sectional studies (US CBO 2005). As the key policy issue is the impact over time of innovation spillovers on productivity and economic growth, the lower time-series estimates are of some concern.

There is consensus on more detailed aspects of knowledge spillovers. Such spillovers flow through a variety of channels (Sena 2004: 318); firms must invest in their own innovation capabilities if they wish to be able to benefit from spillovers (Cohen and Levinthal 1989); and they may be higher between firms in technological or geographic proximity (Jaffe 1986, 1988; Porter 1990). Differences in the magnitude of knowledge spillovers between industries are also reported, with some contributing a high level of knowledge spillover benefits, and others very little (Bernstein and

Nadiri 1991). Clearly the magnitude of knowledge spillovers is variable and contingent.

Overall, then, there is still some doubt about the evidence that intervention in the innovation market is needed because of high positive externalities. Plant and Machlup both expressed considerable reservations that re-allocating resources to inventive activity through the patent system is welfare-enhancing. Plant pointed to the wide range of incremental improvements occurring outside research laboratories as being cumulatively more important to the development of technology than formal R&D (Plant 1934).[12] Machlup was unsure that industrial R&D had a higher pay-off, in terms of economic growth, than other major drivers of growth, such as education (Machlup 1958).

These empirical studies typically use R&D expenditure as a key independent variable. The relationship between R&D expenditure and patenting has changed significantly over the past two decades (Kortum and Lerner 1999; Jaffe 2000; Blind et al 2003; Hall 2005). So they provide only very indirect evidence on the social return to the patent system. They do not begin to address whether the net social return for the whole set of patents granted in a year is positive. To date this question has been asked only in respect of private returns to patenting, and only in respect of US publicly listed firms (Bessen 2006). This study showed a negative private return, except for pharmaceutical firms.

2.4 DO PATENTS INDUCE INNOVATION?

Some analysts take a theoretical view that the level of investment in innovation will be sub-optimal unless the innovator is able to capture the *full* benefits of each innovation (e.g. ACIP 2008: 7). Baumol shows that this is not a realistic position and that in practice benefits need to be shared between the innovator and society (Baumol 2000). This is well illustrated in an interesting study of private seed research. The alleged difficulties in appropriating a return to investment in innovation apply more strongly in agricultural than industrial markets. But Pray and colleagues have shown that both the innovator and the user can simultaneously benefit. In a study of the private seed industry in India they find that the private return to R&D was 17 per cent while farmers, distributors and dealers received between 61 and 86 per cent of the total benefits from the seed research (Pray et al 1991: 321). A delightful win-win outcome.

From a policy viewpoint, the critical question is whether the patents *which are induced by the patent system* create sufficient social benefits to offset the social costs attributable to all granted patents. It is wasteful from a policy perspective to provide the innovator with a return greater than that needed to induce the invention. This, of course, would include a risk-adjusted profit on the capital invested. Effectively there is an exchange of society's power to create an artificial monopoly for an adequate share of the consequent economic benefits. Spillover benefits from innovations which were not induced by the patent incentive – which would have happened anyway – cannot be regarded as benefits from the patent system.

The substantial empirical research on appropriability and reasons for patenting can be used to develop rough estimates of the proportion of patented inventions that might be induced by patent policy.

The 1994 CMS asked R&D performing firms why they patented their most recent patented innovations. Firms were asked to choose from a list of seven reasons and multiple choices were allowed (Cohen et al 2000: 17). Naturally most firms reported prevention of copying as a reason.[13] The next most frequently given reason was to block rivals. Blocking involves the use of patents to prevent other firms patenting related inventions (Cohen et al 2000: 17).[14] The next most frequently reported reason was to prevent infringement suits. This was followed by reputation and use in negotiating access to other firms' patented technologies. Reputation was particularly often reported by smaller firms (Cohen et al 2000: 24).

Once the data are weighted by the number of patent applications, the results change appreciably only for two reasons: prevention of infringement suits and use in negotiations (Cohen et al 2000: 18). Both increase in importance, with 79 per cent of product patents taken to prevent infringement suits (63 per cent for process patents). Comparable figures for access to cross-licensing are 58 and 49 per cent. These data indicate that firms which patent frequently are particularly concerned to protect themselves against litigation, and to participate in cross-licensing negotiations. Thus in terms of patent applications, very many are filed for reasons that are dysfunctional in terms of overall economic welfare (blocking rivals) or because of the very existence of the patent system (preventing infringement suits or participating in negotiations for access to complementary or overlapping technologies).

Such strategic reasons for patenting are confirmed by Blind and colleagues, who review a small number of studies on this topic, and add new 2002 data from German firms which actively use the patent system (Blind et al 2006). They suggest that the motives for patenting are becoming increasingly uncoupled from the need for 'protection' from imitation. Their review of mainly European surveys systematically confirms that important reasons for patenting are defensive and offensive blocking and negotiations for exchange of technologies. One of the most interesting surveys they report investigates changes in motives to patent among very large firms over a ten-year period. The most important change influencing increased patenting is patenting by other market participants.[15]

These data suggest that a major factor underlying patenting activity is simply the existence of the patent system (Merges 1997: 129). This is not surprising when one considers that the patent system can inhibit independent invention. As the level of patenting rises, so does the risk that a firm will be found to infringe another firm's patents. The rational response is to insure against this by taking out one's own patents.[16] The only firms at risk of facing a patent infringement suit are innovating firms (Bessen and Meurer 2008).

This is a long way from the goal of inducing more innovative activity. It is not – or should not be – the objective of patent policy to induce more patent applications.

In industries where few firms report patents as important, it seems unlikely that many innovations are induced by the patent system. Mansfield specifically asked what innovations would not have been commercially introduced or developed in the absence of patents. Outside the chemical industries the highest reported percentage was for machinery, where 15 to 17 per cent of innovations would not have occurred.[17] In contrast a small number of firms, particularly those in the pharmaceuticals and fine chemicals industries report that patents are an important appropriation mechanism. For these firms a high proportion of innovations may well be induced by the patent system. Again Mansfield provides data on this issue. He reports that, absent patents, 60 to 65 per cent of pharmaceutical innovations would not have been developed or commercially introduced (Mansfield 1986: 175). So even in the pharmaceutical industry some 35 to 40 per cent of innovations may have occurred in the absence of patents.[18] Mansfield's data suggest that up to 65 per cent of pharmaceutical and somewhat less than 15 to 20 per cent of other innovations may be induced by the patent system.

Drawing on data on defensive patenting from the Carnegie-Mellon survey, between 63 and 74 per cent of innovations are reported as patented to protect against infringement suits. The corollary is that some 26 to 37 per cent may be required for other than defensive purposes.[19] A generous assumption about induced inventions is therefore that between 25 and 40 per cent are induced by the patent system.

Two dimensions are used to develop some fairly rough estimates of innovations induced by the patent system. Firstly inducement rates are estimated separately for pharmaceuticals compared to all other industries. Secondly market size issues are considered as a basis for estimating whether a national patent system induces innovation in foreign firms.

Considering first the industry dimension, granted patents are separated into a group where a very high proportion of patents may be induced and a group where a much lower proportion are likely to be induced. The first group is the pharmaceutical and fine chemicals industries, as the survey data show unambiguously that these firms systematically report patents as important in ensuring a return to innovation. I assume that *all* patented inventions in these fields are induced by the patent system. This substantially over-estimates induced patents in this group, as the survey data (and real world experience) show that some pharmaceutical and chemical innovation would occur absent patents.[20]

In most countries, the bulk of patents are owned by overseas-based companies (Bates 2003). So in making estimates of induced innovation in any specific country, it is important to consider whether the patent system in one country will induce innovation overseas. The probability will vary with the size of the market where the innovation is being patented, in comparison to the size of the market in the innovator's home country. The size of the US market may well mean that US patents induce innovation in overseas firms. In smaller markets such as Australia it seems unlikely that the patent system induces foreign innovation except in even smaller countries. If an innovator's domestic market is sufficiently large for the full investment (including a risk-adjusted profit margin) to be recouped domestically, obtaining monopoly prices from overseas consumers does nothing to induce the investment; it simply provides a rental stream from overseas.[21]

In making estimates of induced patents in Australia, it seems improbable that Australian patents would offer much of an inducement effect for innovators from the North American, Japanese or UK/European markets – the Australian market is only 2 per cent of the OECD market.[22] The small proportion of additional sales in Australia is unlikely to make a critical difference to the investment decision except in unusual circumstances. I assume no innovations patented in Australia by innovators resident in the G7 countries are induced by the Australian patent system. In contrast, a New Zealand innovator might take into account the possibility of an Australian patent monopoly in determining whether to proceed with a costly innovation, as the Australian market is much larger. In estimating what patents in Australia are induced from firms' resident outside the G7 countries, I treat all these in the same way as domestic patenters. That is, I assume that all pharmaceutical patents are induced and that in all other technology areas between 25 and 40 per cent of patents are induced by the Australian patent system – again clearly over-estimates.

Combining these two sets of assumptions provides an estimate that between 10,030 and 13,090 of the 203,815 patents granted in Australia

Table 2.1 Estimated induced patents: USA and Australia

	USA, 2001–2005		Australia, 1990–2006	
	lower estimate	upper estimate	lower estimate	upper estimate
	Assumed % of patents induced			
Pharmaceuticals				
G5/G7 countries	50	50	0	0
Other countries	100	100	100	100
Other industries				
G5/G7 countries	12.5	20	0	0
Other countries	25	40	25	40
	Estimated induced patents			
Number induced	238,150	325,880	10,030	13,090
% of total granted	29.4%	40.2%	4.9%	6.4%
Induced patents:	Induced patents providing domestic spillovers			
Owned by residents	89,000	122,000		
Owned by non-residents but produced in USA	104,680	143,000		
Total with domestic spillovers	193,680	265,030	6,750	8,810
% of total granted	23.9%	32.7%	3.3%	4.3%

Notes: USA: Total grants for 2001–05 are 810,487. Calculated from USPTO data for "Life and Agricultural Sciences and Testing Method" and "Compositions and Synthetic Resins; Chemical Compounds." Classes are as described in the U.S. Classification System (Arranged by Related Subjects) June 2006 version from http://www.uspto.gov/web/offices/opc/documents/classescombined.pdf, and http://www.uspto.gov/web/offices/ac/ido/oeip/taf/tecstc/classes.htm (accessed 5 March 2007).

Australia: Total grants for 1990–2006 are 203,815. Calculated from data formerly available on IPAustralia website (accessed 19 July 2008): (http://www.ipaustralia.gov.au/about/statistics.shtml, Table P31 (Feb08) Countries of Origin of Granted and Certified Patents). Pharmaceutical patents are taken to be those from technology groups "organic fine chemicals" and "pharmaceuticals, cosmetics" (from http://www.ipaustralia.gov.au/about/statistics.shtml, Table P61 (Oct07) Standard Applications by Technology Real standard patent applications).

between 1990 and 2006 may have been induced by the patent system. This is some 4.9 to 6.4 per cent of granted patents (Table 2.1). This low figure should not surprise. It has long been clear that a patent system is unlikely to induce much innovation in a small economy, especially where the proportion of activity in high-technology areas is low (Penrose 1951).

In contrast, given the size of the US market, US patents might well induce innovations from innovator firms in many other countries, including those with large domestic markets. Here I assume innovation is induced for 50 per cent of US patented innovations from innovators in the five large G7 economies outside North America (Japan, France, Italy, Germany and the UK),[23] and for 100 per cent of patents from other countries. These figures are then modified by technology-specific inducement factors. I again assume that for pharmaceutical and fine chemical patents,[24] 100 per cent of patents might be induced. For all other classes I assume that between 25 and 40 per cent of patents are induced.

These rather brave assumptions (set out in the top block of Table 2.1) provide an estimate that between 238,150 and 325,880 of the 810,487 patents granted in the USA between 2001 and 2005 are induced by the US patent system.[25] In other words some 29 to 40 per cent of US patents may reflect induced innovation.

It is these induced innovations which are responsible for any positive benefit attributable to a patent system. Such positive externalities and dynamic efficiency gains flow from the patent-induced re-allocation of resources. But if an induced patented product is imported, the resource re-allocation will be in the country of origin. And so will most spillover benefits. Where knowledge spillovers depend on local working for the transfer of the important associated know-how, then knowledge spillovers will not flow from that proportion of patented goods which are imported, even where they are induced by the patent system.

There are, of course, few data on the proportion of patented products locally produced.[26] But it is only these locally produced induced patents that provide spillover benefits to offset any costs of the patent system. Given Australia's small market size and low tariff barriers, many products patented in Australia are imported. A rough proxy has been adopted for locally produced patented goods: those where the patent is owned by an Australian innovator.[27] On this basis some 6,750 to 8,810 patents granted between 1990 and 2006 are induced inventions owned by Australian residents (3.3 to 4.3 per cent of all patents). It is this set of patents which must generate the dynamic efficiency gains to offset any social costs created by the 203,815 patents granted in the same period. Each of these domestically produced induced patents must generate sufficient benefits to offset the costs of between 23 and 30 granted patents. This implies a need for quite large average knowledge spillovers for the Australian patent system to confer a positive economic outcome.

In the USA about 37 per cent of induced patents are owned by non-residents of the USA. But it may well be rational for overseas firms to locate production in this large market. This effect is enhanced by US buying practices which can make it difficult for overseas producers to sell into US markets. Consequently some overseas owned induced patents will be produced in the USA generating spillover benefits there. In the absence of any direct information on the proportion of overseas-owned patents made in the USA (rather than imported) I assume that 50 per cent are manufactured in the USA. This gives a final guesstimate of the number of patents which might generate dynamic efficiency gains for the US economy of between 24 and 33 per cent of granted patents. The non-induced granted patents may generate static welfare losses, but cannot generate any benefit attributable to the patent system. Each domestically produced induced innovation needs to produce benefits to offset the costs of only between three and four granted patents.

2.5 WHAT ARE THE COSTS OF GRANTING PATENTS?

While the percentage of granted patents which might give rise to dynamic benefits in the USA is ten times the magnitude in Australia, to conclude that the net impact of the patent system in the USA is positive would be to make some important assumptions about costs. The idea that patent policy is the most efficient available mechanism for inducing a higher level of innovation is at least partly based on the assumption that the costs of a patent system are trivial (Andersen 2003). In fact there are few data on the costs of patent systems, particularly the social costs. There are certainly no empirical data to support the standard assumption of low costs.

Indeed there is very little literature on patent system costs and what there is focuses on the private costs incurred by patent holders (Macdonald 2002: 31). Even here it has been extremely difficult to quantify costs, as demonstrated by Mooney and Oppenheim (1994a, 1994b) in their work on the British patent system. Taking an indirect approach, Bessen has estimated the net private cost of patents for publicly listed US firms and finds a net private loss among US publicly listed firms, once pharmaceutical firms are excluded (Bessen 2006). Indeed Bessen and Meurer estimate that over two-thirds of the private return from global patents systems flow to chemical and pharmaceutical firms. They further estimate that over half of the private return from global patents systems is highly concentrated, flowing to a small number of large pharmaceutical firms (Bessen and Meurer 2008: 108). There is a reasonable academic literature on patent litigation (for example Lanjouw and Lerner 1997; Graham and Somaya 2003; Bessen and Meurer 2007), but there do not appear to be any good data on the payments made. There are however a number of well-known stories about specific cases. The E-Data case involved a "point of sales" kiosk. Some 16 years after this invention the CAFC reinterpreted "point of sales" kiosks to include the internet – not in existence when the invention was made. E-Data successfully sued more than 100 parties including small businesses and individuals (Bessen and Meurer 2008: 1–9). Kodak's 1976 instant photography products were found to have infringed Polaroid's patents and the final payment was US$873.1 million (Quillen 2008).

A few authors discuss the social costs of patent system but tend to the view that detailed empirical estimates are impossible (for example Machlup 1958; Cole 2001). Other authors note positive or negative impacts, generally with no empirical support other than anecdotes. Moir (2009b) makes an initial attempt to codify the types of social cost imposed by a patent system and to bring together the available information on the social costs (and benefits) of patent systems.

Of course, apart from noise, information search costs and the potentially questionable efficiency of resources allocated to obtaining patents, patents that are not used are unlikely to impose significant external costs. So the issue of the proportion of patents used becomes central to the question of the social costs of patent systems.

Some argue that very few patents are used – perhaps as few as 5 per cent (see, for example, Lemley 2001; Blonder 2005). But neither cites any evidence to support this figure. Likewise a European Union study on small firms and patent enforcement provides no supporting evidence or citations for the statement that it "is well known that the majority of patented inventions are never used in practice, either because they are overtaken by further advances, or they are seen by their owners to be uneconomic, or for some other reason" (European Union 2000: 30).

These claims of very low use run counter to the empirical data. Firestone found that 50 per cent of Canadian patents were used to support production. He also reported figures from the UK and the USA: in the UK 30 per cent of patents were worked (Firestone 1971: 14), while in the USA large firms worked 49 per cent of their patents and small firms 71 per cent (Firestone 1971: 149). These estimates are consistent with reports from a 1957 US study that 41 to 55 per cent of patents were used commercially, with up to 71 per cent used among small firms (Griliches 1990: 1679). While this evidence is dated, it does suggest that at least a substantial minority of patents are used in commercial production.

Patent renewal data suggest that many patents continue to have value for their owners, implying some form of use. Griliches (1990: 1679–80) summarises the early evidence as indicating that about half of granted patents are renewed beyond year 10 and about 10 per cent to the maximum limit.[28] Renewal rates in the USA do not show the smooth curves evident in other countries as US renewal fees are payable at only three points over the 20 year potential life. The percentage of US patents renewed to their full term is estimated at nearly 40 per cent (Thomas 1999b). These data show that while many patents lose any value quickly, a substantial minority retain value for some time – their private value at least appears to exceed the costs of renewal.

The concept of patent use has changed radically since Firestone's study. Since the success of the patent lobby in eliminating local working as a condition of patent grant, interest in the use of patents to support product production has waned. However as the CMS data cited above show, patents are now used for a variety of purposes, many involving strategic uses. These include enhancing reputation, a use which likely has little impact on third parties, and insuring against infringement suits, where the main use may well be passive. In contrast blocking patents may impose substantial costs on other firms. And in industries where whole portfolios of patents are exchanged to gain access to essential and closely related technology, high costs are imposed on all parties.

Some of the literature presumes that because of the existence of close substitutes, very few patents have any real degree of monopoly power and so argue that they impose few costs (for example Gans et al 2004). If this is the case then very few patents can be induced by the patent system: if the patent holder cannot achieve higher prices there is no incentive to increase investment. A brief review of legal cases shows that many apparently obvious patents – the kind of innovations that might have many close substitutes – can impose significant costs on other innovators. Amazon's 1-click case is well known and initially imposed substantial costs on competitors. The patent was issued in September 1999 and Amazon obtained an injunction preventing barnesandnoble.com from using their independently invented system over the end-of-year major shopping season. The injunction was lifted 14 months later because of doubts about the patent's validity. Amazon settled out of court, presumably compensating barnesandnoble.com for their losses. The patent remained on the books until late 2007 when, after an independent request for re-examination, the USPTO rejected 22 of the 26 claims. Amazon then amended claims 1 and 11, restricting them to a shopping cart model of commerce and the revised patent was confirmed in March 2010.[29] There is no process to recompense any other party for any license fees extracted during the decade when the invalid claims held sway.

In the Australian *Welcome* case, the core inventive concept in the consumer loyalty card was agreed by all parties to be well known. Despite this the judge upheld its validity. The respondent, who had independently developed a similar smart card use, has gone out of business. It would be preferable to have systematic data on the outcomes of patent litigation rather than such individual stories. But in the absence of systematic data such individual cases show that it cannot reasonably be presumed that obvious patents cannot do real economic damage to competitors. The very real possibility that patents impose substantial social costs should not be dismissed without proper investigation. Indeed a cursory consideration of the impact of high pharmaceutical prices in low-income countries makes it evident that the costs can include preventable deaths. A very high price for those so affected.

Even if a patent is not used it adds to noise in the system. Most patent infringement cases involve inadvertent trespass (Bessen and Meurer 2008), and this is in part due to the difficulty in determining what has already been patented. Patent applicants play strategic games, where the key objective of a patent specification seems to be to hide rather than disclose information. Stallman (2001) provides an interesting case for a method of recalculating the values in spreadsheets where the essential technical terms were completely missing from the specification. Large volumes of potentially trivial patents make the search for those that involve genuine technological advances more difficult and expensive. This imposes higher costs on other innovating firms who need to know what grants and applications are close to their own technology.

Where patents are used, one of the most important social costs is any negative impact on subsequent innovation (see for example David 1993; Macdonald 2004). Decades ago Penrose suggested, "[b]oth within and between countries the greatest social cost of patents arises from the restrictions they put on the right to imitate new ideas" (Penrose 1951: 99). Cohen provides one of the more detailed assessments of the technological hold-up problem, discussing the negative impact of the patent system on airplane development and radio technology. He concludes that "[i]f the technology in question is sufficiently important, only one or a few instances of [restricted access or an anticommons] may impose considerable social cost" (Cohen 2005: 63). As noted above, there is a fine line between imitation and improvement and consequently subsequent innovation. Not only can negative impacts on subsequent innovation create direct losses, but also – because innovation is cumulative, evolutionary and path-dependent – it can change the direction of future technological development.

Other social costs include the direct welfare losses due to reduced (monopoly) output and reduced competition. Investigating these issues is complex. Analyses of welfare losses from reduced output tend to be theoretical, but provide some useful insights into the quite different welfare impacts of alternative types of innovation (see, for example, Tisdell 1981; Deardorff 1992; Winter 1993). Cost-reducing innovations are most tractable for economic analysis, but their welfare implications are quite different from those of new product development, particularly radically new products. Few would question the strong positive externalities arising from the introduction of penicillin (which was not induced by patents) or the birth control pill (which probably was induced by patents).

From a national economic perspective a particularly concerning cost is where patents reduce market competition by excluding new entrants. Cockburn and MacGarvie (2006) have investigated the role of patents as barriers to or facilitators of entry in the software industry and find *direct* evidence hard to find. In their study of 27 narrowly-defined classes of software products they find that entry is lower in industries where there are more software patents, suggesting that patents do operate as a barrier to entry. But they also find that firms holding software patents are more likely to enter these markets, suggesting that patent ownership assists entry, at least in markets where patents are prevalent. The results are very sensitive to the assumptions (Cockburn and MacGarvie 2006: 35).

It is a matter of considerable concern to effective patent policy development that so few data are available to properly measure the costs, or benefits, of patent systems. In 1984 the committee reviewing Australia's patent system recommended that periodically, on patent renewal, the government ask for information on how the renewed patent is being used (IPAC 1984: 10). This recommendation has never been implemented. Nowadays patent offices hand out tens of thousands of patent monopolies a year yet none collects any information on how these monopolies are used. This is the antithesis of evidence-based public policy. It suggests a blithe disregard for the public interest.

Indeed there appear to be some concerted efforts to prevent the collection of data on the impact of the US patent system. Kahin reports that, subsequent to the *State Street* case, the White House Office of Science and Technology Policy commissioned the Science and Technology Policy Institute at RAND to undertake a study on software patent quality and business effects. He goes on to report that "it was suspended at the request of a U.S. multinational company concerned that the study would undercut efforts to secure greater international acceptance of software patents" (Kahin 2003a). Bessen and Meurer comment that the FTC recommendation most prominently rejected by the Intellectual Property Owners Association (dominated by patent lawyers from large firms) was recommendation 10: "expand consideration of economic learning and competition policy concerns in patent law decisionmaking" (Bessen and Meurer 2008: 293–4).

2.6 ARE THERE NET BENEFITS FROM PATENT SYSTEMS?

This discussion confirms that patent policy is a very blunt instrument. The empirical data suggest that patents are effective in achieving a higher level of innovative activity only in a narrow range of circumstances. It is a minority of patented innovations that are induced by the patent system, though in the USA it may be a substantial minority. The owners of the majority of patents may therefore receive windfall profits. Spillover benefits are lower than often alleged, and are contingent on a number of factors including location of production and industry depth. While costs cannot be quantified, there are some potentially serious costs that incur high risks though hopefully with a low probability. History has shown, however, that technological development can be impeded by patent systems.

The conclusion that patent policy does not confer clear net economic benefits is similar to that reached, by different routes, by many others. Granstrand concluded that "the patent system . . . has been neither necessary nor sufficient for technical and/or economic progress at country and company level historically" (Granstrand 1999: 44). Encaoua and colleagues suggest that if the policy interest is the incentive to invest, then patents should not be the default policy choice (Encaoua et al 2006). Boldrin and Levine (2004) suggest patents should be used only when the innovation investment is large and indivisible.[30] Winter, using an evolutionary model, demonstrated that both R&D investment and total surplus would be higher without patents (Winter 1993). Dutton (1984) and Mandeville (1996) both concluded that the most balanced (welfare-enhancing) patent policy was a 'weak' patent system. More recently, in a theoretical assessment of a situation where government has the opportunity to subsidise R&D and where imitation takes time, Bonatti and Comino (2011) find that social welfare is higher in the absence of patents.

Despite the lack of a sound and substantiated theoretical basis, and a complete lack of empirical evidence on its effectiveness, patent policy has been strengthened in ways that seem to reduce net positive externalities and increase social costs. Jaffe, for example, reports "widespread unease that the costs of stronger patent protection may exceed the benefits" (Jaffe 2000: 555). In part, the strengthening has been due to decisions by individual judges, a story investigated in more detail in Chapter 3. In part it is due to successful lobbying by the small number of firms which are major beneficiaries of the patent system (Landes and Posner 2004).[31] In part it is due to a general shift in the pendulum towards viewing patents in a more positive light (Granstrand 1999).

How patent system balance works out in practice is an empirical question and the answer may vary depending on the industry structure of an economy and market size. Another very important factor in patent balance is the quantum of new knowledge required for a patent grant. All other things being equal a higher new knowledge requirement makes it more likely that there will be spillover benefits. This would also reduce the proportion of trivial patents, thus reducing noise and transaction costs.

The data presented above suggest that innovation markets are most likely to fail where relative imitation costs and the overall investment cost is large compared to the time taken to imitate. These conditions are found in the pharmaceutical industry, but in few others. In pharmaceuticals, innovations are highly codified, making imitation faster, and Phase III clinical trial costs are very high. Generic companies can avoid the full costs of Phase III trials, thus radically reducing their development costs. In most other industries patents are less relevant to obtaining a return on R&D investment and are much less likely to induce investment that would not otherwise occur. This brings the discussion full circle to Arrow's seminal article (Arrow 1962). He concluded that markets were most likely to fail where the innovation cost was large and lumpy and suggested that the appropriate response was public financing.

In the post-war period most industrialised countries introduced substantial programs of public subsidy for industrial R&D investment. In addition in some countries there is substantial direct government investment in R&D. But there has been no simultaneous review of patent policy to consider whether in this new world of public subsidy to R&D patent monopolies continue to be effective economic policy.[32] It is apparent from the material presented above that the real-world existence of spillover benefits from patented innovations is both highly variable and contingent on the location of production and the depth of industry. Obviously it is also dependent on the height of the inventive step.

It is also apparent that, even in the best of circumstances, only a minority of patented innovations are induced by patent policy. At a minimum each induced innovation may need to generate spillovers that exceed the cost of three to four patents if the overall system is to generate benefits. While the costs of granted patents cannot be quantified, neither can they be dismissed as negligible, at least without some data to support this assumption. So on both the benefits and the costs side appropriate data are wanting. There has been more progress on the benefits side. The substantial data now available raise considerable doubts about the alleged benefits of patent systems. Further work is needed on patent system costs and a useful starting point would be for governments to collect data on how the monopolies they grant are used. This should be complemented by better data on the impact of patents held by one firm on other innovating firms. Such data could readily be collected through the National Innovation Surveys.

3. Who determines patent policy: judges, lobbyists or legislatures?

3.1 INTRODUCTION

Patent Acts generally do not state any objectives. They simply set out the conditions for patent grant and the benefits to the patent-holder. The European Patent Convention (EPC) states no purpose except to "to strengthen co-operation between the States of Europe in respect of the protection of inventions" (preamble). The Australian *Patents Act 1990* states no objective, simply limiting the grant of a patent to an invention which is "a manner of new manufacture". In the USA, Article 1, Section 8 of the Constitution gives Congress the power to "promote the Progress of Science and useful Arts, by securing for limited Times to Authors and Inventors the exclusive Right to their respective Writings and Discoveries." While not repeated in any form in their patent statute, legal decision-makers in the USA sometimes refer to this authoritative statement of purpose, though not all agree that 'useful arts' means technology.[1]

What patent statutes do say is what criteria must be met for grant: novelty, inventiveness and utility. They also say that the grant of a patent monopoly is conditional: information about the patented invention must be disclosed. Because the objective of patent policy is not specified in the legislation, but the disclosure conditionality is, disclosure is often given weight in legal circles as the objective of the system (Ghosh 2004). Some therefore argue that patents lead to higher economic growth, not by inducing more invention, but because of information disclosure. While this theory is strongly held in legal circles, it has not generally been well regarded by economists and has not been empirically tested (Mazzoleni and Nelson 1998b). There is substantial evidence from national innovation surveys that patent information is little used by technology innovators. One reason is that applicants hide critical technical information when drafting patent specifications (Labich 1988; Stallman 2001).

It is within this environment that individual patent disputes come before the courts. In disputes about patentable subject matter the patent office is usually involved. But case law about other eligibility criteria is often determined in disputes between private parties. A standard response to being charged with infringement is to counter-charge that the patent in question is invalid. Cases which revolve round aspects of the policy rules affecting the key eligibility criteria of novelty, inventiveness and utility often do not involve any consideration of the public interest. Yet the judgements in these cases define and refine the policy rules that constitute the patent system.

This chapter looks first at decisions which change the boundaries of the patent system – what kinds of things can be patented. When patent policy was first designed, and during its early centuries, mechanical invention dominated and most patents were for artefacts. However during the nineteenth century the rise of the chemical industries posed new challenges for patent policy – especially whether chemical compounds were patentable. Germany deliberately chose to exclude chemical compounds from patentability, but in many common law countries such decisions were left to the courts. In the later part of the twentieth century the computing industry raised similar challenges with respect to software. In the USA, the UK and Australia government reviews recommended against allowing patents for software. In the USA and Australia no specific exclusions were written into the patent statutes and courts ignored these reviews (and their acceptance by governments) and started granting software patents.

In Europe governments decided to specifically exclude software from patentability. This legislative exclusion applies to software "as such" but legal semantics are used to re-classify what others would consider to be software as not-software for purposes of the EPC (Bakels and Hugenholtz 2002). Some authors have pointed out the business incentive for patent offices to expand their scope, and this is particularly possible where patent offices also act as judge and jury (Thambisetty 2009: 12; Drahos 2010). As a consequence the EPC has granted 40,000 or more software patents (Miceli 2005), providing a considerable revenue stream. In some jurisdictions courts have begun to question whether any technology basis is needed for an invention to be patentable. The story of these changes to patentable subject matter is briefly reviewed in Section 3.2.

The focus in telling this story is on key policy decisions and how these arose. This overview of legal doctrines is not a legal history. The objective is to provide, for a non-legal audience of policy analysts, an insight into the changing balance of the patent system. The legal decisions are presented from an economic viewpoint – a quite different perspective from a legal analysis of the same material. This is not to say that legal analyses cannot also be useful for policy. Particularly interesting is Thambisetty's documentation of doctrinal incoherence (a range of silly outcomes) in patent law (Thambisetty 2009). Understanding how the law has changed over time is important to understanding the current state of balance in the patent system.

Attention is then turned, in Section 3.3, to how policy in regard to the eligibility criteria of novelty and inventiveness has changed. How these qualitative criteria are dealt with by courts provides a fascinating story about efforts to turn a subjective decision into an objective one. During this process the focus has shifted from the benefits provided by the invention for which a patent is sought to a focus on whether a patent can be refused. The question has become "is it obvious?" rather than "what benefits are contributed?" The definition of obvious is tied up in many rules about what existing knowledge can be considered and how the person defining obviousness would approach the issue. This story indicates the key role played by judges, largely in determining private disputes. It also suggests that the effort to make a subjective judgement objective has resulted in throwing the baby out with the bath water.

A final issue in assessing these two parallel stories is how judicial decisions flow between countries and influence each other. At least in this area, common law countries tend to look to each other for legal precedent. Sometimes this cross-national referencing can be quite complex; for example Canada's statute law is modelled on US law, but case law tends to follow the UK (Bochnovic 1982). The tendency, especially in smaller countries, to look overseas for precedents reinforces the concept of *stare decisis* – that any specific decision acquires a strong precedent-setting force for future decisions.[2] Before the development of good written records this concept had less impact, but its formal adoption in the late eighteenth century solidified this approach (Walterscheid 1995b). This contrasts with the European approach as can be seen in the nonchalance of the EPO to the apparently conflicting decisions made by EPO Appeal Boards (Pila 2011). Where new doctrines are not independently reviewed the *stare decisis* rule means that economically dysfunctional rules can become firm policy. This is particularly the case where there are no divergent voices from the bench. Quillen (2008) argues that the pre-CAFC situation in the USA provided sounder and more balanced interpretation of patent law. This suggests that common law countries might do well to develop sound review procedures in areas where important economic policy is being developed by lawyers.

3.2 PATENTABLE SUBJECT MATTER

The *Statute of Monopolies 1623* severely curtailed the English royal privilege of granting monopolies. It made only three exceptions of which inventions were one. This exception was highly qualified:

> the sole working or making of any manner of new manufactures within this Realm, to the true and first inventor and inventors of such manufactures, which others at the time of making such letters patent and grants shall not use, *so as also they be not contrary to the law or mischievous to the State, by raising prices of commodities at home or hurt of trade, or generally inconvenient.* (*Statute of Monopolies 1623*, S.6, emphasis added)

Effectively this codified existing common law on monopolies (Bochnovic 1982; Pila 2001). The qualifications in S.6 are more succinctly phrased in the 1641 Massachusetts code of laws, which limits monopolies to "such new inventions *as are profitable to the country*" (Article 9, emphasis added). While the US statutes did not refer to the *Statute of Monopolies*, through the common law heritage of the States they borrowed its terminology and concepts. For example, US patent law has always granted patents of invention only to the "first and true inventor" (Khan 2010).

Given the context of the 1623 Statute, drafted to prevent monopolies which interfered with the common law right to carry on a trade, the focus was on newness.[3] Walterscheid reviews Lord Coke's 1628 discussion of the qualities required for a patent to be valid at law, and identifies a strict prohibition against the patenting of improvements ("so as also they be not contrary to the law") (Walterscheid 1995a: 878). In the first major extension of patent law scope this prohibition was removed in 1776 (Walterscheid 1995b: 779).

3.2.1 Extension to Processes and Chemicals

The second extension to patent scope affected the kinds of things ('subject matter' or kinds of technology) that could be patented. Section 6 was initially read as covering only products – applications for processes were treated with doubt if they did not involve a machine. But in 1842 in *Crane* the English courts granted a patent for hot-air blasting for iron smelting, a case which ". . . has settled for all time that a process as such may be valid subject-matter for a patent" (Curtis and Lahey 1954: 2). This issue, of the extension of patents from products ("manufactures") to processes that were not themselves machines, is central to recent extension of patents to software and business methods (Merges 1999; Stern 1999). Courts have often had difficulty in dealing with process applications.

The third significant subject matter extension was to chemical entities. The role of the chemical industry in the development of patent law is well told elsewhere (Dutfield 2003). There was significant controversy over whether chemical products should be patented. The first (1877) German patent law, adopted only after substantial analysis of the impact of patent law elsewhere, excluded food, drink, medicines and chemical substances from patentability. The availability of patents for chemical products was considered to have caused considerable harm to the development of the French and British chemical industries (Dutfield 2003: 78).

Indeed most European countries excluded chemical substances from patentability until quite recently (Boldrin and Levine 2008: 244). The UK and France were significant exceptions but in 1919 the UK changed its statute to exclude chemical products. This was done both to assist the development of the British chemical industry, which lagged that in Germany (Pitkethly 1999), and to deal with the shortages of medicine (Boldrin and Levine 2008: 249). The exclusion continued until the 1949 Act.[4]

Italy too excluded chemical products from patentability from 1939 until 1978, when a legal challenge by a consortium of pharmaceutical companies led to a ruling that this exception was unconstitutional. This change became possible as Italy had joined the EPC, which provided for patents in all fields of technology.[5] Italy had been a major centre for generic pharmaceuticals, supplying among others the US military (Scherer and Weisburst 1995). But the legal change meant Italy lost competitiveness – every available indicator suggests that the impact of the 'stronger' patent regime on this industry was negative and the percentage of global new chemical entities from Italy actually fell (Boldrin and Levine 2008: 222–3). India, whose patent statute excluded chemical products, took over as the global leader in generic pharmaceutical supply.

During the eighteenth and nineteenth centuries US patent law addressed similar issues. US patent law has never listed any specific subject matter inclusions or exclusions, but as in the UK, some fundamental exclusions have been created through case law. These are that laws of nature, natural phenomena and abstract ideas are not patentable. These exclusions were recently restated, unanimously, by the Supreme Court in *Mayo*.

Case law tends to define what is not patentable rather than what is. But in Australia there was a view that patents could not be granted for mere schemes or plans, new uses of old substances (unless some alteration was needed to put this into effect), principles or ideas (Curtis and Lahey 1954). The then Commissioner of Patents, speaking at a major scientific conference, also noted that "the discovery of an unknown property in a known material is not patentable, primarily because no manufacture in the sense of a physical thing is disclosed" (Wilmot 1954: 3).

This view was overturned in a highly influential High Court decision in 1959. The case involved the application of a known chemical to selectively destroy weeds, refused by the patent office as the mere use of known substances which therefore "does not result in any vendible product" (*NRDC* at 4). The decision dealt with a number of issues: an unknown property of a known substance; inventiveness in the idea rather than the application; what a "manner of manufacture" was; and whether horticultural and agricultural processes were patentable. On all these issues the Australian High Court found in favour of the applicant. The court was very impressed with the value of the process: selective eradication of weeds. It reviewed (mostly English) cases from 1795 to 1957 seeking the essence of the "manner of manufacture" concept. It also reviewed several recent refusals of patents for the agricultural use of chemicals but decided not to follow these precedents, determining that the invention created an artificial effect within the general sphere of patentability (*NRDC* at 25). Subsequent decisions have interpreted the *NRDC* judgement as defining a "manner of new manufacture" as any "mode or manner of achieving an end result which is an artificially created state of affairs of utility in the field of economic endeavour" (*CCOMb* at 128).

Christie argues that the *NRDC* decision effectively eliminated any technological boundaries to what is patentable in Australia, given the ease of drafting acceptable implementation claims (Christie 2000: 20). But the radical influence of *NRDC* in extending patent scope was not evident for some years. The 1984 review of the Australian patent system paid little attention to the decision and clearly considered that patents were only for technology-based artefacts and processes. But *NRDC* has subsequently been very broadly interpreted and seems to have removed the requirement for a tangible output (or re-defined it to include intangible outputs such as curves on computer screens).

In most countries it was still the view, at least until the early 1980s, that certain things remained outside the bounds of the patent system, including computer programs (as they were simply mathematical algorithms) and business methods (mere schemes and plans). In some countries methods of medical treatment were considered non-patentable.[6] Another fundamental exclusion was discoveries. The discovery exclusion is important because patents for discoveries "could give rise to unreasonable barriers to potential competitors or to those who wished to use the 'discovery' in other fields of endeavour" (IPCRC 2000: 152).

The discovery exclusion has been sorely challenged in respect of genetic research where patents have been granted for things found (e.g. gene sequences) as well as things created (e.g. methods for determining gene sequences). At the EPO, the USPTO and in Australia it was patent offices which determined that such patents could be granted, notwithstanding that they might well be discoveries not inventions. There has been litigation over gene patents but the private parties involved stay well away from the issue of whether such patents involve discovery rather than invention (Palombi 2004). The EPO's actions were endorsed in 1998 by European Commission (EC) Directive 98/44/EC. Why this would provide any legal basis for such patents is unclear as the EC has no official role with respect to the EPC. The first court decision on this issue in the USA was in March 2010[7] and the matter is yet to be heard by any court in Australia.[8] Important as the gene patenting issue is,[9] the more central subject matter extension from the perspective of the story told in this book is the software exclusion, to which I now turn.

3.2.2 Extension to Software

In 1972 the US Supreme Court, in the *Benson* decision, specifically held that computer software constituted unpatentable mathematical algorithms (Chin 1998). But this decision was partially reversed by the Supreme Court in the 1981 *Diehr* case. This split (5–4) decision has been widely analysed and remains controversial. The dissenting judges considered the majority substantially misinterpreted the invention, which on the face of it seems to simply computerise an existing process for curing rubber. Even the algorithm used to determine when the process was complete was not new either in itself or in the context in which it was used.[10] Despite this, the majority held that the claimed process for curing rubber was patentable subject matter, even though its sole element of newness was a computerised algorithm. The only issue they considered was the patentable subject matter one (§101) and they actively chose to ignore any novelty or obviousness issues.

Legal decisions can seem strange from an economic policy viewpoint, and this carving up of the patentability requirements into discrete sub-issues, not all of which are considered in a single hearing, seems designed to result in the grant of questionable patents. This contrasts with normal executive government administration where *all* eligibility criteria must be met in each case. In *Diehr* all the judges agreed that computer programs themselves were not patentable. It was also clear (at least to four Supreme Court judges) that the *only* new element in the process was the computerisation. Yet the manner in which §101 was interpreted by the majority – specifically that the word "new" in the §101 definition of patentable subject matter was not relevant to interpreting §101 – meant that a patent for a probably uninventive 'invention' was upheld by the Supreme Court. This contrasts with a 1997 decision by the Australian High Court which rejected a claim for a patent for a light-bulb invention that had passed the novelty test but which the court considered was not sufficiently new to meet the Australian definition of patentable subject matter – a "manner of *new* manufacture".[11]

The *Diehr* decision spelled a radical break in patent policy – and one that was inconsistent with the advice of the 1966 President's Commission on the Patent System (*"To Promote the Progress of . . . Useful Arts" in an Age of Exploding Technology*). This Commission considered that there was no evident need for patent intervention in the software market, and that there would be considerable practical difficulties in administering patents for software (Samuelson et al 1994: 2362). Similar views, based on very similar reasoning, were expressed in the 1984 in Australia (IPAC 1984: 40–1). Both governments accepted these recommendations, though neither considered it necessary to take action to specifically exclude software from the patent system.

What they did do was to take action to change copyright laws to include software.[12] Protection of the expression but not the function of software would allow innovating firms a period of market exclusivity while not preventing competition in the market. The TRIPS Agreement, which came into effect in 1995, makes it clear that even a decade later there was no general acceptance of software patenting – Article 10 requires that *copyright* be provided for software. It is disingenuous to claim that software and business method patenting are not listed as specific exclusions in TRIPS (Diallo 2003). Software and business methods were not listed as specific exclusions from patentability as the consensus at the time was that business methods were not patentable as they involved no technology and software was appropriately 'protected' by copyright. "The TRIPS agreement was negotiated at a time when most countries did not allow patents for business methods and computer software as they were thought to be inherently unpatentable" (New Zealand Ministry of Economic Development 2002: 51).

Technically software in itself remains unpatentable in the USA unless it is used in a process that creates a tangible outcome. It must not be claimed as a computer program. But rewording the claims avoids both exclusions and there are several such examples in the cases discussed in later chapters. Following the *Diehr* decision, patent lawyers kept pushing the software envelope (Merges 2003) and the "doctrine of magic words" was used to ensure that software applications would meet the eligibility requirements (Cohen and Lemley 2001).[13] The most significant of a series of CAFC decisions broadening the scope of software patentability was *In Re Appalat* which endorsed the legal fiction that software in use changes a general purpose computer to a special purpose computer.[14] Fiction is a poor basis for important economic policy.

This particular fiction derives from the fact that "software can easily be demonstrated to produce physical changes in a machine, since each step in the program causes a different hardware stage. . . . [but] this applies for any piece of software, even the storage of data collections" (Brödner 2003: 159). Depending on the drafting, claims which are for computer software are regularly referred to as apparatus claims. This fiction is also widely used by the EPO to permit software patents, despite the fact that the EPC specifically excludes computer programs. Brödner notes such claims are drafted as "integral parts of a machine or process" (Brödner 2003: 160). From an economic or policy viewpoint, if the essence of the invention lies in the software then it is a software invention. Re-labelling an invention as an 'apparatus' or a 'device' does not change the fact that the sole inventiveness lies in the software. But such re-labelling has become sufficient to achieve a patent.

The EPO's argument is that patents are for inventions and if an invention has a 'technical effect' then it is patentable despite the specific exclusions in Article 52. Article 52 *starts* by saying that patents are for *inventions*. It then lists the kinds of inventions which are non-patentable. To then argue that patentable inventions are those with a technical effect, so that if a specifically excluded invention has a technical effect it is patentable has no basis in logic or ethics. Nor does it show any respect for the governments which agreed the EPC. Indeed, it appears to undermine the EPC.

While the "as such" qualifier of 52(3) could be (and has been) interpreted along the lines of the *Diehr* decision – that a program creating a technical effect outside a computer is patentable – the EPO has taken a much narrower approach to the as such exclusion. The EPO's technical effect approach seems to deem all software patentable as software runs on computers which are technical (Archontopoulos 2011).[15]

Under European law there is no *stare decisis* rule so individual decisions can and do offer different interpretations of the law. This is clearly evident in the series of decisions on the patentability of software emerging from the EPO Appeal Boards. The EPO Technical Boards of Appeal are not in fact courts of law, but rather a parallel mechanism to national patent office hearing/review mechanisms. Their members are bureaucrats and they are paid by the EPO. But these quasi-judicial bodies give scant regard to decisions by duly constituted courts in member countries (Thambisetty 2009: 12). National courts have been more courteous, attempting to follow the EPO Board leads except where this creates particular difficulties. Such difficulties have been experienced both in Germany and the UK in respect of the EPO's decisions on software.

Faced with this inconsistency the UK patent courts have extensively analysed EPO Board decisions on software, comparing these with UK precedent. Mr Peter Prescott, QC, sitting as Deputy Judge in the British Patents Court, found that the exclusions for computers and business methods were a matter of deliberate policy, and deserved very strict application: in particular patent offices should not allow these exclusions to be undermined by simple drafting (*CFPH* at 36).

This view – that extensions in patentable subject matter should be a matter for policy makers not judges or officials – aligns with the minority view of the US Supreme Court in *Diehr* and with the views of Lord Cooke in New Zealand in *Wellcome*. But it differs strongly from the expansionist approach exhibited by Australia's High Court in *NRDC* and the majority Supreme Court judgement in *Diehr*.

Prescott referred to the difficulties of working with inconsistent EPO decisions and this issue was taken further in a 2006 UK Court of Appeal hearing (*Aerotel*). The Appeal Court also undertook a lengthy analysis of EPO and UK precedent before adopting a four-step test proposed by the UK Patent Office as the equivalent of the earlier "technical effect approach". In considering this test the court refreshingly commented that it asked the question: "What has the inventor really added to human knowledge?" Despite this, the court found that Aerotel's claim that its software telecommunications process (for pre-paid phone cards) effectively created new hardware and so was a valid patent.[16] They did however reject Macrossan's application to automate the processes for creating a company on the grounds that it was both a business method and a computer program.[17]

The Appeal Court recommended that several questions be considered by an EPO Enlarged Board of Appeal to resolve the inconsistencies of the individual Appeal Board decisions. Unfortunately the EPO refused to consider the substance of these questions arguing that the very basis of the referral, by the then President of the EPO Alison Brimelow, was invalid – a claim roundly refuted by Pila (2011). It is unfortunate that the EPO is unwilling to address a problem reported by so many.[18] Indeed since then the EPO Boards have made several further contradictory decisions. These three EPO cases (*Duns Licensing Associates*; *Gameaccount Ltd* and *File search method/Fujitsu*) are discussed in the 2008 *Symbian* decision in which the UK Court of Appeal found that the EPO's jurisprudence was not yet settled. The Court therefore followed UK precedent. Nonetheless the Appeal Court concluded that if a program caused an improvement in the operations of a general purpose computer then it was patentable. This substantially narrows the software exclusion as applied in the UK, bringing it closer to the very narrow interpretation of the EPO.

In Australia the Patents Act was extensively re-written in 1990 to modernise and simplify the system, but not change any of its essential features. Despite the preceding major review of the patent system (IPAC 1984) there were only two changes to patent policy. There was a marginal increase in the novelty and inventiveness standards by changing allowable existing knowledge, and the ability to extend patent life was removed, except for pharmaceutical products. The issue of extending patentability to software-based industries had been considered by the review committee, but rejected as unnecessary. The option of a specific exclusion was considered unnecessary. This matter had bi-partisan support but was not actively discussed during passage of the legislation as there were no consequent changes.

In 1991 the Full Federal Court allowed a software patent for use of two algorithms which produced an improved representation of a curve on a computer screen. The decision made no reference to either the Australian Industrial Property Advisory Committee (IPAC) review or the 1966 US President's Commission. The court referred extensively to US precedents on the issue of whether an algorithm was fully pre-empted in a software program, but did not discuss the precedent breaking nature of their decision to allow a patent for any computer program. The application of the known method within computers was seen as new in computing and therefore inventive (*IBM* at 16). In 1994 this expansive approach was extended, in the *CCOM* case, to allow a patent for translation software. The first *CCOM* decision rejected the patent as invalid – simply using a computer in a conventional manner to reproduce the mental steps in translating Chinese ideograms (*CCOMa*). This decision appears very sound from an economic policy perspective. It was overturned by the Full Federal Court, which drew on pre-EPC UK legal reasoning but did not refer to the Banks Commission's recommendation not to allow patenting for software (*CCOMb*). Van Caenegem summarises their argument as being that "more than a mental process was involved in claiming the process of application of certain steps represented by a computer program on a standard computer, since the method as claimed was incorporated in the program and in apparatus in a physical form" (van Caenegem 2002: 46).

This 'logic' follows the EPO's argument (it can hardly be called reasoning) that when software operates it ceases to be software. In reading patent judgements one is constantly prompted to ask whether the Emperor has any clothes.

Overall the situation is that in all jurisdictions computer-implemented inventions which have their effects outside of computers are patentable. Such inventions include electronically operated washing-machines, cars etc. In Australia all other software 'inventions' are also patentable. Elsewhere if the "beyond a computer" effect occurs in a service industry the issue of patentability becomes complex as the effect of the program may be in a further area traditionally excluded from patent monopolies – business methods. Where software does not have any effect outside a computer, it appears that, at least in Europe and probably also in the USA, it is patentable if it improves the general operations of a computer, but not otherwise.

This confusing situation underlines one of the reasons why economists are so opposed to unnecessary intervention in markets. Whenever such intervention occurs, there will be parties who lose or gain depending on the specific rules and they will pour considerable resources into seeking to bend and change the rules. A whole industry can arise to advocate how borderline issues are interpreted. This is not generally regarded as a welfare-enhancing use of resources. In the days of high tariff barriers there was a bevy of tariff consultants. In Australia the number of patent attorneys has increased from around 75 in 1991–95 to over 250 in 2006–10.[19] Barton (2000) provides data on the growth in the USA in the number of 'intellectual property' lawyers per billion R&D dollars and finds this number has increased from 45 in 1970 to 75 in the late 1990s.

3.2.3 Business Methods: Piggy-Backing on Software

In the USA the CAFC's widening of patent scope eventually led to the 1998 *State Street* decision which took the view that nothing was excluded from patentability. There has been a voluminous literature on this decision, discussing either its legal basis, or the pros and cons of allowing business method patenting.[20] This new patenting opportunity was given widespread publicity by Amazon's 1-click patent, granted in 1998 and immediately used to limit their competitors' activities. There was widespread disbelief at the time that the Amazon patent had been granted, and a large and vociferous debate on the electronic airwaves and the press. From a policy viewpoint the fundamental issue would seem to be whether this did not simply computerise decades-old customer systems such as having a store account, or running a 'tab' at the local pub.

Going even further than the extension to business methods there has also been a suggestion that no technology is required for patentability. In 2005 the USPTO Board of Patent Appeals and Interferences (BPAI) reviewed a case that an examiner had rejected as lying outside the 'technological arts' (*Lundgren*). The majority reversed this decision, finding it no statutory basis for this "new test". Only Smith J dissented, finding it reasonable to interpret the term "useful arts" in the Constitution as 'technological arts', and noting that "the process as claimed is not tied to any known science or technology". Thambisetty suggested this is "a radical signal that [the USPTO] intends to steer away from the limiting notion of 'technology'" – a major change in policy (Thambisetty 2009: 18).

Since then the US shift to remove the longstanding tradition that patents are for artefacts and processes based on technology has been wound back though not completely over-ruled. In 2008 the CAFC rejected a claim for hedging risks in commodity trading (*In re Bilski*) and, on appeal, the Supreme Court supported the rejection but made it clear that "machine-or-transformation test" as the *sole* test of process patent eligibility was not correct (*Bilski*). The Supreme Court avoided commenting directly on another issue canvassed in the CAFC discussion of Bilski – that equating the "useful arts" with technology was inappropriate. The reassertion of Supreme Court patentability standards was reinforced by the 2012 *Mayo* decision. Although *Mayo* was about a method for medical treatment it emphasised again the need for genuine inventive transformative activity for something to be patentable. Referring to its earlier *Bilski* decision, the court found that abstract ideas cannot become patentable by limiting their use to a particular environment.

In the meantime however the *State Street* decision has affected the reach of patent systems in other jurisdictions. In Australia a major review of the patent system in 2000 concluded no action would be needed to prevent such unnecessary patents as most "will not pass the general tests for patent grant" (IPCRC 2000: 153). This sanguine view has not been borne out – over half the business method applications filed in any year have been granted.[21] In a consumer loyalty case (that was determined not to be a business method but rather a method and device usable in a range of businesses) Heerey J said he found the *State Street* decision persuasive. This aside has been taken to authorise business method patenting in Australia. No reasons were given and there is no evidence that the judge considered the economic impact.

Australia also quickly followed the BPAI approach of questioning the need for any technology basis. In a judicial aside when rejecting a business method for hiding one's assets from one's legitimate creditors, the Full Federal Court referred to an opinion of the patent office expressed in the *Szabo* case that an "artificially created state of affairs" required some material application of science or technology. The Court went on to say that "[w]e are not sure that this is correct" (*Grant 2006* at 38). Further, the judgment questioned the Deputy Commissioner's view that patentable inventions should lie within the area of science and technology.

The EPO has been more inclined to enforce the EPC exclusion from patentable subject matter of business methods compared to software. There is only a very small literature on business method patenting at the EPO as EPO data are particularly hard to search for research purposes. Wagner overcame this problem by matching granted US business method patents with EPO applications and found 1,901 applications of which half were pending. Among the 1,015 completed cases two-thirds were granted and only 5 per cent refused (Wagner 2008: 180).[22] Four of the cases in this study have been granted by the EPO. Of these three were initially rejected as neither technical nor inventive, but when a few words were moved from dependent to independent claims the objections disappeared and the patents were granted.

3.3 NOVELTY AND INVENTIVENESS

The business method literature raises the serious question as to whether patents have been extended to the new field of business methods solely, or largely, because of deficiencies in the novelty and inventiveness standards (Whitmeyer 1991; Merges 1999; Barton 2000; Freedman 2000; Ullman 2000; Gladstone 2002; Evensen 2004). There are two aspects to this proposition. One strand suggests the difficulties are practical: identifying the pre-existing body of knowledge (Dreyfuss 2000; Krause 2000; Bakels and Hugenholtz 2002; Noveck 2006). The other strand suggests actual novelty and inventiveness standards have fallen across the board, either through the procedures implemented by patent offices, or through case law (Harris 1989; Lunney 2004; Lawson 2008).

This section provides a brief history of the novelty and inventiveness criteria for patentability. As was the case with patentable subject matter the major policy parameters have been set by judges. Patent offices simply adopt new case law rules into their examination manuals. With varying degrees of speed new policy rules are adopted into statute law through amending legislation. What is unknown is whether patent offices brief executive government about the falling standards. Certainly there is little evidence of legislation being introduced to reverse the negative effects of doctrines which at times appear to lean over backwards to grant patents.

It is somewhat surprising to the innovation policy analyst to find that, under patent law, inventiveness is not a single test for how much new knowledge or know-how is contributed. After all inventiveness is not a discrete variable but rather covers a continuum from none to radically inventive. The issue for a balanced patent policy is where along this continuum to draw the line – at what point will there generally be sufficient benefit to the nation to merit the monopoly grant? If this point is passed a monopoly should be granted to induce the invention. But if there is insufficient new knowledge the nation will be worse off if a patent is granted.

What is surprising from an economic perspective is that over time legal doctrines developing proxies for "any manner of new manufacture" have separated the proxy for "sufficient to benefit the nation" into two quite separate elements of novelty and inventiveness.

3.3.1 Novelty and Existing Knowledge

In early UK patent law the only issue along the novelty/inventiveness dimension was "new". But there was no clear distinction between degree of newness, invention and manner of manufacture. Rather the invention was considered as a whole against public interest considerations which were basic to common law and the *Statute of Monopolies* (Bochnovic 1982).

Testing for newness obviously involves a comparison against what already exists or is known. Newness was originally defined in relation to whether an invention had been publicly worked within living memory. Following the 1778 *Liardet* requirement for patent specifications to be published, newness was also to be tested against publications. A century later an English court established the precedent that in determining novelty *only one piece of previous knowledge could be considered at a time* (*Von Heyden*). This changed the newness test: it was no longer a test of how new, but for difference compared to individual documents. The difficulties this limitation posed are clear in the repeated challenges to the doctrine. But judges have been unsympathetic and reaffirmed this 1880 decision in the UK Court of Appeal (1952) and the House of Lords (1956) (Bochnovic 1982: 21).

This legal doctrine has been adopted into British and Australian statute law. The 1984 Australian review of the patent system recommended that, except for explicit cross-referencing, the prohibition on combining evidence for the novelty test should remain. No reasons were given. If much existing knowledge is ignored, it is easier to claim newness. The very low standard set in the novelty test is evident in the 1993 Australian *Mirabella* case where the High Court held that a light-bulb 'invention' that had passed the novelty test did not constitute an invention – it was insufficiently inventive to meet the definition of an invention as a "manner of *new* manufacture".

3.3.2 Emergence of the Inventive Step

The inventive step test emerged from case law at around the time that the novelty test was emasculated, though it was not adopted into statute law until much later. Bochnovic indicates that the first British case where a patent was held invalid for want of an inventive step was *White* in 1868 (Bochnovic 1982: 15). In the USA the concept appeared earlier – in the

1850 *Hotchkiss* case. Kitch argues that the "substantial novelty" test disappeared in the USA between 1885 and the 1920s, and was replaced by the less clear-cut non-obviousness test (Kitch 1966, 1977). Beier, comparing the development of the inventive step test in the USA, the UK, France and Germany in the period 1850–1960, finds a major difference in approach between the USA and the European countries. He suggests a major difference between the USA – with its focus on the kind of creative process and the skills of the inventor – and Europe, where the focus was principally on the technical and economic effects of the invention (Beier 1986). The US approach is also evident in Australia.

The new inventive step test increasingly revolved around the word obvious, which raises the follow-on questions of "obvious to whom?" and "how obvious?". This approach, the so-called "Cripps question", was introduced as a test in the UK in 1928, and embodied in UK statute law just four years later. The appropriate judge of the inventive step is a "person with ordinary skills in the relevant art". Confusingly, the patent world uses the eighteenth-century term 'art' to mean technology. Legal doctrine has determined that this person must be "an ordinary worker in the field *not endowed with any special inventive skills*" (van Caenegem 2007: 84, emphasis added). The lack of imagination doctrine was recently overturned in the USA when the Supreme Court determined that this person should have ordinary imagination (*KSR*). Empirical analysis of CAFC decisions suggests that once the Supreme Court decided to hear the *KSR* case, the CAFC raised its obviousness threshold before reducing it slightly – though not to the previous low level – once the decision was announced (Mojibi 2010). Nowatarski (2007), on the other hand, argues that *KSR* need raise few concerns for Patent Attorneys as it appears to have had little impact on the BPAI.

As in the novelty test, the existing knowledge that can be used to determine inventiveness is highly circumscribed. The person skilled in the 'art' (PSA)[23] is assumed to have all knowledge that is common and general within the field. Depending on the jurisdiction s/he might be allowed to combine this common general knowledge (CGK) with other published material, usually under highly prescribed circumstances. Once the relevant body of permissible knowledge has been determined, the issue becomes whether the PSA would deem the invention obvious.

But how inventive must something be to be patentable? Dreyfuss notes that US law says a lot about the process to determine obviousness but nothing about the standard (Dreyfuss 2008). In British (and therefore Australian) law a very low standard has been set – a scintilla. Like the policy rule that the PSA must have no imagination, it is hard to trace the origin of this doctrine. Potts was only able to trace it to a 1912 text where it was presented as a summary of case law.[24] Potts concludes that the scintilla doctrine actually devolves to a test of obviousness, where the "spark of invention" is just perceptible to the skilled workman (Potts 1944: 117).

In contrast Quillen suggests, that at least in respect of litigated patents, there was a reasonable inventiveness standard in the USA prior to the establishment of the CAFC in 1982 (Quillen 2006). He compares Koenig's analysis of data from the period 1952–77 showing that two-thirds of appealed patents were over turned by courts as being invalid (Koenig 1980) with current data that the CAFC finds only 40–45 per cent of patents to be invalid. Quillen argues that while these data clearly show that the USPTO has always issued many invalid patents, the court-applied standard of inventiveness has fallen since the establishment of the CAFC.

The CAFC's PHOSITA is very different from that of the Supreme Court in *Graham*. While the Supreme Court's PHOSITA was aware of ever-widening knowledge fields, the CAFC's PHOSITA is "a literalist, without imagination or creativity, unaware of developments pertinent to his or her work" (Quillen 2006: 213). By narrowing the knowledge considered by the PHOSITA, the inventiveness standard is lowered. Further, the CAFC has elevated so-called secondary indicators[25] of inventiveness above the statutory criteria that the 'invention' not be obvious compared to the allowable existing knowledge. These two doctrines alone suggest a substantial reduction in the quantum of inventiveness required for a US patent. Lunney (2004) has pointed to a change from the synergy to the suggestions test for combination patents as also reducing the height of the inventive step.

Many inventions combine different elements that are already known. This view has led to considerable concern among some CAFC judges that one should not be too ready to deem a combination of known elements obvious. Similar concerns are evident in Australia. In Europe a combination of known elements is required to have an outcome greater than the sum of the parts or an unexpected result to be deemed inventive. This "synergy" doctrine is the standard used by the US Supreme Court but has been abandoned by the CAFC (Harris 1986).[26] It was overturned in Australia in 1980 (*3M*). The new policy rule in the USA and Australia is the "suggestion" rule – a combination of known elements cannot be rejected by an examiner as uninventive unless there is clear written evidence (a suggestion) that that combination has already been thought of. But obvious ideas are not usually written down (Ullman 2000; Bakels and Hugenholtz 2002). In Australia the patent examiners' manual goes further, advising that a combination is obvious only if it is the *sole* option. If a PSA might come up with several closely similar options, then the claimed option is inventive even if it is one of the set identified by the PSA.

In regard to "how obvious", the USA and Australia seem to be competing for the lowest quantum. Notwithstanding the evidence on the USA, Australia seems to be winning this race with even IP Australia commenting that Australia's inventive step is lower than that in the USA (IP Australia 2009a: 6). Drawing on several High Court cases,[27] Lawson demonstrates that the Australian standard of obviousness is that "an inventor would be *directly led as a matter of course* to the invention *in the expectation of success*" (Lawson 2008: 56, emphasis added). This creates a very low threshold. It means outcomes from normal experimentation among a range of likely options will always be regarded as inventive. Such a low standard has a negative impact on the balance of the patent system.

During 2009 IP Australia issued a series of discussion papers with the objective of raising the standards required for patenting in Australia. The "led directly . . ." doctrine was raised in the first of these papers (IP Australia 2009a: 12–13). Following submissions from the patent community, IP Australia advised it would "address concerns through restating the guidelines for inventive step in the Examiners' Manual and through more rigorous application of the inventive step tests during examination, rather than through changes to the law" (IP Australia 2009b: 12). Just how greater care by examiners can in any way offset a bad doctrinal rule is unclear. Examiners are required to follow precedents set in case law.

Several US analysts are critical of the CAFC for not following the standards set by the Supreme Court (Harris 1986; Lunney 2004; Quillen 2006). Lunney, finding a series of changes in the legal rules in appeal cases over the period 1944 to 1995,[28] notes a number of areas where the decisions of the CAFC run counter to those of the Supreme Court. He concludes that at times the CAFC has shown a "reckless indifference" to upholding the law (Lunney, 2001: 380). Quite recently the Supreme Court has, after a gap of many years, considered a number of patent cases and has reversed some aspects of CAFC decisions. In *KSR*, the Court indicated that the PHOSITA should be considered to have normal creativity (Dreyfuss 2008): 433). The main difference between the CAFC and Supreme Court considerations of the *Bilski* case was the Supreme Court clarification that the machine-or-transformation test was not the *sole* test of patentable subject matter. *Bilski* also reinforced earlier rulings that abstract ideas are not patentable.

Because inventiveness is such a subjective judgement there are few empirical studies which attempt to measure the actual height of this critical variable. Some researchers have used proxy variables such as patent citations or the number of claims as measures of inventiveness (e.g. Hirschey and Richardson 2001; Gandal 2002; Hunter 2004), but there are no studies showing that these proxies actually do measure inventiveness. The best of these administrative by-product variables is perhaps forward citations but this too is asymmetric – it theoretically identifies more inventive patents rather than less inventive patents. But there are no independent empirical studies demonstrating that forward citations identify more inventive inventions. There is one detailed study of the quantum of inventiveness in the 50 'best' (most cited) software patents granted by the USPTO, but this study uses the USPTO's allegedly low standard. All cases in the study are found to involve only incremental inventiveness and two are found to be obvious (Campbell-Kelly and Valduriez 2005). In an initial consideration of financial patents Lerner (2002) also found a very low standard for patentability.

In contrast to Australia and the USA, the EPO is often considered to have a higher standard for the inventive step. This conclusion is partly based on its lower grant rate (Jensen et al 2006). Despite this general view there are some who are more sceptical. Bakels and Hugenholtz comment that "[t]he Examination Guidelines of the European Patent Office leave no doubt that the test of non-obviousness will present an obstacle to patentability only in exceptional cases. For instance, a new but trivial combination of known techniques would be considered 'obvious'" (Bakels and Hugenholtz 2002: 36–7).

3.3.3 Other Patent Policy Rules

A number of legal doctrines were developed to try to ensure that patents are not granted for 'inventions' that have little merit. These are the tests regarding analogous use, new use of old substances and mechanical equivalence (IPCRC 2000: 154). In policy and practical terms these three doctrines are very similar.

The earliest rejection of an invention on the grounds that it was simply an application of a well-known thing to a different purpose for which its properties were well-suited (analogous use) was in 1838.[29] The principle was considered by the House of Lords in 1865, where the Lord Chancellor confirmed:

> Upon that I think that the law is well and rightly settled, for there would be no end to the interference with trade, and with the liberty of any mechanical contrivance being adapted, if every slight difference in the application of a well-known thing were held to constitute a patent . . .[30]

This doctrine is very sound from an economic perspective. Entrepreneurial initiative is often founded in taking a simple idea from one field and applying it in another. In cases like Amazon's 1-click patent – where the centuries old concept of a customer running an account was applied in an internet environment – there are no high investment costs to impede the innovator and the analogous use principle is clear. There is no economic case for a monopoly. However, where development costs can be substantial – as for example in the case of Velcro – then a monopoly grant may be required to induce the investment. From an economic perspective, therefore, great care needs to be taken in accepting an invention which applies a known thing or process in a new environment or for a new use.

Despite the analogous use precedent, in 1930 the English courts overturned the refusal of a patent for use of a known product (hardened glass) for a suitable purpose: vehicle windshields. The court acknowledged that this was contrary to prior authority (Brennan and Christie 1997: 242). But as late as 1959 the Australian High Court upheld the analogous use principle in *Microcell* (Brennan and Christie 1997: 243).

The doctrine of analogous use seems highly relevant to both software and business method 'inventions'. Many patented business methods use well-known processes in a computerised or networked environment. On the face of it, they would often seem to fail the patentability criteria on the ground of analogous use. Brennan evaluates the famous priceline.com patent for an internet-based reverse Dutch auction system and concludes it is "a claim to a use for which the Internet's then known properties indicated exact suitability" (Brennan 2002: 27). The well-known Amazon 1-click patent was discussed in Section 2.5. Again it seems odd that the analogous use principle did not apply – the essence of the invention is the use of a customer account in an on-line environment. The essence of the invention in *Welcome* was the use of a well-known software technique (dynamic storage) applied in a smart chip. The judge considered the analogous principle but held that it did not apply because the limited memory space on the smart card "presented difficulties which were overcome only after much time and effort" (*Welcome* at 130). A detailed reading of the material in the decision suggests that the real difficulty was in the attitudes of retailers. No evidence was presented about any technical difficulties which had to be overcome. The only issue was consumer loyalty specialists finding the available technology. From the perspective of the goals of the patent system, the lack of any new knowledge or know-how from using known methods in slightly new fields would not merit grant of a patent.

3.3.3.1 Mechanical equivalents and workshop improvements

The mechanical equivalent principle – designed to set a minimum quantum of difference that is not deemed novel – should also be operating to ensure that uninventive patents are not issuing. It is particularly relevant to 'inventions' which are combinations of known elements. If one element is varied, but the invention as a whole is functionally equivalent, then the 'invention' is not novel. If, however, the replacement element is itself novel and inventive, then the mechanical equivalence doctrine does not apply. The parallel doctrine under the inventiveness test is whether the combination is technically equivalent to a previously known combination. Again the essence of the test is whether the essential character has been changed.

If an 'invention' is a "mere workshop improvement" – something that the ordinary person skilled in the technology would come up with – then it is not inventive. But much hangs on the word mere. In the cases examined and reported in this book, examiners do raise issues of technical and mechanical equivalence and workshop improvements. In Australia, the applicant seems simply to argue that this is a wrong interpretation for examiners to simply grant the patent. But patents granted both in the USA and Australia seem to be very trivial variations from processes that have already been granted patents.

3.3.3.2 New uses of known things or processes

From an economic policy perspective it is unclear why a monopoly needs to be granted to someone who develops a new use for a known substance. Such experimentation is part of normal life. Unless the development costs are substantial, normal market mechanisms should ensure a good return on any investment. The product is already developed and the only additional cost is marketing. Again the word "mere" is critical to how this doctrine operates. In Australia the new use of old substances exception was held not to operate in *NRDC*. The High Court was very impressed by the economic value of the new use – far more efficient eradication of weeds. A "mere" new use depends heavily on the lack of any ingenuity in the underlying idea or its development.

The principle that one cannot obtain a patent for new uses of old substances is currently being further unravelled through trade negotiations. The 2004 Australia US Free Trade Agreement requires patentability for new uses of old substances (Lawson 2007: 145). The new use must pass normal novelty and inventiveness tests, but these standards are low. New uses of old substances and processes are taken a step further in the currently proposed, but highly controversial, Trans-Pacific Partnership (TPP) Agreement. A leaked draft of the TPP, currently being negotiated, states:

> patents shall be available for any new forms, uses, or methods of using a known product; and a new form, use, or method of using a known product may satisfy the criteria for patentability, *even if such invention does not result in the enhancement of the known efficacy of that product.*[31]

It is clear from the phrase "known efficacy" that this push derives from the pharmaceutical industry. India requires a demonstrated improvement in efficacy for a pharmaceutical drug to be granted a patent (Sampat et al 2012). The TPP proposal seeks to make such an approach unlawful. This aligns with the private interests of a few large corporate entities to the detriment of everybody else. A current strategic game in the pharmaceutical industry is patenting enantiomers when the patent on profitable drugs expires. Enantiomers are almost identical mirror-images – rather like a person's left and right hands. Indeed these pairs of chemical compounds are also referred to as left- and right-hand molecules. Frequently the therapeutic effect is identical.[32]

These doctrines – designed as they were to stop every trifling variation from being granted a monopoly – created an important balance in the patent system. Their winding back is part of the process that has unbalanced current patent policy.

Finally, a set of doctrines about the rules used to make decisions also affect the actual inventiveness standard. In most jurisdictions the patent application is deemed to be inventive and it is the patent office which has to demonstrate that it is not. In Australia this rule was imported from the UK, where it developed through case law. US patent procedures also place the onus on the examiner to demonstrate that an application fails to meet the statutory requirements for patentability. This "reverse onus of proof" rule contravenes normal economic policy principles that applicants for government interference in the market should demonstrate a clear benefit to the nation as a whole. This would require a *beyond reasonable doubt* standard of proof that the threshold of sufficient inventiveness has been passed.

But the rules in patent policy are defined from a legal not an economic perspective. From a legal perspective *beyond reasonable doubt* is the standard for criminal not civil law. Hence most patent jurisdictions not only place the burden of proof on the government to demonstrate that a monopoly should not be issued, but also set the determining rule as either *benefit of the doubt* or *balance of probabilities*.[33] The introduction of the *balance of probabilities* test in Australia in April 2002 brought it into line with the UK (Pascarl 2002). In the USA the bias in favour of patent applicants is compounded by a rule that anyone challenging a granted patent for want of novelty or inventiveness must prove their case *beyond reasonable doubt* (Jaffe and Lerner 2004).

3.4 CONCLUSIONS

Patent policy is fundamentally economic policy. Yet it has been driven by judicial decisions often made in the context of private commercial disputes. In some jurisdictions there is no provision for public interest implications to be considered when new doctrines that impact on public law are introduced. A further problem is that, in many countries, governments are advised about patent policy by patent offices. As Drahos (2010) has shown, these offices have become isolated within a narrow community and their economic interests are closely aligned with patent system expansion. There is little evidence of any evaluation of the economic impact of new doctrines emerging from case law before these are incorporated in statute law. In one of the few examples of such monitoring IP Australia played the key role in amendments which removed a restriction on including patent documents in existing knowledge for low (or no) technology 'inventions'. A second problem – a very narrow view of how obvious – was raised, but after submissions from interested parties no action was taken.

Patent law is a pre-eminent example of the operation of public choice theory (Olson 1971; Landes and Posner 2004; Scherer 2006). A small number of attorneys and firms capture a very large part of the benefit if patent volumes increase through ever broader subject matter reach or ever lower inventiveness standards. Those who pay are widely dispersed through society, and not well placed to organise to defend their interests. It rests with parliamentarians to protect the public interest. But legislatures have not intervened to overturn these judgements.

There are three important reasons for this. Firstly, because the policy changes are driven by legal changes, legislatures could be presented as the ones actively making a change: 'attacking' the newly established standards for the 'protection' of 'property', rather than defending the public interest. The second reason is the decades of propaganda that all creative and inventive efforts deserve rewarding through patent (or copyright) monopolies, and that anyone who benefits from anyone else's ideas is a 'pirate'. It is this propaganda which allows protection of the public from undeserved monopolies to be framed as an attack rather than a defence of the public. A third difficulty is that patent law is presented as complex. Those not deeply immersed in it are warned, often by patent attorneys, against interfering. It was the American patent bar which successfully lobbied against the inclusion of a US Government Accountability Office (GAO) study of business method patents in the *American Inventors Protection Act* of 1999 (Kahin 2003a). As a body outside the patent community the GAO would have taken a dispassionate approach, based on evidence.

The complexity of patent law is often used to hide the simplicity of the underlying bargain. Complexity is an active strategy used to hide systems in which a small number of parties gain substantial economic benefits. "Legal entrepreneurship when economic stakes are high does not work simply by exploiting change and complexity that is inherent in post-industrial societies. It also works by contriving change and complexity" (Braithwaite 2005: 148).

In the patent system complexity hides a series of decisions which may be innocuous individually, but which add to such a severe narrowing of the critical threshold requirements of 'novelty' and 'inventiveness' that many commentators consider they have lost all meaning. This raises the question of whether the patent system is out of balance. Both in Australia and the USA there is considerable comment on the very low quality of many granted patents. Some of the patents emerging from the EPO suggest similar problems.

Perhaps because the economic objectives of patent policy are not clearly stated in patent statutes, judges seem to pay little attention to the public interest. There are exceptions such as the *CFPH* and *Aerotel* decisions in the UK, Lord Cooke's analysis of patenting methods of medical treatment in New Zealand (*Wellcome*), and recent decisions by the US Supreme Court, particularly *Mayo*. In Australia the patent policy goal remains embedded in the provisos of the 1623 definition of a patentable invention. In a recent case involving an 'invention' to move assets into a trust structure so they cannot be claimed by legitimate creditors, Branson J drew on these provisos. She determined that the critical principle in the case was that "an invention should only enjoy the protection of a patent if the social cost of the resulting restrictions upon the use of the invention is counterbalanced by resulting social benefits" (*Grant 2005* at 20). As an additional reason for rejection she noted that the invention might shield the owners from laws enacted in the public interest. This is one of the few recent patent cases that seems sound from policy and public interest perspectives.

It was strongly criticised by the Full Bench on appeal:[34]

> we do not find it necessary to discuss the requisite economic benefits of the alleged invention . . . Nor is the Court in a position to determine the balance between social cost and public benefit. Parliament has already made that judgment, as its predecessor did in 1623, by rewarding innovation with time-limited monopoly. (*Grant 2006* at 43–5)

From an economic viewpoint this is an extraordinary statement. It shows a lack of awareness that a positive outcome for the patent system as a whole depends on the majority of patents *each* delivering a benefit to the nation. The Australian legal definition of a patentable invention is spelled out in the words of S.6 of the *Statute of Monopolies*, hedged with qualifiers designed to ensure patents are not granted where they do not benefit the nation.

Whether the inventiveness standard is very low can be tested. The central contribution of this study is an in-depth investigation of a set of recently granted business method patents. These are analysed for their inventiveness, but not in terms of the patent law definition. Within the context that a good patent system is a balanced patent system, where the social benefit exceeds the social cost, they are assessed in terms of what new knowledge or know-how they contribute. After all it is new knowledge and know-how which creates potential spillover benefits and so benefits to society. If most granted patents make such a contribution it is likely the patent system overall will produce a positive economic outcome. But if most do not, then the few inventive patents will have to create sufficient spillover benefits to offset the costs of the many uninventive patents.

In a subjective area such as inventiveness there are always likely to be errors. A key policy question is whether to err on the side of granting uninventive patents or take the risk of occasionally refusing patents for inventive inventions. All jurisdictions offer a series of appeal rights against adverse patent office decisions. Challenging a granted uninventive patent places the costs of the challenge on just one firm, while all competitors will benefit if the challenger is successful. Of course, where the costs of challenge are minimal – as in EPO pre-grant oppositions – challenges are more likely. But where challenges require formal court action the asymmetric incentive structure together with the high cost discourage challenges to uninventive patents. Such challenges are extremely rare unless there has first been an infringement suit. Placing the doubtful case onus on the would-be monopolist would be fairer than placing it on the affected innovating firm. This suggests that a preferable public policy standard would be to err on the side of refusing inventive inventions. Another reason for opting to err on the side of refusing good patents is that this would increase the certainty of granted patents (Jensen and Webster 2004).

4. In the national interest: defining patentable inventions

4.1 INTRODUCTION

The economic discussion in Chapter 2 shows that patents will serve the national interest if they are granted for innovations which would not otherwise take place and which have spillover benefits that more than offset their cost. This is a far cry from the rigid set of prescriptive rules that currently constitute patent policy.

But while it is easy to describe in general terms the kinds of inventions that should merit a patent grant, it is far more difficult to set up simple and robust rules that are capable of easy implementation. This chapter begins by discussing in more detail the kinds of inventions where there would be a national interest in providing a patent incentive. The discussion includes the issues of inducement, the quantum and measurement of spillover benefits, whether a technological basis is needed, issues involved in patenting mathematics and software and the separation of ideas from artefacts based on them. The discussion concludes with a consideration of the particular issues raised by combinations of known elements or processes and whether the yardstick of contributed new knowledge or know-how can be used to determine patentability for such inventions.

In Section 4.3 the bases on which cases were selected are discussed. The set of selected cases is reviewed in terms of representativeness, particularly inventiveness. Other characteristics of the selected cases are also discussed to provide a feel for the dataset. This section concludes with a discussion of how cases are assessed to determine what new knowledge or know-how is contributed by each case. This approach to evaluating inventions is radically different from the legalistic rule-bound approach of current patent law. It is diametrically opposed to the approach which patent examiners must take. Examiners are effectively required to prove that an application is obvious if they are to reject it. The approach of asking what is the new knowledge or know-how contributed takes a positive approach of requiring that such a contribution be clearly evident.

The chapter concludes with a discussion of a small number of the cases. Cases discussed in Section 4.4 are selected to show the range of service industries which are now attempting to use the patent system. The material presented on each case focuses on identifying the core of the inventive contribution and considering what new knowledge or know-how each contributes.

4.2 WHAT SHOULD BE PATENTABLE?

A fundamental principle of good policy is that it should achieve its goals. In the case of patents this is to achieve a higher level of investment in innovation than would otherwise occur. The critical issue for patent policy is therefore whether it induces innovation which would not otherwise occur. Ideally patents should be granted only where the innovation is induced by the patent system. This is most likely to be where the initial investment is large and imitators can rapidly enter the market. If sound data on speed of market entry were available, this could be combined with data on the size of the investment to determine patent eligibility. Such data are not available, so a second-best option must be sought. It is always useful, however, to keep first-best options in mind, lest second- or third-best options move too far away from the overall policy goal and call into question the effectiveness of the policy.

A next place to look for the critical variable to determine patent grant is among variables which could be used to indicate that an innovation delivers a benefit to the nation. This benefit must go beyond the benefit to the patent owner. National benefits take the form of net consumer surplus and/or spillovers from new knowledge or know-how. Using net consumer surplus increases as an administrative tool is challenging. Apart from the difficulties of applying this theoretical construct in the real world, one would also need to measure consumer surplus lost through products displaced in the market. There is a real difficulty in readily measuring *net* consumer surplus from any innovation.

New knowledge or know-how is the other source of benefit to the nation. The first principle for there to be a knowledge (or know-how) spillover from an innovation is that the innovation must contain some new knowledge (or know-how). If it has no new knowledge it cannot be the source of any spillover benefits. If there is new knowledge it may not necessarily be useable by others, but at least the possibility of such use exists.

New knowledge may also operate as a proxy for innovations contributing to the quality of economic life through higher net consumer surplus. Imagining the kinds of innovation which add significantly to the quality of life, the list might include air travel, mobile phones, contact lenses, pharmaceuticals, Velcro, refrigeration, micro wave ovens. Clearly some of these innovations have negative side-effects, particularly on the environment. But they all also embody real advances in knowledge and know-how. It may well be that new knowledge and know-how can be a useful indirect measure of the benefits provided through net increases in consumer surplus.

The next question is how much new knowledge is sufficient. It needs to be enough to more than offset costs. If 'enough' only balances costs then society would be as well off without a patent system as with one. There is a *continuum* of inventiveness ranging from "mere workshop improvements" to radical breakthroughs. The challenge is to determine at what point along the continuum there is a sufficient net benefit, and a patent should be granted.

This type of difficult boundary problem is a characteristic of all systems of market intervention. Such difficulties, and the resources which are drawn to arguing about them, are one reason why economists consider market regulation inefficient. But, given market regulation, they have to be dealt with. The challenge is to identify some 'bright line' rules that will ensure balance in the patent system, and will not be amenable to manipulation by those who make a living out of the regulatory intervention. If clear rules can be developed and maintained, this will reduce the quantum of resources wasted on arguing about boundaries.

An economic policy analyst would set the new knowledge requirement at a sufficiently high level to achieve genuine spillover benefits. At a minimum this would exclude minor modifications and the simple transfer of ideas between broadly related technologies and industries.

Going beyond a minimum knowledge contribution, and recognising that the grant of a patent involves a variety of resource costs, the standard should require a 'reasonable' contribution to new knowledge or know-how. Historically there have been legal doctrines (policy rules) attempting to implement such view. One is the exclusion of "mere workshop variations". Another is the exclusion of analogous uses – clear parallel uses of known elements. A third is the doctrine of excluding new uses of old substances.

Given the implicit assumption that patents were always intended to be about technological advances, their extension to business method patents highlights a number of other issues that need to be considered in setting standards for granting patents. Firstly there is the question of whether a technology base should be explicitly required. Secondly, many business method patents are written at a very high level of generality so issues about patenting ideas as opposed to specific applications of ideas also become important. And thirdly, rules about combining known elements also become critical as business method patents often involve combining known elements or using known processes in marginally different configurations or environments.

4.2.1 Should there be a Technology Basis?

Traditionally, to be patentable an invention had to add to knowledge in the fields of science and technology. This assumption was so basic to the patent system that it was rarely written down.[1] Such shared basic assumptions are so obvious within a society "that they are never fully or systematically articulated" (Hirschman 1977: 69). The assumption is implicit in the TRIPS Agreement's prohibition on discrimination between fields of technology (Article 27). Reading parliamentary debates on patent legislation makes it clear that parliamentarians still assume patents are granted only for relatively significant technological advances. In some ways the EPO's requirement for a technical effect is a search for a science/technology base to patentable inventions.

There is a lively debate about the technical effect approach: some consider that, in the area it is most frequently called on (software), most of the many patents granted by the EPO have no real technical effect (Miceli 2005). Others suggest that this issue diverts attention from the problem that quasi-courts such as the EPO Technical Boards of Appeal have virtually eliminated the inventive step (Bakels and Hugenholtz 2002). There is also some variation within Europe in the technical effect approach. The differences between the UK and the EPO were discussed in Chapter 3. German courts have been strong defenders of the technology boundary. Pilch reports the German Federal Court of Justice as commenting that:

> The patent system is also not conceived as a reception basin, in which all otherwise not legally privileged mental achievements should find protection. It was on the contrary conceived as a special law for the protection of a delimited sphere of mental achievements, namely the technical ones, and it has always been understood and applied in this way.[2]

Before electronic computing, mathematics was a branch of science largely divorced from the world of patents, other than via its use in other branches of science or engineering. It was widely considered that mathematics, based largely on logic, was simply a set of ideas and as such unpatentable. Indeed there is no consensus as to whether mathematics is an art or a science.[3]

A direct corollary of the non-patentability of mathematics was that computer programs were not patentable (Bauerle 2002). In addition to their mathematical basis prohibiting software patents on subject matter grounds, it was also considered that software 'inventions' were so incremental that they would not pass the inventiveness threshold (Samuelson et al 1994).

Computers run on electronic signals and are effectively ever-larger sets of on/off switches. All computing languages eventually have to convert to a set of binary (on/off) instructions or they cannot be implemented. This means that the maths involved in programming is quite straightforward – the simple application of logic to the problem in question. Care is needed in designing efficient programs for large systems. Efficiencies can be achieved by importing ideas from elsewhere into this new realm. For example data compression techniques, important for speedy transmission, are based on long-standing methods for documenting knitting patterns.[4] Rewarding use of such known ideas in a clearly suitable new environment with a government monopoly grant requires careful consideration in relation to the goals of patent policy. While larger programs can be expensive to write, the costs of doing so are production costs not R&D costs. There cannot be any argument that they can be cheaply imitated, except by copying and copyright provides protection against this. There is not therefore any evident market impediment to such innovations, nor is there any new knowledge in transferring ideas from one realm to another. Providing patent monopolies for such 'inventions' is not justifiable on any sound economic ground.

Software patenting raises the further issue of whether there should be a requirement for more than the simple use of mathematics or logic to solve a problem. Because mathematics is so inextricably tied in with philosophy and logic, it is also reasonable to consider whether mathematics-based inventions should be treated differently from other inventions. For example if the only inventiveness lies in the mathematics, perhaps a very substantial new contribution to knowledge might be required.[5] Alternatively, the system could be returned to the *status quo ante*, where mathematical algorithms were considered unpatentable, whether or not they tied up all uses of an algorithm.

4.2.2 Ideas and their Implementation

Another issue underlying the extensive argument about software patentability is separating the idea from its implementation. There are two issues here. The first is public access to any particular algorithm. This limitation to software patentability was removed in the USA by a new doctrine that the application of an algorithm could be patented if it did not claim all uses of the algorithm. This new approach was imported into Australia in 1986 (Stoianoff 1999: 503–4). Similar issues were considered in the UK. For example in *IBM Corp* the UK Patent Appeal Tribunal considered the

1972 US Supreme Court *Benson* decision that one cannot have a patent if it fully pre-empts a mathematical formula, but considered it did not apply to the case under consideration.[6]

The second difficulty is the level of generality. Many software 'inventions' are written at such a high level of generality that they really only disclose the idea rather than the implementation (Kahin 2003b). Such high levels of abstraction also allow for strong exclusive monopolies if a patent is granted (Bessen and Meurer 2008). The Signature Financial Group patent at the heart of the *State Street* case involved the simple computerisation of Internal Revenue Service (IRS) guidelines for minimising tax on an investment product. As the lower court pointed out in invalidating the patent, this meant that no other party could use computers to follow these IRS guidelines. Due to the complexity and tight deadline for the process, it would not be possible to follow the IRS guidelines without using a computer. The CAFC overturned this decision, and held the patent to be valid.[7]

This patent challenges the longstanding policy doctrine that ideas may not be patented. In 1874 the US Supreme Court determined that where there was no distinguishable difference between an idea and its implementation, the idea was not patentable.[8] The ideas/artefacts distinction helps to ensure that patent eligibility focuses on those things where some experimentation and development cost is incurred – where there may actually be a market failure. The distinction – that knowledge should remain in the public domain even while specific uses of that knowledge are tied up in proprietary artefacts – also plays a role in balancing costs and benefits in a patent system, and thus ensuring a patent system benefits society as a whole.

At this point it is useful to return to the purpose of a patent system: to induce a higher level of inventive effort. Clearly the application of logic to solve a problem may well be possible with quite minimal resources (depending on the problem and the underlying technology). Further where the 'invention' is expressed only in very general terms it is not at all clear that it actually has been developed. Where the R&D cost is low, there is little likelihood of market failure. In such situations there seems little need for intervention and no need for grant of a patent monopoly. So focusing patent eligibility on technology would focus on inventions where there are significant development and commercialisation costs, making it more likely that a patent incentive is actually needed.

This focus on lumpy investment costs is also relevant when considering combinations of known processes or elements. In discussing how invention occurs, Magee (2002) notes the importance of combinations and using ideas from one context in another. A wonderfully inventive example of such thinking is Velcro. While removing burrs stuck to his trousers, Swiss inventor George de Mestral thought about the marvellous qualities the burrs would make in a fastener.[9] So certainly taking an idea from one context and applying it in another can lead to an invention that would almost unanimously be considered very inventive. In the Velcro case, there were a variety of technical issues that needed solving and this contributed new knowledge and know-how. Converting the idea into a manufacturable product involved real costs suggesting that a patent may have been needed to induce this investment.

This example contrasts starkly with many patents issuing today, particularly, but not exclusively, in the field of business methods. There are many examples of ideas taken from one area and applied in another. They appear very obvious, yet have been granted patents. The current patent rules fail to recognise that we now live in a world where inventiveness is the norm in most lines of business. As Bagley has pointed out, "[i]n business, as much as anywhere else, solving problems in one area by application of business principles or models from another area is clearly the norm" (Bagley 2001: 274).

One reason why patent offices are granting patents for obvious combinations is the shift from the synergy to the suggestion doctrine in the USA and Australia. The synergy test can be satisfied if there is an unexpected result – which implies new knowledge or know-how. It can also be satisfied if the new combination produces a result which is greater than the sum of the parts. Again this implies new knowledge or know-how. The synergy test reflects the economic goal of new knowledge. It contrasts with the suggestion test which makes it virtually impossible to reject an application for a combination of known elements. A return to the synergy test would do much to raise the quantum of inventiveness required for grant of a patent. This could also be achieved by redefining the inventiveness test to its positive form – a requirement to demonstrate new knowledge or know-how. At present the test takes a negative form – can the examiner show that the 'invention' is obvious?

A particular form of combination 'invention' found in the business method field is simple computerisation of a known process or use of a known process on modern electronic networks (Hall 2009: 2). Businesses have been using computers to automate previously manual processes since at least the early 1970s. Given the power of modern computers and software languages, the business equivalent of the null hypothesis is "why not computerise?" rather than "why computerise?" There had been substantial computerisation of business processes before patents were extended to business methods. There was no evidence of any market impediment to such initiatives. Provision of patents in this field therefore seems entirely unnecessary. The only benefit of this extension is to those intermediaries whose income is related to the volume of patenting.

Modern electronic systems are now ubiquitous and provide a very powerful platform for delivering commercial goods and services, as well as for a range of non-market uses. Networks offer interesting new possibilities as to how to deliver a range of goods and services, with geography now playing a less constraining role. Business was quick to seize on these new opportunities and e-commerce applications have been around since at least the early 1990s. Patenting of such methods has proliferated only since the *State Street* case in 1998.

As with simple computerisation 'inventions', it is difficult to see what inventiveness is involved in transferring a known process to the internet. There are not usually any contributions to knowledge or know-how. So why should a government intervene and limit competition around such business initiatives? The business method cases assessed here include three where networks are critical to the success of the invention. But there are a number of other cases where networks are used and provide a useful commercial edge even though they are not central to the core 'inventive' concept. In the market, network advantages reinforce first mover advantages further undermining any case for government intervention.

Many other business method 'inventions' seem no more than trivial variations on existing themes. Indeed some of the variations seem to relate more to design than to function. Other business method patents simply link various databases to generate useful service outputs. There are several old legal doctrines that were designed to prevent the grant of patents to such trifling 'inventions'. Doctrines such as technical and mechanical equivalence and workshop variations operated to set a floor to the quantum of novelty or inventiveness required for grant of a patent. The prohibition on granting patents for analogous uses also operated to reinforce if not raise this minimum standard. Somehow these doctrines seem to have become less effective in recent decades.

If very trivial patents are granted this raises particular problems for software 'inventions'. Richard Stallman makes a very useful analogy between software programming and orchestras. In both the challenge is producing a new work, on a large scale, using a multitude of features that are not new in themselves, but which may well be combined differently. He asks us to imagine what would have happened to orchestral music if patents were granted on individual musical ideas, then goes on to imagine the impact on Beethoven:

> To write a whole symphony, you are going to have to do lots of different things and at any point you could be using an idea that somebody else has patented.

> Of course, if you do that, he'll say "oh! you are just a thief, why can't you write something original". Well Beethoven had more than his share of new musical ideas. But he used a lot of existing musical ideas. (Stallman 2001)

One issue not usually discussed in considering the height of the inventive step is where the onus of proof should lie. As noted earlier it is usual in a democracy for the seeker of special privileges to have to demonstrate that there is a net benefit to the nation before such privileges are granted. Unfortunately in the patent system it is the patent office which is required to demonstrate lack of inventiveness rather than the potential monopolist who must demonstrate a genuine contribution to knowledge.[10] If the onus of proof lay with the applicant, the height of the inventive step would inevitably increase and many very trivial patents would not be granted. If this were combined with the normal economic standard for regulatory intervention in markets – that it is clear *beyond reasonable doubt* that there is a net benefit – the standard would be more robust to semantic games playing.

With a *beyond reasonable doubt* test and a change in the onus of proof, most combinations would be deemed obvious, unless the applicant could demonstrate particular challenges raised and solved through a genuine contribution of new knowledge. Further, if one asks that this new knowledge be in a technology field, then the technical requirement test is operationalised in a new way, effectively raising the standard for patentability. This new standard is well aligned to the requirement for a benefit to the nation.

4.3 SELECTING THE CASES FOR STUDY

There are several criteria which need to be considered in selecting a set of patents for investigation. The first is the choice of business method patents as the class of patents to be studied. This choice was made because it aligns with my own expertise. It also has the advantage of being more accessible to a wide range of readers than real technology fields would be.

It is notoriously difficult to use official patent databases to select patents of a given subject matter, despite the International Patent Classification (IPC) system. Patent classes can be extremely heterogeneous (Desrochers 1998). The most often quoted example is that water pistols and devices for distributing holy water are found in the same class (Griliches 1990: 1666). Side by side with this class heterogeneity, any given type of invention might be assigned to many classes. Sorensen and Stuart, for example, searched 2,400 patent subclasses to ensure a complete identification for semiconductor inventions (Sorensen and Stuart 2000: 91).

Layne-Farrar (2005) compares several studies of software patents to investigate the impact of identification methodology on the findings. The studies used keyword searching, IPC classifications, or IPC classifications followed by a keyword search.[11] She concludes that the soundest method is to combine a classification-based approach with a detailed review to weed out inappropriate cases. This approach is used here: cases were selected based on relevant IPC classes and then cases that are not business methods are weeded out, by reviewing the patent specifications.

With the massive growth in the volume and scope of patent systems the IPC is currently updated continuously. IPC8 was introduced on 1 January 2006, replacing IPC7.[12] In IPC7 business methods were defined in sub-group G06/17/60. But in IPC8 they had expanded to five sub-groups in the group G06Q.[13] IPC classifications are not very robust. Exploration of a set of 404 Australian applications filed from 1993 to 1999, and classified as business methods under IPC7, found that 189 (47 per cent) were not in the IPC8 business method classes. However applications for the same period defined by IPC8 business method classes contained 93 applications which were not defined as business methods under IPC7. In this study cases were selected if they fell into either the IPC7 or IPC8 business method classes.

The second criterion relevant to selecting cases is their representativeness. Patents are very diverse in character. Unless many cases are examined, there is a reasonable chance that they will be unrepresentative. However reading patent claims is both tedious and time-consuming: the average number of claims in the selected dataset is 30, with a range from four to 115. A balance thus needs to be drawn between a sufficiently large set from which to be able to generalise, and a sufficiently small set to be manageable.

A third important issue in selecting cases for study is the desire to look at the *substance* of granted patents, particularly at how inventive they are and what new knowledge they contribute. This means the priority date of the invention is of critical importance. This date determines the body of existing knowledge against which the inventiveness of the claimed invention should be assessed. Clearly the more recent the priority date, the less likely there will be errors of hindsight.

But it takes a long time for a cohort of applications to progress through a patent office as considerable leeway on timing is granted to applicants. For the cohort of Australian business method patents filed in 2001, 32 per cent were still in the system in March 2007 (compared to 2 per cent for the 2000 cohort). Clearly a random sample from the 2000 cohort would contain many cases with quite old priority dates relative to 2007. Selecting cases that have recent priority dates therefore requires selecting granted cases from incompletely processed cohorts. This places constraints on the method of selecting the cases from the cohort.

Balancing these conflicting factors, the cases selected were from the cohort filed between 1 January 2003 and 31 December 2006 and accepted or sealed by 30 June 2007. That is, the initially processed applications from a four-year cohort were selected in full. This yielded 94 patents, most with priority dates of 2002 or later. Two were misclassified cases and one concerned pure software processes, rather than computer-implemented business methods. These three cases were dropped. A further case, converted to a patent of addition during the examination process, was also dropped.[14]

Of the remaining 90 cases, 18 belong to a single applicant, Silverbrook. Silverbrook is Australia's most prolific patenter, with 837 Australian and 3,666 US patents granted as at the end of 2010 (Moir 2011). Its underlying technology involves a small high-speed printer. The patents classified as business methods do not represent genuine business processes but rather are part of the strategic game of exchanging "truckloads of patents" in the electronics industry. Silverbrook has a number of in-house patent attorneys charged with completing one application a day.[15] All the Silverbrook cases were excluded from the study, giving a final set of 72 cases.[16]

Effectively the selected cases are a universe of recently granted cases, at a brief point in time. They are 4 per cent of the 1,678 applications filed in 2003–06 and 8 per cent of the 908 grants from this cohort. This cohort has not yet been fully processed: as at 18 July 2012 there were 69 cases still pending, all PCT cases. Patent processing is notoriously slow and the 2003 cohort was not completed until 22 September 2009.[17] The 2004 cohort has also been fully processed, with the last acceptance published on 31 May 2012.

How representative are these cases of the cohort of all 2003–06 filings? Applicants determine the speed at which an application moves through the process: they can ask for early (expedited) examination, or can wait until they are directed to request examination. They also have 21 months to respond to adverse examiner's reports, and can choose the speed of response. There can be a number of examiner's reports: usually there are only one or two, but for one case there were four. Those patents which are granted quickly have been pushed through the system by their owners, probably because they are seen as more valuable. Within this set of 72 cases there are 30 where the owners asked for expedited examination. Seventeen gave reasons: 11 mentioned commercial development and six the need to stop potential infringers (others developing the same idea).

The cases are therefore unrepresentative in terms of their speed of passage through the patent office. Over half were accepted within two years of filing, seven within six months of filing. This is remarkably speedy processing.[18] These unusually speedy cases are offset by 14 cases with relatively old priority dates – between May 1998 and July 2001. Nine cases have more than four years between the filing and priority dates, of which seven are from the USA, where continuations abound.[19]

In general, companies dominate patent systems: 82 per cent of US grants between 1964 and 2003 were to companies. In Australia 92 per cent of patent grants are to organisations, mostly companies (Moir 2008). Individuals are over-represented in the selected cases, at about 18 per cent. Australian applicants are even more over-represented – 54 per cent of the selected patents have Australia-based owners, compared to 8 per cent among patents generally. This is attributable to the PCT process – those wishing to pursue overseas patenting through the PCT route often want a quick result on their first application, and the selected cases are among the first grants in the cohort. The country of first application tends to be the country of residence (Bosworth et al 2003).

While the selected cases are unrepresentative in terms of processing speed and ownership characteristics, there is no reason to think that the degree of inventiveness is related to either of these variables. Processing speed is related to the strategic goals of the owner, and it is clear from the dominance of Australian applications that moved through the PCT route that the owners considered them marketable overseas. Nearly 20 per cent of the cases have quite old priority dates.[20] There is no evidence of any difference in inventiveness between cases with older or more recent priority dates. Nor is there any difference in inventiveness between those owned by Australian applicants and those owned by overseas applicants

The analysis of these cases is based on a reading of the patent specifications, with a particular focus on the claims, that is, on the knowledge claimed as invented, and for which a monopoly is sought. In legal parlance this is called construing – the content of the specification is assessed to identify the inventive contribution (Stoianoff 1999: 501). The initial assessment of all cases, particularly the comparison with existing knowledge, was completed during 2007. Where no contribution to knowledge is found, the analysis moves on to identify what aspect of patent rules contributed to allowing the grant. This draws on a reading of the correspondence between the examiner and the applicant.[21]

There is little previous literature for this approach:[22] in fact only one previous qualitative assessment of patent quality in a scientifically selected set of cases has been found. That used the low USPTO obviousness standard as the basis for assessing inventiveness in software patents (Campbell-Kelly and Valduriez 2005).[23] This contrasts with the approach in this book. Here inventiveness is assessed from the economic perspective of whether there is a contribution to new knowledge or know-how compared to previously existing knowledge.

Patent claims are often written in obscure and complex language. As an aid to assessing the substance of the claims they were all 'translated' from legalese into English by the author. In discussing each individual patent, some examples are presented of the actual claims, usually in 'translation'. So that the reader may get a feel for these patents, for seven cases the original wording of the claims is provided in the Appendix.

Patent examiners are bound by the detail of patent law, as set out in the examiner manuals. All the cases assessed here are applications accepted or sealed in Australia. In other words they have all been deemed sufficiently inventive to be patented under current Australian law. Some have been accepted at the EPO, in the UK or in the USA so have been judged by examiners to meet inventiveness standards in those jurisdictions. The standard used here in judging patent quality is quite different – it is operationalised in terms of the positive question: "what is the contribution to knowledge or know-how?" Using this yardstick some radically different conclusions about the inventiveness of the granted patents are reached. This should not be taken as a criticism of the work of patent examiners. They are bound by the law. The completely different approach used here turns the normal examination question: "can I prove it is obvious?" on its head. Different outcomes are only to be expected.

The 72 patents in the selected dataset cover a diverse range of business methods and/or service sector products. Some are support mechanisms common to all businesses, such as marketing, accounting, audit, customer management, purchasing and transport as well as back-office administration. Others are service products, though as the products are intangible, the claims are drafted as a method or system for producing the product (for example financial products). The processes involved in delivering a particular outcome do not align well to the patent system assumptions as to what constitutes a single invention. In many cases examiners separate out elements of the process requiring that sub-sets covering a "single inventive concept" be selected. Applicants then have the right to file the deleted sub-sets as separate divisional applications.

Three-quarters of the cases with overseas applications (49 out of 64) have filed through the PCT route. The PCT process allows an applicant to reserve the option of submitting the same application in a range of countries, using the priority date of the first application. The owner has up to 12 months to apply in other countries. The owner then has a further 16 months to obtain an International Search Report (ISR). National phase entry can occur up to 30 months after the first application, depending on

Table 4.1 Cases by progress through EPO and USPTO

	USPTO	EPO	UKIPO	IP Australia
Granted, no objections	1	1		27
Granted, after objections overcome	19	3		44
Granted after appeal	2			
Total granted	22	4 [a]	6 [a]	72 [b]
Refused	3	10 [c]	3 [d]	
Of which, appeal pending	2	2		
Actively withdrawn		5 [e]		
Abandoned	26	12	4 [d]	
Pending	3	7		
Key data missing	4	1	10	3
Total applications	54	38	13	72

Notes: Includes closely similar parent applications. Does not include applications which did not enter National Phase. Sixteen cases had no US or EPO application, but only eight had *no* parallel overseas applications.

a. One granted both by the EPO and the UKIPO.
b. Includes one case accepted but lapsed before sealing.
c. Two refused after appeal; includes one case actively withdrawn after a continuation was filed (the continuation was refused).
d. Cases noted as abandoned may well be subject matter refusals – all were terminated approximately two years after requesting examination.
e. Two of these were withdrawn before any examiner's reports were issued.

circumstances.[24] The PCT route is a highly efficient means of taking out an *option* on patenting in a number of countries, but monitoring is easier meaning greater disclosure. Eight applicants have filed in more than two countries, but directly rather than through the PCT route. Another seven have filed in only two countries: Australia and either New Zealand or the USA. Altogether 190 separate overseas applications have been identified. There are 54 parallel applications in the USA, 38 at the EPO, 35 in Canada, 29 In Japan, 23 in New Zealand and 13 in the UK.

Tracking overseas outcomes has focused on the EPO and the USPTO as both offices provided on-line access to correspondence between examiners and applicants.[25] As at July 2012 overseas applications at the EPO and USPTO are still pending for 10 cases (see Table 4.1). The EPO has granted patents in four cases but has refused 10,[26] four of which appealed the refusal. Two of the appeals have been resolved and both were rejected. The UK has granted patents in six other cases, including one where the EPO Appeal Board refused a patent. All cases where the EPO has granted a patent have also gained a US patent. In all the USPTO has granted patents in 22 cases and has refused only three, two of which are waiting

Table 4.2 Cases by type of 'invention' and USPTO/EPO outcomes

	AU	USA					EPO				
		G	R	A/W	P[a]	T	G	R	A/W	P[a]	T
Pure computerisation	21	7		9	2	18	1	7	4	2	14
Networks central	3			1		1			1		1
Databases linked	4	3		1		4	1		2		3
Analogous use	3			1		1			1		1
Combinations	20	4		9	1	14			5	3	8
Trivial variations	18	6	1	4	2	13	2	1	3	4	10
Simple idea	3	2		1		3			1		1
Total	72	22	1	26	5	54	4	8	17	9	38

Notes: Includes closely similar parents. G: grants; R: refusals; A/W: abandoned or withdrawn; P: pending; T: total applications.
a: includes cases waiting appeal outcomes.

appeal outcomes. Two of the US grants followed successful appeals (see Section 6.2). In many cases an applicant abandons or withdraws their application after receiving a negative report from the examiner. Such cases also provide useful information – altogether there are 56 cases where there is some useful information from overseas applications.

Among the 72 patents there are six cases of multiple patent ownership. Contentguard has four patents on writing contracts for purchasing digital material, and Accenture has three patents for office support systems. There are two companies and one individual who each have two patents in the dataset. US-based etalk Corporation has two closely related patents on performance evaluation. Within the sub-set of six betting patents, two are owned by an Australian individual and two by Cantor Index LLC. Cantor Index is a subsidiary of Cantor Fitzgerald, which itself has a patent among the selected cases.[27]

The selected cases can be classified along a number of dimensions: industry of use; the type of 'inventiveness' and the main reason why a patent was granted. The analysis of cases in Chapters 5, 6 and 7 focuses particularly on reason for grant, though in the case of computerisation and combination patents there is an overlap between reason for grant and type of 'inventiveness'. Table 4.2 shows the cases by type of 'inventiveness' and progress at the EPO and USPTO. For example many of the simple computerisation cases have overseas applications. Of the 18 with US applications, seven have been granted, nine abandoned, one is pending and one is waiting an appeal outcome. There were 14 with EPO applications and only one has been granted though two cases are pending (both waiting appeals). Seven have been refused, two after appealing. Four cases were abandoned or withdrawn.

A small number of cases are presented in the next section to give a flavour of the diversity of industries claiming business method patents and an introduction to the inventiveness standard.

4.4 SOME INITIAL CASES: PATENTS BY INDUSTRY OF USE

The *State Street* decision and the virtual removal of any technology basis from patentability requirements have opened the patent door to a wide range of industries never previously affected by the patent system. The 72 cases studied here include five real estate patents, 14 trade or logistics systems, 14 finance patents, eight e-commerce patents, six from marketing and advertising, nine covering aspects of organisational or business performance, six betting patents and four for selling digital products. A final six cases could not be readily classified by industry or type of support service. A small cross-section of these cases is discussed here.

Interactive property tour (AU2003250595, priority August 2002) is an example of a real estate 'invention'. It is a website providing a set of electronic images of a property, including images of a map and a plan. Icons are located on the plan. If the icon is clicked you see the view from that location. Templates, in several pre-determined styles, are provided for creating standardised web pages. Each image and associated description form one page, and the 'tour' is a group of pages. The sole feature that has any possible difference from pre-existing websites may be the icon on the map. But as pre-existing property web pages provided photos, 360° video tours, maps, and so on, this seems more a workshop variation than an invention. There is no contribution to knowledge of any kind. The claims are set out in full in the Appendix. The Australian examiner raised no novelty or inventiveness objections. At the EPO and the USPTO examiner's reports cited existing knowledge to show obviousness and the application was abandoned.

Frequently trade or logistics 'inventions' simply take existing processes and computerise them or use them on modern electronic networks. A prime example of combining old methods with the advantages of electronic networks is *System and method for selecting a service provider* (AU2003200220, priority May 2002). This is a networked system for comparison shopping for services. Traditionally, larger companies use tender processes to select service providers, balancing quality and price to select a preferred supplier. This patent includes quality-weighting of prices in a computerised tendering process. As with other business method patents, there is a large ambit claim from a small base. This system was developed for the purchase of surveillance services, and includes only the two quality dimensions of distance and cost, yet the claim is for selecting a wide range of service providers. With networks, multiple buyers can share common databases, thus reducing costs in managing the purchase of services, and it is this well-known feature of networks which creates the potential market for a system such as this. Once established, such a system would be likely to have significant network advantages over later entrants.

The calculation of quality-weighted price estimates is mere computerisation of old manual (mental) methods. Claim 1 specifies a computerised method which processes an enquiry by retrieving cost data, processing this and capturing and updating further cost data. Claim 8 provides for the retrieval, processing, capture and update of quality data. Other claims cover weighting of "performance attributes" and provision of a comparable index for each service provider. Clearly there is no new knowledge or know-how.[28]

The financial services industry has long been noted for its high level of innovation and players in this industry have been quick to grasp the new opportunities provided by patents (Lerner 2002, 2004). There are 14 finance cases in this study. One is unusual in that it does not use any computerised methods at all. It is a system for teaching children about finance revolving around the age-old concept of the child working for her pocket money (*A Financial Education System*, AU2003203582, priority April 2003). Many elements that could be found in any textbook on financial education are included. There are options that simulate tax, sickness insurance, cheque or savings accounts, credit cards,[29] and purchasing shares and/or real estate. Materials for implementing these options, e.g. pretend cheque books, are illustrated. The application was rejected as lacking any inventive step. The claims were re-written, and the patent granted.[30] There is no evidence of any contribution to any kind of knowledge.

Rivalling the finance sector in its eagerness to take advantage of the new breadth of patentable subject matter is e-commerce. The internet offers substantial new reach in delivering both goods and services, and digitisation allows a range of old business methods to be adapted to internet use. Sometimes this involves combining several old ideas and developing an internet version.

E-commerce had been around for some time when these applications were filed. The Australian government, at least, was involved in initiatives to create single business gateways in the early to mid 1990s. While the web has been around for at least as long,[31] different uses have developed at different speeds. Some of the earliest commercial uses of the web have been airline travel,[32] retailing and banking. The earliest priority date among the eight e-commerce patents is February 2000. This was after the dot.com boom of 1995–2000 so it seems unlikely that putting old ideas on the web would then be either novel or inventive even within the very narrow definitions used in patent law.

Transaction verification system (AU2004252925, priority June 2003) lies at the boundary between finance and e-commerce. This patent addresses the risk of financial fraud by requiring independent authentication of financial transactions. The core concept is use of a second, independent, communication channel to authenticate a transaction before approval. Separate authentication is fundamental to any system requiring high accuracy levels, for example the invention of double-entry book-keeping in Tuscany in the late thirteenth century (Boldrin and Levine 2008: 185). Where there is a high probability of fraud in financial transactions an obvious solution is to use the centuries old concept of independent verification. The means of sending data and receiving a return authorisation parallels systems and methods in widespread use for electronic authorisation of credit card purchases for well over a decade. The messages are encrypted, using code-hopping techniques. None of the claims covers any technical aspects of encryption or code-hopping. They simply describe a software process combining these known processes. There are no contributions to knowledge. There are no surprising results from the combination.

While there were parallel overseas applications, these were abandoned (at the EPO after receipt of the supplementary search report). The USPTO found there were two distinct inventions in these claims and the application was restricted to nine claims. These were all considered obvious in relation to existing patent and non-patent documents. The US examiner drew on common general knowledge to advise that associating a user identity with an electronic serial number was "old and well known in the art because it is used to uniquely identify each mobile communication device".[33] The applicant did not reply and the application is deemed abandoned.

Also at the borderline between finance and e-commerce patents is *A system and method for electronic commerce* (AU2005210510, priority February 2004). This prevents fraud when e-commerce orders are placed over insecure networks. It deals with ordering processes, focusing on ensuring that critical data in the order are not altered before the merchant accepts the data. This is done by use of a digital key automatically validated against a secure database. The 'advance' is that the order data do not need to be checked. If the digital signature is correct, the order is assumed valid. In other words the 'inventive' concept is identity authentication. The 39 claims do not claim new processes for setting up a digital key or encrypting this. The key is simply downloaded then used in the order and checked on receipt. At best this 'invention' takes a number of elements from known systems and combines them in a logical manner to address a specified 'problem'. There is no evidence of any contribution to knowledge in any field.

Parallel applications were abandoned at the EPO and the USPTO after negative reports. The EPO's adverse first report commented on the "notorious and commonplace features" in the claims.[34] No specific existing knowledge was cited. The application was amended but abandoned after a second negative report. There was a similar experience at the USPTO (10/588275). The claims were amended after a first rejection (lack of novelty and inventiveness). The application was abandoned after a second rejection on obviousness grounds.

The next case illustrates a market research and advertising patent. It also demonstrates both the narrow semantic arguments involved in obtaining a patent and the high level of generality of the written claims. *Ad market system and method* (AU2003235214, priority May 2002) uses extraordinarily complex and obtuse language (even for a patent) to describe a method for collecting personal data from internet users, and for advertising to them. Consumers receive unspecified incentives to provide data and watch ads. Advertisers can target selected consumers, and estimate costs based on the frequency of viewing. Underneath this it is simply software for collecting, aggregating and analysing data. The system calculates who will watch what and how often so that advertisers can look at anticipated costs and choose how to spend their budgets. It provides graphic and numeric displays.

The Australian examiner rejected the patent as not inventive, citing a single US patent. This was despite the fact that the Japanese International Preliminary Examination Report (IPER), on which he relied, listed six Japanese documents. The examiner also advised the applicant that the features in the dependent claims were either disclosed in the cited patent or were mere matters of design. The claims were amended by bringing five of the dependent claims into the independent claims. The remaining claims were simply re-numbered. The attorney argued that the "incentive setup means" and the "step of allowing the viewer to select [modules in the software]" were not in the one cited patent. The patent was immediately accepted. In other words, moving elements of design choice into the independent claim created inventiveness where there had previously been none. There is no economic rationale for grant of a monopoly in exchange for such semantic games.

The application was rejected by the USPTO (citing four US patents), amended and then rejected again before being abandoned (10/987622). At the EPO it was rejected, has been amended and remains pending. The EPO rejection followed the usual formula of advising that the subject matter was excluded but that this would not be used as the basis of rejection. As is often the case with very generally drafted business method applications the EPO advised, "the division does not find it necessary at present to refer to any particular art in support of [the lack of inventiveness] due to the paucity of technical definition going beyond the banal".[35] The applicant has responded with revised claims and the application remains pending.

This database management and analysis system makes no contributions to knowledge in either information technology generally, database management in particular, or indeed market research or advertising. Components are described in terms of "interaction means", "display means" and so on, so that it is unclear if the program has even been written. In Australia moving elements of design choice into the independent claim was sufficient to create inventiveness where previously this had been lacking. In the US the applicant has added the element of user specification of conditions – a variation used in several cases in the dataset to create a unique feature in an old combination. Whether the USPTO will agree that this creates inventiveness is as yet unknown.

Turning to organisational and business performance, *A method of determining a target event of a reoccurring event* (AU2006200104, priority May 2005) predicts recurring events such as regular meetings. This is very similar to the capability offered by Microsoft's *Outlook* since at least the mid 1990s. The method determines the cycle for the event, converts this to a numerical format, and determines a later occurrence. Subsidiary claims include periodicity greater than a day, calculations for more than one cycle, application to Julian, Georgian or lunar calendars, and display of outcomes. Nothing about this system was novel in 2005, or indeed 10 years before that.[36] The examiner rejected the patent on novelty and inventiveness grounds, citing two US and two Japanese patents. The applicant amended the claims, moving the step of converting the dates to numbers from claim 2 to claim 1 and adding the words "relative to the origin". A new claim 2, that the period for the events could be greater than one day, was introduced. The attorney argued that this particular conversion process was not noted in any of the four cited documents, and was a significant practical advantage over them. As the language of this conversion (see below) is very general, this assertion is not proven. Given the alleged importance of this element of the invention, it is interesting that it was not included in the initial specification. The patent was granted.

While Australian examiners are not required to justify their reasons for grant, it is clear from the amendments and the sequence of events that the added feature of converting a date to a number prior to manipulation then reconverting it is the basis of the grant. Electronic calculators and computers operate on binary systems and it is therefore *essential* to convert the date to a binary equivalent prior to calculations and then reconvert it to a date for presentational purposes. No detail about the method for the conversion is provided and so it cannot be determined if this method differs from those used in every other electronic diary system on the market well before May 2005. Perhaps the language used – "applying a first format operator to the or each cycle and which converts a format of the or each cycle into a numerical format that relates to the origin" – prevented the examiner from noticing how basic this procedure was.

The applicant also lodged an application at the USPTO. It was examined after the *In re Bilski* decision which emphasised the importance of software inventions being tied to a machine or transforming underlying subject matter. The US examiner rejected the application on a number of grounds, including subject matter. In his obviousness rejection he referred to a single US Microsoft patent (5813013) filed in 1996. This was an earlier patent than the four cited by the Australian examiner.[37] The USPTO report argued in detail that the cited patent included each element in the application. The application was abandoned.

Betting patents raise particular issues about 'inventions' based solely on mathematics and logic. Two cases, owned by one individual and both called *improved betting method*, were each amended before grant to take account of examiner objections. AU2005200780 (priority July 2004) proposes an alternative point at which to cut out the organiser's percentage in a parimutuel system. In such systems a percentage is taken out of the pool by the operator, before the balance is divided between those holding winning tickets. The invention is designed to make parimutuel operators more competitive with fixed odds operators by providing a process for offering a higher share of the pool in winnings to selected customers such as those placing high volume bets.[38] The 'invention' was initially rejected as non-patentable subject matter then as being neither novel nor inventive. The applicant used the previous grant of a betting patent to another applicant to argue that the 'invention' was patentable subject matter. The claims were amended to address inventiveness concerns by moving some detail from the independent to the dependent claims.

AU2005201458 (priority August 2004) deals with the returns to win and place bets. This application was also initially rejected as non-patentable subject matter and as neither novel nor inventive. The applicant amended the claims to overcome the novelty and inventiveness objections, but the system remains a simple process for paying different amounts for win and place bets. The attorney referred to the acceptance of the 2005200780 patent to argue patentable subject matter, but this was not accepted by the examiner. In the interim the *Grant 2006* decision had reinforced objections to patenting inventions with no concrete, tangible, physical effect. Amendments to overcome the objection of lack of tangible effect simply added the phrase "information processing means" at each step of the claimed process. The patent was granted.

Most betting patents are obvious once the desired outcome ('the problem') has been specified. Implementing the desired outcome is simply a matter of knowing probability theory and related branches of maths. Any skilled designer of betting systems would have this knowledge. Neither 'invention' makes any contribution to mathematical knowledge or betting know-how.

One of two medical patents falls into the miscellaneous category. *Emergency communication service providing method and device* (AU2003248001, priority September 2002) is a system for allocating emergency patients to treatment facilities. It operates through a "communications network", possibly a phone system. The network links an emergency services centre, staffed by a doctor, with treatment centres and emergency service vehicles. Data are sent from the ambulances to the centre; the centre checks treatment location availability and advises the ambulances where to go. The advice can include treatment advice.

In any large city, having centralised advice on treatment facilities for emergency patients is sensible, but this was not a new idea in September 2002. Ambulance services are often provided through a single authority and the ambulance call centre knows which hospitals are currently admitting patients, and which are not. The inclusion of medical advice on treatment during the trip may be helpful in some cases, but again is not a new feature. So this system simply combines well-known procedures. It was rejected for lack of novelty compared to three previous Japanese patents. All claims were deleted and replaced. The new claims defined a satellite communication gateway, not a feature disclosed in any of the cited knowledge. The patent was granted. Here an 'invention' making no contribution to knowledge has been granted a patent on the basis of one small feature making it trivially different from previous documented systems. Furthermore, this feature – not in itself new – is peripheral to the core content of the 'invention', though a communications gateway would be essential in its implementation. It was added simply to evade previous existing knowledge and achieve grant.

4.5 REDEFINING INVENTIVENESS

This chapter has provided a bridge between the background economics and law discussion (Chapters 2 and 3) and the analysis of cases in Chapters

5, 6 and 7. For a patent system to deliver outcomes that benefit a nation the spillover benefits must exceed the costs. As spillover benefits most frequently occur when the invention delivers new knowledge or know-how, this seems to be a useful proxy for determining which inventions should be patentable. Judges in the UK Appeals Court have commented that identifying the new knowledge contributed should be an essential part of patent examination.

Unfortunately once the examiner has identified the core contribution of the invention, s/he is then required to address a different question – "is there written evidence to deem this application obvious?" This is quite different from asking, "what new knowledge is contributed?" Requiring that a patent office prove lack of inventiveness rather than that the applicant proves a genuine knowledge contribution contributes to a low inventiveness standard. Further case law sets the amount of 'inventiveness' required at a very low level. In the UK and Australia the standard is a scintilla. There is no specific quantum of inventiveness required in the USA, though the secondary factors used by the CAFC tend to assume that any form of commercial success indicates inventiveness.

Consideration of the factors that would ensure patents are granted only for induced innovations with associated knowledge spillover benefits suggests it would be sensible to reinstitute a technology base for patentable subject matter. This includes re-instituting the exclusion of all forms of mathematical algorithm from patentable subject matter. Requiring a technology basis would be a rough proxy for assessing an R&D cost impediment to the innovation occurring without the patent incentive. An improved outcome would also be achieved simply by requiring a reasonable quantum of knowledge or know-how for any invention to be patentable.

Cases were selected for this study to minimise the age of the 'inventions' (Section 4.3). This means they are unrepresentative in terms of processing speed and ownership, but there is no reason to suppose either of these characteristics is related to inventiveness. The data set includes some cases with older priority dates and a good number from overseas applicants and there is no discernible difference in inventiveness along either dimension. An initial set of 10 cases are discussed in Section 4.4. These indicate the broad range of service industries now seeking monopolies for common processes. None of the 10 cases demonstrates any new knowledge or know-how, either in terms of the business processes involved or in terms of the software generally required for implementation.

The next three chapters discuss the remaining cases, also focusing on identifying any new knowledge or know-how. Where none is found the analysis looks at the exchanges between applicant and examiner to identify the reasons for the grant.

The cases are organised to illustrate how decision-making rules operate in practice and where they vary between patent offices. Chapter 5 looks at issues dealing with identifying existing knowledge. Also considered here are cases where amendment is used to differentiate the 'invention' from existing knowledge thus achieving grant. Interwoven with the story of amendment is the issue of the reverse onus of proof, addressed in Section 5.4. Chapter 6 considers cases where the 'invention' combines known processes, a particularly challenging issue for patent systems. Among the 41 cases where the invention is a combination, 21 involve simple computerisation of known processes. The cases presented in Chapter 7 cover a more diverse range of issues. Cases granted under the EPC, which is considered to have a higher inventive step, are reviewed in Section 7.2. Cases which illustrate the failure of doctrines designed to ensure a minimum standard to the inventive step (particularly the analogous use and workshop variation doctrines) are considered in Section 7.3. Cases presented in Section 7.4 throw light on a range of other doctrines that affect the grant of obvious inventions.

5. Finding and avoiding existing knowledge

5.1 INTRODUCTION

A major strand in the literature on business method patenting suggests that the reason so many obvious patents are granted in this field is that much of the knowledge and know-how in business is not documented. This issue is explored in Section 5.2.

Where the examiner does identify existing written knowledge and uses this to reject an application on novelty or inventiveness grounds a common response is for the applicant to make minor amendments to the claims and then argue that this overcomes such objections. In Australia the ability to endlessly amend specifications was introduced in the *Patents Act 1953*. The economic (and administrative) impact of this policy change has never been assessed. Continual amendment is also a feature of the US system. In contrast the EPO procedures provide less open-ended opportunities for amendment. Cases where amendment was critical to gaining grant of a patent are discussed in Section 5.3.

Examination procedures at the EPO, the UKIPO, the USPTO and at IP Australia set up a process whereby the examiner must disprove the eligibility of the application rather than the applicant demonstrating novelty and inventiveness.[1] Cases where applicants use this reverse onus of proof presumption to challenge inventiveness objections are discussed in Section 5.4.

5.2 FINDING EXISTING KNOWLEDGE

Both the 1966 US President's Commission on the Patent System and the 1984 IPAC report included problems identifying existing knowledge among their major reasons for recommending against software patenting (IPAC 1984; Samuelson et al 1994). Discussion of this issue forms a large part of the voluminous business method patent literature (Hunter 2004). Proposals for improved opposition hearings (e.g. Merges 1999) or for peer review (Noveck 2006) are also implicitly directed to this problem. EPO oppositions lead to high rates of revocation (36 per cent generally and 42 per cent for business method patents), suggesting a widespread problem in the identification of existing knowledge (Wagner 2008). What light do the cases considered here throw on this issue?

In 26 of the 70 cases where there is information about Australian examiners' reports, no novelty or inventiveness objections were raised. Identifying existing knowledge would thus seem a problem in over a third of cases. At the time these cases were examined Australia had a particularly narrow definition of allowable existing knowledge for assessing inventiveness.[2] For 21 of these 26 cases, examiners' reports citing existing knowledge were found at the USPTO (20 cases) and/or at the EPO (five cases). This leaves only five examined cases where no examiner at any office cited any existing knowledge. Among these five cases two were rejected by the EPO without any specific knowledge being cited – the rejection was based on common general knowledge. From this dataset the surprising finding is that existing knowledge, largely in the form of patent documentation, was found for so many of these trivial 'inventions': 65 cases.

Three of the five cases where no existing knowledge was cited in any office are presented in this section.[3] So are two cases contrasting the Australian failure to find existing knowledge with obviousness rejections at the USPTO and the EPO. A sixth case discussed here is one where there were interesting differences between the USPTO and the EPO in the existing knowledge identified. A patent was granted by the USPTO but the case was abandoned at the EPO.

Method and system of exchange (AU2003204406, priority May 2003) involves the buyer and seller of property using the same agent (a very frequent occurrence in Australia). Bids are secret (standard closed tenders) and made through the internet, or through a secure container (locked safe). The buyer pays the agent's commission. This feature is tautological. The buyer is the only party handing over money. Typically the agent's fees are deducted from the gross payment. The applicant requested expedited examination, a clear sign that others are also working in this area. The Australian examiner raised clarity issues but made no novelty or inventiveness objections. There is no contribution to knowledge and the programming is straightforward. Two well-known processes are combined (real estate selling and tendering), and the claims include a non-computerised version. While property sales by tender are relatively unusual in Australia this approach has been around for at least some decades. Patents were sought only in Australia and New Zealand and both were granted. This is a particularly clear example of the effect of a patent statute which presumes novelty and inventiveness. Where a method is so obvious that it is not written up (as everyone knows it and does it), then the examiner will be unable to find documented evidence as a basis for refusing a patent.

Commodities exchange system and method (AU2004219547, priority March 2003) is a system and method for trading physical commodities on spot (current) or futures markets. It includes the capacity for partial order execution (standard in online share trading). Buyers and sellers are warned if their price offer is worse than the current market price (another standard feature). When an order is executed, costs are calculated, inclusive of insurance and delivery. With the possible exception of the automatic insurance and delivery cost calculation, this system is no different from very many other electronic trading systems in use for some years before 2003. The additional feature of insurance and delivery is rather obvious for commodities as compared to shares. Despite the lack of any contribution to knowledge or know-how, no novelty or inventiveness objections were raised by the Australian examiner.

Interactive System and Method for Viewing On Line Advertising (AU2004210528, priority September 1999) was granted in New Zealand, but withdrawn from the EPO after an adverse examiner's report (EP2000962078, no documents cited). Viewers are randomly invited to view advertisements and are compensated with rebates on internet connection time. The rebate value depends on the time spent looking at advertisements. The core independent claim provides an excellent example of the very general language used in business method 'inventions'. Claim 1 is presented in original and translated form in Box 5.1. This shows how unintelligible most patent specifications are. Patent drafting is often designed to hide, rather than disclose knowledge (or the lack thereof). The disclosure is very general, more an idea than an artefact. Subsidiary claims concern design features – the form, location, timing and re-appearance of the ads, that the computer could be a different device, that the consumer provides data to the advertiser. The extent and frequency of flashing ads and pop-ups on the internet has grown extensively since September 1999, but the idea was not novel even then. The core 'inventive' feature is reimbursement for time – an old approach in the marketing and advertising business. There are no contributions to knowledge or know-how.

A financial management system (AU2003271414, priority September 2002) provides a computerised budgeting system with visual representations. Budget items are represented as icons, and re-allocations are shown with blocked out columns on each side and graphics with arrows and numbers in the centre, indicating where funds are flowing. It is designed for use in either an office or a home environment. Helping the relatively innumerate to understand and use budgets is important. There are many financial education materials on the market, and have been for decades, including materials with visual representations. There are also many computerised financial products on the market. This one provides *visual*

BOX 5.1 ONLINE ADVERTISING: ORIGINAL AND TRANSLATED CORE CLAIM

Application AU2004210528; priority date 24 September 1999

Claim 1: An online interactive advertising system which enables viewing of advertising by a person engaged in an activity in which the person receives electronic data and/or images and at the same time and at the option of the person views said advertising; the system comprising;

[translation: someone at a computer (or similar) receives electronic information and chooses whether to look at advertising too]

a consumer station which receives electronic data or images; an information provider which delivers said electronic data or images to said consumer station, a host having a website with which said consumer station communicates and interacts, an advertising provider in communication with said host; wherein the advertising provider communicates via said host with said consumer station via the internet upon election by said consumer station responsive to an invitation from said host; wherein, without requiring software downloaded and installed into the consumer station, the consumer receives said advertising material by responding to a random invitation from the host, which appears at the consumer station wherein, when said consumer elects to view advertising from said advertising provider via said host, the consumer receives rewards, credits or benefits commensurate with the length of time advertising is viewed.

[translation: a consumer uses a computer, connected to the internet, and, in response to an invitation, can choose to access a website with advertising without downloading any software; the invitation is random and if the consumer chooses to look at the ads s/he gets rewards related to how long s/he looks at the ads].

illustrations for a very basic budgeting system, surely a matter of design, not function. There is nothing new in the function of the system. The 'invention' contributes no new knowledge to either finance or information technology fields. The 24 claims are shown in the Appendix. They are relatively simply phrased, and illustrate how business method claims are often repetitive. Here the claims are presented as a system (claims 1–11) and a method (claims 12–22). The final two claims are for a program and a "computer readable medium" version.

This is an Australian PCT application, and the IPER, issued in Australia, identified four patents *and no non-patent material*, and concluded that all claims were novel and inventive. In contrast, the USPTO examiner rejected the application as being obvious in relation to three US patent documents, all dated 2001 or earlier. One of these documents was identified in the Australian IPER. The claims were amended, in particular by moving features from dependent to independent claims. The examiner was not persuaded that this created inventiveness and, using the same documents, again rejected the application. All 25 claims were deleted and replaced with 15 new claims. The new claims were rejected as not novel in relation to a 1988 US patent (Pollalis), and obvious compared to this and two other documents. The applicant successfully argued against the novelty objection as Pollalis was a project management system, but the examiner identified three new documents which, in combination with Pollalis, maintained the obviousness objection. Again the applicant disagreed, but in his fifth rejection the examiner again rejected the application as obvious.[4] A request for continuing examination has been granted and the case remains pending as at July 2012.

This is an interesting contrast between the two offices in identifying existing knowledge and in using this to assess inventiveness. The failure to use non-patent art in either office seems extraordinary, given the subject matter. In the US, at least, this might not have been necessary because of the many relevant patent documents found. The contrast between the Australian IPER, which found no documents defeating novelty or inventiveness, and the USPTO's five rejections also raises issues about international sharing of critical search materials.

System for permission-based communication and exchange of information (AU2003247258, priority February 2002) is a market research/advertising patent, also granted in New Zealand. It was abandoned in the USA and at the EPO after a single rejection by each office. The claims cover the receipt and storage of data from multiple consumers, database searching in response to requests, and providing search results. The method provides 'promotional' material to selected consumers, and aggregated consumer information to the promoter. The promoter is charged for these services and the consumers receive a 'fee' for their responses. The fees can be forwarded to a range of destinations (banks, service providers etc.). All of this can happen in a variety of environments, including email and SMS. The claims specify in detail how consumer data are collected (basically questionnaires with multiple fields) and updated. A wide range of variables can be collected. The owner identifies a critical contribution as consumers identifying what commercial material they are willing to receive.

This is a straightforward system for collecting, analysing and distributing data, via a range of electronic media, with provision for the collection of fees and payments to providers. The claimed advance – consumers identifying relevant material – is framed as allowing consumers to "market themselves to businesses". But in reality this 'invention' simply combines standard market research data and promotional techniques with user choice. In essence it is a database system. Academics have been linking databases for many decades. The addition of the consumer choice feature (the "permission-based" system) is quite straightforward. Focusing on what consumers want is a very old strategy for business success.

The Australian examiner identified two patent documents but concluded that these "citations do not disclose or even suggest the invention as claimed. The citations relate to obtaining data to create customer profiles but do not involve a permission based system. The invention must therefore be considered to be novel and to involve an inventive step."[5] Given the extreme detail in the 115 claims, it would be hard for an examiner, constrained by the suggestion doctrine, to rule out the 'invention' on obviousness grounds. On the other hand, if patent rules required the inventor to demonstrate that the invention was inventive, it is equally hard to see what material could possibly be used to support this application.

Examiners at the USPTO and the EPO both raised objections. The US examiner raised inventiveness problems, citing two patent documents, and subject matter issues (not tied to a machine and not transforming subject matter). The applicant, a British company, did not reply to the examiner's report and the application (US10/504839) was deemed abandoned. The European version was amended before examination, with the 115 claims fully replaced and reduced to ten. In March 2009 the examiner advised that while it seemed likely this was excluded subject matter, conflicting Board of Appeal decisions did not allow a straightforward decision on this matter.[6] Consequently it was rejected for want of inventiveness, noting that the non-technical steps required no ingenuity for their technical (i.e. software) implementation. No specific existing knowledge was cited. Again the UK company did not respond and the application was deemed abandoned.

This case shows how, despite the EPO's reluctance to refuse applications because the 'invention' is excluded subject matter, the separation of claim content into allegedly technical matters (operation of computer or other equipment) and non-technical matters does not prevent refusing uninventive business method inventions. In this case the EPO determined that all matters except programming were non-technical. As the conversion of the business processes into software was straightforward, the application lacked 'technical inventiveness' and so was refused. Simple refusal as a business method would have been clearer to the applicant and required fewer resources. It could also have occurred in 2004 when the European search report was done, rather than in 2009 when the exam report was completed. This, however, would have deprived the EPO of five years of renewal fees.

The next case is another 'invention' for database management. The EPO found substantially different existing knowledge than the US and Australian offices. A patent was granted in New Zealand, the USA and the UK,[7] but the application was abandoned at the EPO. *A system for and method for authenticating items* (AU2003207780, priority April 2002) is one of many cases where a known system and method is applied to a marginally new use. The 'invention' was designed as a database system for tracking items owned by celebrities and used at specific public events. It incorporates an ID into the item(s) before the event, stores the data, and allows updates. Subsidiary claims cover sporting and other events, types of item, data storage, 'identification means', scanning, and online features. ID means includes RFID tags and tamper minimisation, including heat sealed patches. As in other business method patents, the claims do not cover the technical features of these types of ID, but rather the programming for linking the data. Essentially it is a system for storing, linking and updating data.

The 'inventive' feature is use by celebrities at events. Attaching identification to items through a range of means is quite old technology.[8] The specific use scenario seems inadequate grounds for granting a monopoly. Implementation is unchallenging in terms of programming. No contributions to knowledge or know-how about database use are evident.

This 'invention' was granted in Australia less than eight months after filing, a remarkably speedy outcome in the patent world. No novelty or inventiveness objections were raised by the examiner. A request for re-examination was received from a competitor some two years after sealing. The applicant was advised that the fee for this was a hefty A$1,300 and did not proceed with the request.[9]

Although granted in the USA, the US examiner issued three rejections on novelty and obviousness grounds. Following each rejection the claims were amended. In responding to the third rejection the argument was put that the "invention employs an RFID *similar to the way a master craftsman historically used his signature or mark*" (emphasis added). This seems an extraordinary argument to put in trying to show inventiveness – referring to an approach that has been used for centuries. But it does indicate the attitude of entitlement that is evident in many of these applications. The applicant went on to argue the invention was unique in providing authentication "in some way associated with *an event* or with *one or more participants in the event*". The examiner then issued a notice allowing grant of a patent, commenting that existing knowledge did not 'teach' use of a RFID tag "to authenticate that the item has been used at the event".[10] This use of a specific type of ID at a specific type of event was the deciding factor in patent grant. It clearly demonstrates the very narrow definition of inventiveness in the USA.

At the EPO the applicant maintained the application despite a European search report identifying five patent documents challenging novelty and inventiveness. The examiner's report cited four patent documents (only one of which was in the Australian ISR). The patented knowledge cited in the EPO report was also a different set from that cited by the USPTO examiner. The EPO examiner found 50 of the claims to be not novel and the remaining 23 not inventive. The applicant did not reply to this report and the application has been abandoned.

As well as illustrating the lack of new knowledge or know-how, these six examples indicate that in some cases, especially where a number of old elements are re-arranged into a (marginally) new combination, it can be very hard for the examiner to document the exact 'invention'. The last case also illustrates how narrow is the difference required to show 'inventiveness' compared to existing knowledge. These cases also illustrate the use of amendment, which is discussed next.

5.3 AMENDMENT

Where the examiner finds existing documented knowledge and rejects the claims as lacking novelty or inventiveness, claims are often amended to ensure that the *exact combination of characteristics* identified by the examiner is avoided. The EPO has a well-designed system to ensure no more than two considerations by examiners before a final decision. In theory a final rejection at the USPTO should be just that, but in 22 out of 54 cases a final rejection did not terminate the examination process.[11]

Ten cases are discussed in this section. They illustrate a variety of types of amendment. In its ultimate form this strategy can include withdrawal of an application once a divisional has been filed, thus setting up a new opportunity to refine the wording. The EPO version of an application for computerisation of PCT applications provides an example of this. After clear advice from the examiner that the application was considered unpatentable the applicant filed a divisional and a few hours later withdrew the parent.

System and method of attracting and lodging PCT national phase applications (II) (AU2003244578, priority October 2000) has had some difficulty achieving patent grant except in Australia and New Zealand. The Australian examiner considered the claims related to two inventions, one for a system where an application instruction was received by email, and the other via a website interface. The applicant accordingly deleted all email claims. The examiner had limited his search and report to claim 1, the deleted independent claim, and considered this to concern only common business practice in attorney firms. Once the elements which had been examined were deleted, the patent was granted. While there was no effective examination of the website claims that were granted, the process was identical between the two versions. It is unclear why the examiner then issued a patent for what he considered to be common business practice in patent attorney firms.

The patent as granted is for a website where, in response to receiving a PCT national phase filing instruction, a PCT database is searched to identify the application, and costs are calculated based on number of pages and number of claims. An attorney database is checked to identify the instructing attorney and amend this information if necessary. Possible elements in the costing are listed. This is a very clear example of mere computerisation of a longstanding manual method ('mental steps'). By 2000 such simple computerisations were common business practice, a well-known method of raising productivity.

The US application was initially rejected on subject matter grounds (both computer program and lack of apparatus/transformation) as well as novelty and obviousness grounds. The computer program objections were overcome by changing the phrase "an interface" to "a computer system" or a "computer being programmed to" and the transformation objections by adding to claim 1 "display at least part of said cost information on said interface".[12] By the fourth rejection only obviousness problems were raised. Amendments submitted after the fifth rejection were considered non-compliant as they simply repeated earlier argument and the application was abandoned.

The application was actively withdrawn from the EPO after two adverse reports, and only hours after a divisional had been filed. The examiner considered the application had technical character as the software ran on a computer, but could not find any interaction with the non-technical components. The examiner had also pointed out that converting the business process to software was a non-technical matter, saying:

> Writing *computer programs as such* is per se a non-technical activity, it is technically no different from writing a piece of music or a novel. Thus, the writing of

a *computer program as such* does not, in itself, contribute to the solution of any technical problem.[13]

The claims were amended so that each had a technical character ("computer-based interface"). However in the summons to an oral hearing the examiner advised that the method still did not have technical character as "it employs no technical means, causes no technical effect and solves no technical problem".[14] As noted above the applicant then filed a divisional and withdrew this application.

This strategy of lodging a divisional immediately prior to withdrawing an application that will be rejected creates a new fee stream for the patent office and a new grant opportunity for the applicant, but it is unclear what public good function it provides. Processes exist for applicants to appeal negative decisions, and to allow a repetition of the same application is a simple waste of resources. The divisional repeats the same steps as its parent, but the claims are directed to a website for lodging PCT applications (as in the Australian version).[15] The EPO again noted the application had only non-technical subject matter but formally rejected it because it does not involve any inventive step (Article 56). This is in line with the EPO's clear aversion to rejecting applications on the subject matter grounds of Article 52(2) when Article 52(3) applies. The continuation was formally refused at an oral hearing in March 2012.

Another simple computerisation of known procedures is a computerised expert medical system (*Medical data warning notifying system and method*, AU2003281184, priority July 2002). Expert systems involve the conversion of human knowledge into computerised systems. They require programming a highly specific set of rules, which simply translate into binary code the thought and decision processes of the expert(s). This type of system originated in the artificial intelligence field during the 1960s and 1970s and started to be applied commercially in the 1980s.

Expert systems are a useful tool releasing expensive and highly trained labour. Like audit, benchmarking and other common methodologies expert systems can be applied across a wide range of fields. Development of the specific rules in a new field might be time-consuming, but requires attention to detail not ingenuity. So one would think that the use of an expert system in a new arena would not meet the normal definition of inventiveness. In fact this is not the only expert system among the cases reviewed here.[16]

The claims were originally written in general terms covering any set of medical data transmitted from the home and monitored by a professional. They were twice rejected by the Australian examiner for want of novelty and inventiveness. In response to the first rejection the applicant added considerable detail about the specific medical data to the claims, and narrowed the scope to peritoneal dialysis. The Australian examiner again rejected the application for want of inventiveness, arguing that the differences in specific medical indicators listed would be obvious. The claims were further amended, limiting them to a system with a server giving a warning message, then reverting to stand-by mode.

In arguing that the 'invention' now differed from previous patents, the attorney emphasised that the earlier patents *did not include a server reverting to stand-by mode*. This trivial feature – entirely irrelevant to the substance of the 'invention' and a standard procedure in computer operations – made the difference between rejection and grant. The difference in outcome between Australia and Korea – where the application was rejected – indicates the impact of different approaches to inventiveness.[17] Claim 1, which includes this limiting factor, runs for half a page and the limiting factor is embedded in the last sub-paragraph of the claim (see full claims in the Appendix). It may not therefore be obvious to competitors that this patent should have very narrow scope.

A well-known problem in patent systems is that language can be narrowly construed in determining grant but subsequently broadly construed in litigation.[18] Whether the limitation embedded in the lengthy first claims would constrain use of this patent would depend on court interpretation.

The application was withdrawn from the EPO following receipt of the supplementary European search report, identifying two novelty-challenging patent documents (EP2003741375). It was rejected twice by the USPTO (10/521235). In response to the first rejection the applicant submitted amendments similar to those first submitted in Australia – the claims were limited to peritoneal dialysis. The US examiner considered that these details were non-functional elements with no patentable weight and again rejected the application. The applicant did not respond and the application was deemed abandoned.

The amendments in the next case confirm that the distinguishing feature creating 'inventiveness' can be very minor. *Method and system for blocking unwanted e-mail* (AU2003244552, priority September 2003) checks the addresses of incoming emails and allows them through if the address is known, and blocks them if they are from a known unwanted address. For remaining emails the method despatches a query to the sender, such that only a human being can reply. If a correct reply is received this and future mail from that sender is allowed through. Reports are provided. The method depends on interrogating headers, and the contents of blocked or unknown emails are not received onto the server.

The applicant requested expedited examination because of concerns about infringement (independent invention): a clear indication that the approach was sufficiently obvious that others were developing similar products. The patent was accepted in 32 weeks and sealed within a year of filing. The examiner initially considered the main claim to be neither novel nor inventive. The claims were amended "to clarify the invention over the cited prior art". The applicant's attorney argued that this invention was "not a challenge response", and that it had the major advantage of not downloading unwanted emails onto the server. But according to independent *Ferris Research* this patent *is* for a challenge/response system, though the feature that rejected emails are not downloaded does differ from other such products.[19] Interestingly this last feature is *optional* in the marketed product. It is not part of the main claim (claim 1), but shows up in subsidiary claim 11. The programming is straightforward. The business idea not to receive what you do not want would almost seem tautological – the ultimate in the obvious.

However, giving the 'invention' the benefit of the doubt, it may be that the *idea* of not receiving unwanted email *on a server* was new at the time. There had been considerable public discussion about the problem of unwanted spam by September 2003 – Australia's Spam Act was passed in 2003 and preceded by substantial public debate. The best point at which to block spam is likely to have been considered in these many discussions. It is not mere hindsight to identify a range of issues that would have been identified in addressing spam prevention, and the point at which the unwanted email should be queried must be dealt with in writing the software. Although this idea *may* be 'novel' compared to any written documentation, it is likely to have occurred to many experts in the field, as is indicated by the applicant's concern about others working along similar lines. Though unlikely, it is possible that this 'invention' contains a new idea. The possible new idea is buried in claim 11 and is optional in the marketed product. It seems probable it was added to overcome novelty and inventiveness objections.[20]

A patent at the boundary between software, information management and business improvement is *Dynamic Collaboration Assistant* (AU2003264604, priority March 2003). Accenture's specification notes the piecemeal development of computerised systems for supporting electronic teamwork and collaboration (e-mail, groupware (shared use files), mail and message lists, and "team workspace applications" (chat rooms and shared file storage)). The background argues that this 'invention' "integrates collaborative services into business processes to enable partners to share related information".

The 44 claims (summarised in Box 5.2) set up a "knowledge model" of all documents, files, individuals and organisational units each assigned to one or more contexts. Whenever a user creates a new document, the knowledge module is checked and possible applications are displayed. The underlying idea of developing and using classifications is, of course, very old. The EPO examiner considered the essence of the invention lay in the "use of well-known information modelling concepts such as user profile and knowledge module". The economic policy question is, does the new use in a specific environment create any spillover benefits to justify grant of a monopoly?

BOX 5.2 DYNAMIC COLLABORATION ASSISTANT (SUMMARY OF CLAIMS)

Application 2003264604; priority date: 19 March 2003

1 method of collaborating across computer network by: generating a GUI* displaying 1+ collaborative applications; determine use context; adjust display of applications based on use context and list related documents/files
  2 provide links to listed documents;
    3 use context determined by scanning opened documents to see if they are new
      5 if new, does document contain contextual information?;
        6 by comparing user profile with new document;
          7 drawing on contextual matching pattern;
        8 terminal sends message to server if contextual information;
          9 message is read;
            10 context information checked against knowledge model to give list of relations;
              11 including associated user and document lists;
              12 send message re new context to terminal;
              13 GUI# display on terminal consequently adjusted.
    4 use context determined by querying knowledge model where existing documents, files, people and organisations are associated with a use context
14 Repeats claim 1 for a "dynamic collaboration assistant" version: detail on the sub-elements ("text scanning component', "context parser", "context listener") repeated as in claims 15–25.
26 Repeats claims 1 and 14 for a "computer program for use in . . ." version: followed by similar details phrased as computer usable medium, program code, configured in various ways and capable of analysis as per sub-claims above, repeated in claims 27–38.
39 Repeats main claim in terms of a terminal connected to a server, means for generating the GUI*, determining the use context, and means for analysing and adjusting display.
40 As per claims 14–25, where context listener can be placed in active or inactive state by the terminal user
41 As per claims 14–25, contains context selector component allowing manual setting of context
42–44 As per drawing claims.

Note: * *GUI: graphical user interface (i.e. an icon).*

The Australian examiner rejected the application twice. In response to the first rejection the applicant amended the claims to clarify the importance of the *context* in which the terminal was being used. The examiner responded that two previous patents also determined context by using keywords and then adjusting displays. The applicant's attorney disagreed with this interpretation. He argued that displaying group information was not the same as displaying lists of documents, and that keywords did not fully describe context. The patent was granted. Again it was minor differences in design features and the words used to describe them – rather than even a modest difference in substance – which led to the grant. Effectively marginally different methods of determining the context of use of a networked terminal were deemed sufficient to meet patent law's minimalist definition of inventiveness. Amendment was critical in assisting this application to pass the very low inventiveness threshold.

The patent was granted in the USA after five rejections and eight sets of amendments (10/391,680). It has been refused at the EPO, but an appeal is pending. The five US rejections encompassed grounds of lack of clarity, non-patentable (computer program) subject matter, lack of novelty and lack of inventiveness, based on several US patent documents, principally Satoh (US patent 6675197). The initial objection that the claims were nothing more than a computer program was overcome through amendment. The substantive discussion by the examiner across five rejections covered 102 pages of minutiae on the differences between the application and prior patent documents. In the end the examiner redrafted the claims in their entirety then granted a patent. The argument justifying grant encompasses a paragraph-long sentence listing the detailed features of the revised invention, so it is the highly specific detail of the combination which made the grant possible.

At the EPO the examiner relied on a single prior art document – the same Satoh application but in its original Japanese version. The application was originally rejected as unclear as well as lacking in novelty and inventiveness. The claims were amended to address clarity concerns and claim 1 changed the phrase "monitoring a context" to "determining a context" "to clarify that the claimed invention involves a technical process".[21] This change from the passive monitoring to the active determining overcame novelty objections but the application was again rejected on inventiveness grounds. The next set of amendments focused on displaying "a plurality of different collaboration applications" and an argument that the invention reduced the bandwidth required when updating networked terminals. The applicant was summoned to an oral hearing, but declined to attend and asked for a detailed appealable decision. That document provided four pages of argument about the lack of inventiveness in the independent claims. Accenture has appealed.[22]

An Identification Card Production and Distribution Method (AU2004201620, priority April 2004) allows the supplier to obtain appropriate data to populate the fields of an ID card template over the internet. It then displays an image of the draft final product to the client. The process starts by verifying the client's computer's identity. That's it. In other words it takes advantage of modern electronic networks to deliver standard processes for producing ID cards. There is no contribution to new methods of doing business or to software programming.

Although designed specifically for ID cards, the claims cover a wide range of other products, showing how patentees successfully claim larger monopolies from small 'inventions'. The examiner rejected the application twice for lack of novelty and inventiveness in relation to one patent document. In the first reply the attorney amended the claims by shifting details from claim 2 to claim 1. He argued that the amended feature of verifying the identity of the client's computer made the claim both novel and inventive in relation to the cited patent document. The examiner replied that the amendments introduced new subject matter, and that the claim remained obvious as verifying a remote computer location was merely use of the well-known device of a cookie. The claims were amended to remove the implied new subject matter but did not address the inventiveness objection. The patent was granted just five days after this second response was mailed. This seems surprising given that the lack of novelty was not addressed by the applicant nor dealt with in the amendments.

Minor rearrangement of claims wording can also gain a patent at the EPO as shown in the next case. Secure transactions over the net, using fingerprint authentication, is the subject of *Method of conducting transactions over a network* (AU2004203415, priority February 2000). The 'invention' is a computer program that authenticates messages prior to financial transactions by means of encrypted fingerprint data. The idea of using encryption for internet financial transactions was well established by 2000. The claim is not for a new method of encryption, nor for any improved encryption device.

This patent is a child of a US PCT application,[23] with the child being filed only in the USA and Australia. The parent and child applications are very similar: a terminal disclaimer applies to the US child, which was granted after nine rejections. The argument revolved around where the fingerprints are stored and whether this location had been 'taught' by previous knowledge. In the first and second rejections the examiner used an official notice procedure to put the onus on the applicant to demonstrate that encrypted stored fingerprint data was not part of common general knowledge. The applicant argued that in a technical field such a use of the official notice procedure was improper. By the seventh rejection a non-patent document had been added to the cited existing knowledge regarding encryption and the storage location for the fingerprints. After the eighth rejection the USPTO advised there were four different inventive concepts and asked for an election/restriction to one. Following this restriction, the examiner redrafted the claims and issued an Allowance Notice. Unusually, he gave no reason for the change in opinion.

In Australia the child was rejected twice, and at length. The Australian examiner initially raised concerns about fair basis, more than one inventive concept, and lack of novelty and inventive step compared to a wide range of existing knowledge. The applicant made considerable amendments to the claims to meet these objections. The attorney argued that earlier fingerprint authentication systems involved transmitting fingerprints to match against a central database, in contrast to storing the fingerprints in the authentication device so that only the authentication was transmitted. This argument implies that simply storing data in a different location becomes grounds for inventiveness. The examiner demurred, and again rejected the application arguing that the relevant documents disclosed storing the fingerprints in a stand-alone system. The applicant re-argued this point at length, and the patent was granted. Unfortunately Australian patent examiners, unlike their counterparts at the USPTO, are not required to provide reasons for grant.

The closely similar parent was filed at the EPO.[24] In an extraordinary demonstration of the lack of clarity in the term 'technical' and of the lack of substance to the inventiveness test, the EPO granted the parent a patent when nine words were moved from claim 2 to claim 1 (EP2001911157). Before this minor rearrangement in wording the EPO had found no evidence of any technical inventiveness in the claims. The examiner's report noted that the objective was a business method, defined in terms of the steps of the claim. The examiner considered that there was no solution to any technical problem – the technical character of the claim lay in the use of the network to communicate authentication. But the technical system was used for a non-technical process, which could be implemented without any inventive step. Following this rejection the words "wherein the stored fingerprint is in an encrypted format" were moved from claim 2 to claim 1 (and parallel words from claim 34 to 33). Thirteen claims were deleted. These semantic changes – which in no way changed the nature of the underlying software-implemented business method – convinced the EPO that the 'invention' now had both technical character and inventiveness. A patent was granted in June 2007. But the 'invention' remains a computer process to authenticate identity based on receipt of an authentication code from the fingerprint device. The fact that the stored fingerprints are encrypted merely changes the piece of data transmitted but in no way affects the process of authentication covered by the claims. The steps of the claim continue to define a simple business method.

This EPO case highlights the challenges to sound innovation policy posed by delivering innovation policy through the legal system. From an economic or industry policy perspective it is hard to see why semantics should be allowed to determine that others should be prevented from developing similar business systems. This is not the only application in the dataset where deleting subsidiary claims and moving their words into the main claim suddenly made an uninventive invention inventive.

Trading tools for electronic trading (AU2003228606, priority April 2002), a US continuation, has been granted in the USA, Korea and the UK. It is pending at the EPO. The UK patent office provides no online record of the thinking underlying this grant.[25] The Korean grant was preceded by a refusal.

The applicant suggests the disadvantage of existing electronic trading systems is that multiple elements must be entered to place an order (such as commodity identifier, price, quantity, and whether buy or sell order),[26] and notes that taking longer to enter orders can reduce competitive advantage. The 'invention' consolidates these elements in a single control icon, which can be amended while watching other trading information. Effectively the claimed method repositions the buy/sell information into the icon. This is technically equivalent to re-sizing screens and having several open at once. Another technical equivalent would be multiple screens. Given the system shown in the 27 pages of diagrams, it is clearly designed for professional traders, who usually do have multiple monitors. Any computer-literate frequent trader, professional or not, has probably discovered this technical equivalent for themselves.

The Australian examiner considered it was neither novel nor inventive remarking that "[t]he claims relate to a procedure which is well known". The applicant cancelled 56 of the 59 claims, added 18 new claims and replaced all the figures. The applicant then argued successfully that *the precise integers* – largely the repositioning of axes in response to commands – were not disclosed in the cited prior art. The 'invention' remains a trivial design variation on existing systems. There is no contribution to knowledge of trading systems or to software technology.

The USPTO identified three different inventions. The selected method version was then rejected as indefinite and obvious. The examiner also identified double patenting issues and, unusually, also objected to the abstract being "so generic and short that it is of no apparent value". He helpfully advised the applicant that, based on previous patents granted to the applicant, the addition of the limitation "wherein the method in combination includes consolidating the price levels of the common static price axis such that a plurality of price levels are combined into a consolidated price level" to would "render the claims patentable".[27] The applicant amended the abstract and thanked the examiner for his helpfulness but did not amend the claims. The examiner again rejected the application on grounds of double patenting and obviousness. Following a personal interview and a change of examiner, the claims were amended overcoming double patenting and inventiveness concerns. The inventive feature was having two displays of market information (each showing price movements) but controlled by two different software processes. Again this suggests an extremely narrow reading of previous knowledge within a closely related environment of use – not the definition of inventiveness called for by the underlying economic rationale for the grant of patent monopolies.

The EPO examiner rejected the application for lack of inventive step, citing no documents as "the employed technical means are so conventional that they were widely available to everyone . . . and no documentary evidence is considered required because of their notoriety".[28] The claims have been amended and the application remains pending.

A very simple financial product patent is Westpac's *Integrated financial service product* (AU2005204292, priority August 2005). Westpac, one of Australia's four main banks, asked for expedited examination to progress the product's commercial launch. The 'invention' is a computerised system for a package of three accounts (a loan account, a credit card account and any other available account). The loan and credit card accounts have a single credit limit, and are both unsecured loans. They have different interest rates. There is a rewards program associated with how the customer manages transactions in and balances between the two accounts. There are transaction and rewards databases to manage the information, and produce customer statements.

In first rejecting the five (repetitive) main claims, the examiner pointed to lack of novelty and inventiveness, citing two patent documents and three non-patent documents, including competitor Commonwealth Bank's Viridian package. Westpac's attorney replied at length, arguing that "none of the cited documents discloses *each and every one* of the essential features of the present application" (emphasis added). She argued that none of the cited documents would lead a skilled person to develop this particular invention, ignoring the well-known high level of innovativeness in the financial sector. The examiner was unimpressed by the attorney's arguments and again rejected the application as lacking inventiveness.

In her lengthy reply, Westpac's attorney presented a detailed comparison with the Viridian product. This comparison depended heavily on *extremely narrow* readings of specific features: for example the fact that customers *can* link credit cards to the Viridian product, but that they are not *compulsory*, is used as an argument for 'inventiveness'. Similarly the Viridian benefit in terms of reduced loan debt is not "reward currency" and there are no "reward program rules".[29] Although in the context it is clear that benefit and reward are closely similar, these arguments overcame the objections. The patent was accepted within a month.

There is no addition to knowledge. The differences between the two products are at best marginal. They are more like workshop *variations* than workshop *improvements*. Indeed the examiner advised in his first report that the subsidiary claims were merely matters of design. The programming is straightforward.

Another patent effectively rejected in the USA is *A system and method for representation of business information* (AU2004201587, priority April 2004). This links business data and geographic data so that the business data can be mapped and presented visually on a map. The attorney asked for expedited examination as "the applicant has a number of close competitors in the area and believes they are developing potentially infringing systems". This is a clear indication that the 'invention' is obvious within the field, so no incentive is needed.

The claims were subject to extensive correspondence between the Australian examiner and the applicant, with the examiner rejecting the application four times. Initially the principal claims were rejected as neither novel nor inventive and the subsidiary claims as being merely matters of design choice, or typical methods given general knowledge. The applicant requested reconsideration, on the basis that the business information did not have a spatial component and so could not be mapped without conversion. The examiner was unconvinced. The applicant then amended the claims, arguing that while existing systems provided a map application function for business data, in the claimed invention a predefined protocol allowed the user to change the view, update the data and work in the spatial dimension. While this is a different means of generating the mapped data, nothing in the application indicates any software inventiveness. Indeed the differences appear to be design features.

Following a third negative report from the examiner, the applicant modified the claims again to clarify that the two applications (business data and map generation) *interface* with each other, so that the mapping function takes in the data and manipulates it to produce a map. The accompanying argument claimed that the prior art did not discuss an *interface* between business data and mapping techniques (though it did allow users to map business data). By the fourth exchange of views, the examiner indicated a willingness to reconsider the application if the broadest claims were narrowed in scope, and the interface element was written into claim 1. The additional words simply specify an interface which selects business information data and imports this into the mapping module. But given that other known systems allowed users to map business data this interface feature can at best be seen as a technical equivalent to the earlier systems.

Like the expert medical system discussed above, this case shows how a specific, well-known, software feature can be written into business process claims simultaneously narrowing the scope and creating 'inventiveness'. This is a rather hard concept to understand. It seems to say, "if I make this uninventive invention narrower in its scope it can pass the inventiveness test it previously failed". Quite how this contributes to the goal of patent policy is unclear.

The US examiner also had significant problems with this application, raising novelty and obviousness problems, citing one US patent and common general knowledge. He used the official notice procedure to place the onus on the applicant to refute the claim of common general knowledge. No response was received and in June 2008 the application was deemed abandoned.[30]

The USPTO rejected *On-line Interactive System and Method for Transacting Business* (AU2003231594, priority July 1999) four times. This online method for buying, selling and transporting goods reserves goods when a purchase request made. The buyer's credit rating is then checked and the goods are either sold and shipped or returned to inventory, depending on the outcome of the credit check. This approach is hundreds if not thousands of years old, though this version uses electronic network capabilities. In particular shippers' networks are used to gather and assess financial data about purchasers and to collect and forward payments. It was effectively refused by the EPO, though the applicant argued a 'technical' advance to the 'technical' problem of reducing ordering times. The EPO considered any time saving a business objective and noted there was nothing inventive in the software implementation. The application was withdrawn following a summons to oral proceedings. It has been refused in Korea and granted in the USA, Russia and New Zealand.[31]

In granting the patent the US examiner included amendments agreed during a telephone conversation. These focused on the role of the freight carrier. The basis for grant was the role of the freight carrier (shipper) in assessing credit worthiness using a specified range of inputs. As was the case with the virtually identical parent, the Allowance Notice also noted that ". . . none of the art of record, alone or in combination, discloses that *the freight carrier*, in a trade transaction, *that ships the goods* to the buyer *is also playing the role of a financial facilitator . . .*".[32] This variation was added to the parent as an amendment during the examination process. Using shipper's established networks to collect and disburse funds for internationally traded items does not, in itself, appear to be more than a change in design elements.

This case again shows how the legal approach to assessing inventiveness bears no relation to any normal understanding of the meaning of inventiveness. There are no contributions to new knowledge, whether technical or business knowledge. The central 'inventive' concept – reserving stock at the point of order – cannot possibly be considered even novel, given the history of wholesale trade. The distinguishing feature claimed – using shipping agents – seems more of a workshop variation or a design feature than an inventive element. Yet the patent has been granted in three countries and refused only in Korea and at the EPO. Like other patents in this dataset changing the actor in a business process seems in itself to create patent eligibility. This is a very far cry from the objective of increasing investment in technology.

A frequent observation from these 10 cases is that when the examiner identifies existing knowledge demonstrating a lack of novelty or inventiveness, the applicant merely amends features to make a small difference. In some cases the applicant thanks the examiner for finding this existing knowledge. In 50 out of 72 cases the claims were amended at least once during their processing in Australia. Claims were amended more than once in 22 cases and three applicants amended claims six times. These cases illustrate how semantics can be more important than substance in determining grant of a patent monopoly. Such strategic games range from simply rewording the claims where the subject matter is non-patentable (for example, computer programs or mental steps) to the addition of minor design features to ensure that a specific combination of old elements passes the inventiveness test. Such standard features as user specification of conditions, specific actors or unrelated computer processes (going to standby mode) can be added to ensure that the exact combination found in existing documents is avoided. Astonishingly these changes can involve narrowing scope or adding peripheral or optional features. The most astounding aspect of patent law's inventiveness definition is that the simple act of moving words from dependent to independent claims creates inventiveness where previously there was none. This magic happens in all offices and can even overcome EPO objections that an application has no technical element of inventiveness.

These cases show that only very trivial variations to existing knowledge are needed for the grant of a patent in all three jurisdictions. Effectively the patent law definition of 'inventive' has become 'trivially different'. But a marginally different way of producing the same result does not add to knowledge, except in unusual circumstances. As Machlup remarked 50 years ago:

> The production of the knowledge of how to do in a somewhat different way what we have already learned to do in a satisfactory way would hardly be given highest priority in a rational allocation of resources. (Machlup 1958: 51)

5.4 ONUS OF PROOF

From an economic policy perspective a widely accepted rule to prevent special interests reducing national economic well-being is that there should be a very clear demonstration of *national* benefit before any intervention to reduce competition in markets. In Australia, for example, the Federal-State Competition Principles Agreement exemplifies this in guiding principles for legislation. Article 5.1 of the Agreement provides a that "legislation . . . should not restrict competition unless it can be demonstrated that: (a) the benefits of the restriction to the community as a whole outweigh the costs; and (b) the objectives of the legislation can only be achieved by restricting competition."[33]

This principle is economically sound in all nations and at all levels, from national legislation to individual applications for monopolies. Despite this, patent statutes are drafted in such a way that the seeker of a benefit from the government does not bear the full onus for demonstrating their case. Rather the onus lies with the government to demonstrate lack of eligibility. Patent statutes in Australia and the UK set out a presumption of inventiveness[34] which effectively reverses the onus of proof. This is also evident in the USA, though to a lesser extent.[35] The US system also has an "official notice" procedure whereby the examiner can place the onus on the applicant to demonstrate that something is not common general knowledge. This is a useful second-best rule.

A further decision-making rule in the patent system is that decisions should be made on the basis of either *benefit of the doubt* or the *balance of probabilities*, not *beyond reasonable doubt*.[36] But the economic principle for regulatory interference in the market is that the need for this should be demonstrated *beyond reasonable doubt*. Lawyers, however, reserve this rule for criminal not civil law. This is another example of how using legal rules in economic policy can deliver very inferior outcomes.

In negotiations between patent attorneys and examiners, there are seven cases where applicants clearly use the presumption in favour of the novelty and inventiveness of the application to challenge the examiner to either grant a patent or point out where each and every element of an 'invention' is clearly shown in existing documented knowledge.

Browser Plug-ins (AU2003200819, priority March 2002) claims software for automated management of internet bookmarks/favourites and automated up-dating of embedded links. The 11 claims are simply written, covering software that plugs into existing internet browsers, a button for creating bookmarks and the capacity to retrieve and store web pages. There is a structured display for bookmarks. The user can set a schedule for automatic updating. Linked pages can be downloaded to cache while the user is doing other tasks, so they will load more quickly later.

This sounds a useful product, but there are no challenges in the programming. In terms of the business idea itself, once the problem of the mildly tedious nature of setting up bookmarks which are embedded in links was specified, programming would be very straightforward. Parallel processing (here by downloading while other tasks are happening) is a longstanding technique to improve speed and is widely used in all industries.

The Australian examiner rejected the patent twice on novelty and inventiveness grounds, in comparison to Microsoft's Internet Explorer 6.0 and two US patents. He commented that the difference between the invention and an earlier US patent was no more than a workshop variation: "an arrangement that any competent worker in the art would be expected to make directly and without difficulty". He also considered there was no single inventive concept. In their first set of amendments the applicant argued that the claims were united by the technical feature of storage of URL content to cache, a feature not disclosed in the cited knowledge. He also strongly disagreed "that the examiner has provided any evidence whatsoever of the level of skill in this art at the time the invention was made or any other basis from which the cursory conclusion of 'workshop modification' can be drawn". The examiner rejected the application again, specifically citing Explorer's help page. The application was again amended and 14 claims were dropped. In proposing these further amendments, the attorney referred to an agreement in a phone conversation with the examiner "that the presence of the limitation 'update schedule' etc in claim 1 was sufficient to distinguish the invention from the prior art on the basis that these features are not found in the cited art".[37]

There are several interesting aspects to this case. It is a simple software process, protected by copyright. The investment is not large, so there seems no market impediment. The core of the 'invention' lies in specifying a 'problem' (after which simple logic creates a 'solution') rather than any new knowledge or know-how. The applicant challenges the examiner to prove every detail of uninventiveness including his judgement that it is a mere workshop variation. The distinction between this 'invention' and existing knowledge which created patentability is a narrowing of the main claim to include an "update schedule". Whether this narrow interpretation would be maintained in any validity dispute is unknown. The claim language is very abstract and abstract claims can be read widely as well as narrowly. If this were to occur the patent could limit the activities of an independent inventor, at a social cost. It is also unclear, from an economic perspective, why narrowing the scope of an uninventive invention makes it sufficiently inventive to merit grant of a patent monopoly. There are a number of examples in the dataset of this strategy of narrowing the content of an 'invention' to overcome lack of inventiveness.

The US examiner rejected the application on three grounds: that, as software, it was excluded subject matter; that it was not novel and that it was obvious. The examiner helpfully advised the applicant that software is simply functional descriptive material, but "[w]hen functional descriptive material is recorded on some computer-readable medium, it becomes structurally and functionally interrelated to the medium and will be statutory [subject matter] in most cases since use of technology permits the function of the descriptive material to be realized".[38] Despite this helpful advice, the applicant, a small Australian company, did not respond, and the application has been deemed abandoned.

Systems and methods for work list prediction (AU2003204420, priority May 2002) is another patent for a system developed in a particular context (insurance claims processing) where the claim is for a far larger scope. Again it is written in very broad terms, with "receiving modules", "step determining modules", "a step definition module" and "execution modules". These are simply different parts of the computer program.

The application was abandoned in the US after six rejections. Initial amendments took care of technical objections, but in the third rejection, the examiner raised subject matter problems (lack of transformation as the 'invention' merely generates a work list and is not tied to any particular apparatus). One claim was rejected as being software. The applicant amended the claims inserting the words "computer system implemented" before "method" to overcome the lack of any tie to an apparatus. Rewording of claim 8 also overcame the computer program exclusion, though the 'invention' remains simple business process software. Through all the extensive correspondence the parties disagreed as to whether a system which predicted due dates for workflow elements clearly indicated identifying when workflow elements became due.

The examiner made use of the official notice procedure which places the onus on the applicant to provide evidence that something is not common general knowledge. The applicant then argued that "it is not aware of any evidence or authority indicating that 'predicting when work items are expected to become due' was well known [in May 2002]".[39] This is an astonishing allegation. For decades, if not longer, most managers in most effective organisations were using a variety of systems to track and monitor work and identify problem areas. Constrained as the patent system is to written documentation, the examiner calmly responded that "Tarumi does not explicitly disclose predicting when work items are expected to become due. Rather Tarumi provides a deadline for each work item".[40] This semantic minutiae highlights the lack of any height to the inventive step in the current patent system.

In Australia the claim was initially rejected as neither novel nor inventive, citing a single US patent. The attorney replied at length, arguing that the cited patent focused on workflow rearrangement to meet predefined goals or deadlines. Project management and workflow analysis are, of course, *fundamentally* about completing work on time, and predicting completion dates is integral to these management techniques. The attorney went on to say that unless the examiner could provide a detailed explanation of exactly where in the prior art the 'invention' was anticipated, the patent should be granted. For example he argued the prior art did not suggest an "execution module" to calculate an expected completion time. This minor workshop variation (if that) does not add to knowledge of workflow management, nor are there any technical challenges in implementation. The patent is owned by a British company, and the patent has been withdrawn from the UK Patent Office, possibly because it was deemed to be excluded subject matter.[41]

System for Ordering, Tracking and Payment of Goods and Services (AU2003200960, priority September 2002), with 68 complex claims, is a detailed back-office process for checking and paying invoices. The Australian examiner initially rejected the application as lacking novelty and inventiveness. The claims were amended, but the examiner maintained inventive step objections, commenting, "[t]he claimed invention represents *no more than a workshop modification* of the prior art" (emphasis added). Accompanying a second set of amendments the attorney argued, "*it has not been shown by the Examiner* that the addition of a payment processing system *in the context of the management interface hub* as disclosed in the present application, was part of common general knowledge in Australia" (emphasis added). He also argued that the added key 'differentiating integer' of the third-party consumer, distinguished this 'invention' from the cited existing knowledge which involved suppliers, participants and customers. Three parties by other names. The case was accepted within two weeks.

This back-office process for handling invoices was clearly designed for the insurance industry as the insured (the third party) presents an invoice to the insurer who then deals with the service provider (specified as medical practitioners, repair services, employee reference services, or suppliers of labour). The claims repeatedly specify that the processes deal with data supply, and payment depends on factors like speed of supply and communication method (rewarding digital communication). While the claims are written in extremely complex language, and cover a wide range of very basic design features, they are simply for computerisation of well-known manual procedures: what lawyers would refer to as 'mental steps'.

The examiner at the USPTO also had problems with clarity, novelty and inventiveness, referring to five US patent documents. The applicant never replied to this 13-page report and the application (US10/528231) was deemed abandoned. It is interesting that there is no overlap between the seven patent documents cited by the Australian examiner and the five cited by the US examiner.

It is difficult to identify any contributions to knowledge or know-how, either in business methods, or in programming. Even from a patent law perspective there is clearly only a narrow differentiating factor from previous systems. If the inventors had been required to demonstrate that the system went beyond common general knowledge or practice in the insurance industry, they would have found this very difficult.

The US examiner raised novelty/inventiveness objections for *System for Confirming the Presence at Home* (AU2003204139, priority May 2002), a software conversation between online diaries designed to determine an agreed delivery time. Following a second rejection advice (neither novel nor inventive, citing two US patent documents), a notice of appeal was filed. In relation to the appeal the attorney argued, "[the] Examiner has failed to show that each and every element as set forth in claims 1 and 2 is found in . . . Further, the Examiner has failed to make out a *prima facie* case of obviousness . . ."[42] In the event the appeal was not followed through and the application has been abandoned. But this language confirms that US examiners also face a reverse onus of proof situation.

Presence at Home is an extraordinary patent. It is a computerised link between electronic diaries, rather like a series of phone calls to make an appointment (see full claims in the Appendix). Through networked terminals the subscriber sets a "presence at home" indicator, and the deliverer's terminal receives and interprets this data. Further steps include the capacity for the deliverer to enquire and the subscriber to respond. Notices of outstanding deliveries can be sent. While a phone conversation might be quicker, one advantage is input at any time (as with email). But the sense of a patent is not at issue, only its inventiveness. It appears to be a simple system: the mere computerisation of the mental steps involved in a scheduling process. Again if it were the applicant who had to demonstrate novelty (in the ordinary sense of the meaning) and inventiveness (again against a standard of a reasonable quantum), it is hard to see how any case for a patent could be made. There is no contribution to either business process knowledge or to any of the technological arts. The Australian examiner raised neither novelty nor inventiveness objections.

Online fare booking method and system (AU2004202066, priority March 2004) handles queries for air travel, including varying numbers of passengers by checking enquiries against travel databases. The customer is offered available options around the desired date. The system prints a travel document and/or a receipt. This was naturally rejected for want of novelty or inventiveness. The rejection was based on only one US patent document (6304850, Keller et al). No non-patent websites were cited.[43] The attorney's response illustrates the very minute differences that suffice for grant of a patent monopoly. For example he argued, "Keller teaches how a *fare availability search* can be conducted, whereas the present invention goes beyond this by *combining* a *fare search* with an *availability search*."[44]

Clearly this 'invention' involves no contributions to knowledge in any field. The differences compared to existing systems are trivial, and largely matters of design not function. It appears that counting the scintilla of inventiveness required under current Australian patent law starts from a base of 'not identical' rather than some modest degree of inventiveness such as a workshop variation. A patent was also granted in New Zealand, the only other country where it was filed.

A Method of Commerce (AU2004203807, priority May 2004) effectively turns a magazine into a lottery ticket. The claims centre on the identifier for the magazine copy and the purchaser, selection of the winner from the database, and publicity about the winner. In other words it parallels well-known systems for lotteries, including subscriber registration. It links the idea of prizes to the sale of magazines, so at best it combines two well-known business processes. There are no software challenges and no contributions to knowledge or know-how.

The examiner raised inventiveness objections, citing five patent documents and common general knowledge in the field. The attorney thanked the examiner for drawing this material to their attention, indicating clearly that neither applicant nor attorney had done an adequate 'prior art' search before filing the application. He went on to argue that the five steps in the patent claim, viewed in their entirety, did not constitute common general knowledge, even if individual steps such as purchasing a magazine were well-known. He argued there was no evidence of any magazine with these features and went on to say, "we are totally unaware of any system containing all the features of the claim". He further argued "that unless the Examiner can prove what constitutes common general knowledge in Australia . . ., the examiner should withdraw reliance on the common general knowledge in combination with the citations raised".[45] Australian lottery systems have all the features of these claims, except that one buys a ticket not a magazine. Despite the copying of an exactly useful process from another field, the patent was granted.

This Japanese PCT 'invention' did not enter national phase in Europe but was examined in the USA. The US examiner rejected it as ineligible subject matter, a process not linked to any particular apparatus (11/579125). It was also deemed obvious compared to two US patent documents, one website and common general knowledge. The applicant did not respond and the application was deemed abandoned.

Cantor Index[46] has two betting patents in the dataset. One, discussed in Section 6.2, is designed to allow a bet against a particular outcome – that the favourite will not win (like short-selling in financial markets). The other (*System and method for generating customized odds bets for an event*, AU2003257910, priority July 2003) is for calculating the odds for combined event outcomes, such as quinellas and trifectas. The examiner rejected this twice on novelty and inventiveness grounds. The second rejection included subject matter problems, following the *Grant 2006* decision requiring a physically observable effect for something to be patentable. Cantor deleted the first 35 claims to overcome the subject matter objection, leaving 12 claims directed to a "system for managing bets". Cantor also argued that "the Examiner has failed to provide any documentary evidence to support his assertions that the differences between the current application and the cited art are merely matters of design choice. Additionally we note that the Examiner has not demonstrated any motivation for the skilled person to look to combine the teaching of the cited reference with the common general knowledge in the art at the priority date to arrive at the solution claimed."[47] The application was accepted two weeks later.

The application has been rejected in the UK as excluded subject matter.[48] It has been granted in New Zealand and by the USPTO. It is pending at the EPO, where as yet there is no examiner's report. The US grant followed four rejections (all based on lack of novelty) and two appeal notices. There were seven pages of redrafted claims in the notice of allowance, but the statement about the reasons for allowance is uninformative. It simply cites a large chunk of the complex independent claims and states that existing knowledge does not teach this or make it obvious.[49]

Betting on a combination of winners (two in a quinella and three in a trifecta) is a decades-old process. To generalise such bets to a wider range of combinations is within the normal competence of anyone skilled in designing betting systems. Implementation of such a broader system involves the use of probability theory and programming but requires no ingenuity. It certainly does not add to knowledge.

The degree of inventiveness in the cases presented here is so very low that if the onus of proof lay with the applicant it would be difficult to argue the case for grant of the patent. From a policy perspective it is concerning that a situation has been allowed to arise whereby it is the government that has to demonstrate cause for refusing a monopoly, rather than the applicant showing cause for its grant.

5.5 SUMMARY

The data presented here suggest that the common view in the business method literature – that examiners are unable to find relevant documented knowledge on which to base obviousness rejections – may not be the most important factor in the grant of trivial patents. Among the 72 cases there were only five examined cases where no examiner at any office cited any existing documents. The surprising finding is that there is so much existing patenting of well-known business processes. The data confirm a particularly low inventive step in Australia. There were initial examiner objections on inventiveness grounds in 44 of 71 cases, while in the USA there were obviousness objections in all but one of the 54 parallel applications.

In the majority of cases claims were amended before grant. As indicated in the discussion on legal doctrines in Chapter 3, it is a simple matter to overcome a novelty objection – one merely makes a small change in the claims. This usually includes adding or deleting features as necessitated by the existing processes identified in the documents cited by the examiner. This is why the full weight of determining patentability falls on the inventiveness test. But the ten cases discussed in Section 5.3 show that amendment usually also makes it possible to pass this test. The quantum of inventiveness required seems to be a very small difference rather than any ingenuity or demonstration of new knowledge or know-how.

Indeed none of the cases discussed in this chapter shows any contribution to knowledge or know-how. The degree of inventiveness in the cases presented here is so very low that if the applicant had to prove inventiveness – especially on a beyond reasonable doubt basis – this would clearly be impossible. Applicants rely on and actively use the reverse onus of proof doctrine, as demonstrated in the cases discussed in Section 5.4. This doctrine reduces the height of the inventive step.

There is one case which might contribute a new idea – though it seems likely others would have identified this idea and it certainly would have been an issue that came up in writing any software for blocking unwanted emails. Implementation of this idea does not contribute any new knowledge or know-how.

During the amendment process a number of applicants narrowed their claims. Outside the patent world the idea that a process which is not inventive might acquire inventiveness by reducing its scope seems laughable. Often the scope is narrowed by adding a normal feature of computer operations – a server going to standby mode (system for allocating patients to emergency treatment facilities); an interface (mapping business data and back-office invoicing process); an update schedule (internet bookmarks); or converting dates into binary code (diary event management).

The cases discussed in this chapter also show how helpful examiners can be. Particularly at the USPTO examiners often assist applicants to redraft claims so that they become patentable. USPTO examiners also provide applicants with clear advice as to how to reword their unpatentable software claims so that they become patentable. In the isolated world of the patent community – where gaining a patent seems to trump all other matters – there does not appear to be any concern that using semantics to get round a legal prohibition is a form of undermining the law.

Another difference in perspective found in the patent world is illustrated in three of the 24 cases discussed in this chapter. In these cases, where the ordinary person would find the inventions obvious, the patent world not only finds inventiveness but *multiple* inventions.

But the most startling case in this chapter is the case where encrypted fingerprint data are used to authenticate identity prior to making a financial transaction. The claims are actually for a software process for checking identity and then allowing access to the financial system. They do not cover any aspect of fingerprint encryption. The way in which the claims treat the encrypted fingerprint material is simply as a piece of data – an authentication code. Indeed the argument during examination in both Australia and the USA was over the location of the encrypted fingerprints. In both jurisdictions grant finally revolved around the fact that the encrypted data were stored at a location different from that identified in previously patented systems. This seems like an argument that a simple change in location generates sufficient inventiveness for a patent monopoly.

Astonishing as this outcome is, it is trumped by how this case gained a European patent. The EPO rejected it as being simply a business process with no element of technical inventiveness. But when the words "wherein the stored fingerprint is in an encrypted format" were moved from claim 2 to claim 1 a patent was granted. These words simply define a key piece of data in the business process. It is astonishing that this simple re-wording of the claims passed the allegedly high inventive step at the EPO. From an economic perspective it is astounding that moving words from a dependent to an independent claim suddenly achieves inventiveness where this was previously lacking. This is not the only case in the dataset where this has happened.

The degree of inventiveness in the cases presented here is extraordinarily low. If it were applicants who had to demonstrate the case for grant of the patent, it is hard to see how they could have succeeded. From a policy perspective it is concerning that a situation has been allowed to arise whereby it is the government that has to demonstrate cause for refusing a monopoly, rather than the applicant showing cause for its grant.

6. Combining known elements

6.1 INTRODUCTION

Inventions which are combinations of known elements pose particular problems for grant of a patent monopoly. All the elements are known, so a new use or rearrangement of the elements would surely fall into normal business practice. In general it is unclear why there would be any argument for government intervention to restrict competition. However if there are unusual challenges – particularly challenges incurring a high R&D investment – then there *may* be a case for intervention. The traditional synergy doctrine required that there be something extra from a combination for it to merit the privilege of a patent. This was specified as either an unexpected result or a result greater than the sum of the known parts. If either of these conditions is met then a new combination may well confer at least some new knowledge or know-how. A simpler approach would simply be to require a contribution to new knowledge or know-how as the condition for grant of a patent.

The synergy doctrine remains in effect in the UK and other EPC countries. But in the USA and Australia it has been overturned in favour of a much lower threshold: the suggestion doctrine. Although the Supreme Court recently changed the emphasis in several of the new doctrines introduced by the CAFC it has only partially addressed the relative priority of the Court's synergy test compared to the CAFC's suggestion doctrine. The suggestion doctrine makes it virtually impossible for a patent examiner to maintain an obviousness objection to a combination 'invention'.

Among the cases selected for this study there are 41 which are best categorised as combinations of known elements. Of these 41, 21 cases involve the mere computerisation of known processes while 20 are other forms of combination, though usually in a computerised environment. A further three cases centre on the use of modern electronic networks and two of these are the simple adaptation of known processes on modern networks. Some of the combination cases illustrate other aspects of patent policy rules and are discussed elsewhere. Seven computerisation cases are discussed in Section 6.2 and six other types of combination cases in Section 6.3.

6.2 SIMPLE COMPUTERISATION

One of the simplest examples of computerisation of a well-known business method is *A method for performing an asset valuation* (AU2005203023, priority July 2005). The 19 claims are summarised in Box 6.1, which shows no differences from the mental steps that any valuer would traditionally perform. The specification does not point to any technical contribution and it is clearly a straightforward computerisation of well-known methods. The application was rejected twice for lack of novelty and inventiveness. In replying to the examiner's objection that the method was common general knowledge, the attorney agreed that valuers used computers and calculators, but suggested they often cut corners and failed to keep computer records. The "structured approach" in the 'invention' would overcome these problems. The claims were amended, but still do not appear to be anything other than simple computerisation of well-known steps. Although clearly designed for real estate, the claim has been broadened to apply to any asset. There were no overseas applications.

System and Method for On-line Analysis and Reporting of Financial Operation Data from Community Pharmacies (AU2003204214, priority June 2002) simply computerises well-known accounting methods – even the specification says this. It is a networked computer system for analysing operational/financial data from pharmacies, with a server to receive, store and analyse data, a monitor for viewing, an access box for transfer, a firewall, an internet service provider and wireless transmission – a very standard combination. The operational and financial data are specified as including the current ratio; the acid test ratio; inventory turnover rate; periods for accounts payable collection, accounts receivable collection and net working capital turnover; and percentage figures for gross margin, net income, and return on equity and assets. One could go back decades and find all these measures in any business accounting textbook. It does contain elements of benchmarking, but financial ratios were developed precisely for the purpose of comparing the performance of different entities (benchmarking). In describing previous knowledge, the applicant notes that pharmacies have previously had to collect and analyse these data themselves or pay someone to do this for them, thus disclosing this as simple computerisation with no other 'inventive' elements.

The US application provides a very clear example of how the theoretical exclusion of computer programs from patenting is regularly undermined through semantics. The first US rejection report advised that 10 of the 15 claims were not statutory subject matter as they were simply computer program claims. They were re-drafted as "computer-readable storage medium"' claims, and the examiner agreed this change in wording made

BOX 6.1 A METHOD FOR PERFORMING AN ASSET VALUATION (SUMMARY OF CLAIMS)

Application 2005203023; priority date: 12 July 2005

Claims:

1 method for asset valuation, comprising:
  (1a) putting 1+ queries to valuer;
  (1b) receiving responses;
  (1c) use responses to computational device to decide if inspection needed.
  2 step 1a includes queries about adequacy of relevant information;
  3 step 1a relates to: availability of mandatory data; information about calling the client; data reliability; whether comparable sales data are available
  4 step 1b includes receiving input into computational device from valuer
  5 between steps 1b and 1c an inspection flag is set, based on responses
    6 flag set if valuer finds available information inadequate
  7 step 1c determines if inspection flag is set
    8 flag set if valuer finds available information inadequate
  9 receive asset valuation from the valuer using the computational device
    10 create the valuation report including received asset valuation
  11 if inspection needed, message sent advising valuer
  12 step 1c includes deciding if internal inspection needed
    13 step 1c includes calculating loan to valuation ratio
  14 electronically storing record of data when valuation done
    15 including valuer's notes (using computational device)

16 computer readable instructions for the above
17 computational device loaded with these instructions
18 valuation report generated by this method
19 method as per accompanying drawings.

the non-patentable computer programs patentable. However in his second report the examiner rejected all claims as obvious in the light of US 5991741, a magazine article and public use of a software system.[1] The application was then abandoned. The Australian examiner accepted the application in August 2004, raising no novelty or inventiveness objections. The patent cited by the US examiner was filed in 1997 and granted in 1999. It is unclear why the Australian examiner did not find this.

Accenture's second patent in the dataset is *Change navigation toolkit* (AU2003255356, priority August 2002), a software product for implementing new computerised operational systems. Getting this process right requires considerable attention to detail, a fact well illustrated in the 128-page application with its 72 claims. Many of the well-known problems encountered when migrating to new business IT systems are identified and addressed using rules stored in a software library. Claim 3 specifically refers to processing insurance claims, which suggests this software was developed in that environment. Other subsidiary claims detail such design features as what is stored where; sample forms, correspondence, tasks and file notes; generation of messages; that the new system should be trialled. Subsequent claims require that the new system include internet connection, that training includes remote audit training and that a work plan and project timeline are developed. These are all well-known elements of established best practice in implementing major new software systems. They have been in use for some time by many organisations. Several Australian government agencies, including IP Australia, implemented major new financial management systems in the mid 1990s using these elements.

This simple computerisation of the complex process of implementing new IT systems in large organisations could also be characterised as an expert system. The important thing about installing major new systems is to get multiple elements right. But from a patent law perspective this creates difficulties as the total required system can look like a complex combination. Few of the elements are optional if a good outcome is to be achieved. With such a detailed set of claims it is improbable that this 'invention' could fail the rigidly defined novelty test with its use of only a single document or artefact. Similarly, with the suggestion doctrine for combinations, rejection of such a detailed process would be challenging.

There is a public interest in having efficient and effective businesses and public organisations. Such organisations are very likely to replace major computerised operating systems from time to time, and this poses challenges. There are many ways to address these. Often organisations hire specialist companies to assist in this process and a good reputation and track record is critical in winning such business.[2] If any such company develops a computer program to support such a change, this program is copyright protected. Beyond this, the prime public interest would seem to be in the effective *dissemination* of good change management systems. There is no evidence of any impediment to the development of such organisational improvement methods: as demonstrated by the simple and logical nature of the steps claimed in this patent. But there are some questions about whether such techniques are sufficiently widely disseminated. So not only does this patent not add to existing knowledge in any field; it may act as an impediment to dissemination of known techniques. The claimed 'invention' merely computerises known methods and process steps.

An application was lodged at the EPO but was refused for want of inventiveness (EP2003766384). The EPO did not reject this as an unpatentable method of doing business. The identified 'technical problem' was seen as the "automatic configuration of a computer system" – but as is clear from the application the problem with installing major new IT systems is a complex process requiring a concerted effort across an organisation and its staff. The EPO examiner simply noted that he was unable to determine such a configuration outcome from the transfer of sets of rules between memories. There was no parallel US application.

SAP's patent for a computerised risk evaluation system (*Method and system for risk evaluation*, AU2003200483, priority February 2002) offers no advances in either approaches to risk evaluation or to software engineering. The claims are written in unhelpfully complex and legalistic language and repeat themselves as method, system and computer program product claims. But the approach is identical to risk management approaches in use since at least the mid 1990s, and probably well before that. Indeed I recollect an almost identical process being used in what is now called IP Australia when I worked there in the mid 1990s. The 'invention' takes a set of measures relevant to strategic business planning and forecasting, and assigns risks, threat levels and associated probabilities to each. An aggregate risk-weighted score for the business is then calculated. There is no development in methodologies for assessing risk. The patent does no more than computerise a known approach to assessing business threats and risks. In Australia the examiner raised no objections and it was granted without amendment.

The EPO's examination division considered there was no technical issue meriting a prior art search due to "the paucity of technical definition going beyond the banal for the person skilled in the technical art".[3] The application was refused. At the USPTO the application was abandoned after five rejections (each followed by amendments). The early amendments re-wrote the process claims to be acceptable as statutory subject matter (though the substance of the 'invention' did not change). Other amendments addressed objections of want of novelty and inventiveness, largely by adding specific business details and then arguing these were not fully disclosed in the cited existing knowledge. The applicant also argued that "'[i]n rejecting claims under 35 U.S.C. § 103, the Examiner bears the initial burden of presenting a *prima facie* case of obviousness. Thus when an Examiner relies on general knowledge to negate patentability, that knowledge must be articulated and placed on the record."[4] This is another example of the reverse onus of proof issue discussed in Section 5.4.

By the third rejection the grounds were solely obviousness. The amendments attempting to overcome this objection involved addition of such 'inventive' features as sales prospects, potential clients, non-conflict risks and weightings based on a "plurality of questions" – as though one would need weightings with only one question. Because the final amendments came after a final rejection and raised new matter not in the initial specification, the USPTO refused to examine the application further. It was deemed abandoned in February 2011. Across the five closely argued rejection notices the examiner provided the applicant with 55 pages of careful argument showing why this self-evidently trivial and well-known process would not be granted a patent. This hardly seems a rational use of resources.

Contentguard's *System and method for supplying and managing rights expressions* (AU2003240981, priority June 2002) has also been granted in Korea and the USA. Like its other three patents in the dataset Contentguard asked for both expedited examination and postponement of acceptance.[5] Despite the complexity of the 101 claims this is mere computerisation of the terms and conditions of various sale options. The claims detail alternative uses and how conflicts can be resolved using pre-specified rules. They cover digital and non-digital goods, content and services. The Australian examiner objected that the 'invention' was technically equivalent to an earlier US patent. The attorney argued that the previous patent concerned purchase and possession of goods, not purchase of a 'rights expression' (though the 'rights expression' generates access to the goods and so is technically equivalent to a sale). Much was made of the possible variations in the manner of using the purchase – these are of course design details. The attorney also argued that there were differences in how buyers and sellers were matched. The patent was granted.

Although there are 172 family members, overseas applications were readily split into 17 sub-families based on the patent title. The patent is still pending at the EPO. The EPO examiner rejected the application in March 2005 as there was no technical solution to a technical problem. No specific existing knowledge was cited. The applicant deleted and replaced all the claims in August 2005. The EPO database shows no further action as at mid July 2012 (EP2003783515).

The parallel US application was rejected six times, principally on novelty grounds. Five sets of amendments were filed. Contentguard then appealed. The appeal hinged on whether the limitation "determining what action said repository is to take when said repository processes said item based on a combination of said repository rights expression associated with said repository and said item rights expression associated with the said item" was anticipated by US 5629980 (Stefik). The BPAI determined that the claim limitation required that the repository action be based on some combination of a "repository rights expression" and an "item rights expression". The BPAI considered that Stefik disclosed "item usage rights", repository security levels and "user specified rights", but not the exact combination "repository rights expression" and "item rights expression" in the Contentguard claims. The BPAI did not address the issue of whether this minor variation (of language not substance) met the non-obviousness requirement.[6] The patent was granted. But in the context of these two 'inventions' it seems clear that "item usage rights" and "user specified rights" are the technical equivalent of "rights expressions".

Contentguard's very similar patent application *System and method for granting access to an item or permission to use an item based on configurable conditions* (AU2003290930 priority 18 November 2002)[7] was refused at the EPO in July 2012 largely for lack of inventiveness compared to a 1995 European patent jointly owned by Contentguard and Xerox. The claims were amended several times during this process, including in the middle of the oral hearing at which the patent was refused.

It was granted in the USA, also after appeal to the BPAI. Again the BPAI focused on whether "rights expressions" were disclosed in patent document US 2002/0099544 A1 (Levitt). The BPAI noted the applicant claimed rights expressions included "expressions of licences, license components and/or fragments thereof, such as the grant element, principal element, right element, resource element, and/or condition element, as well as any other suitable expressions". The BPAI went on to note that Levitt was a computer program for speech recognition and that it disclosed grammar expressions that can be recognised, prioritised, compared to a database and otherwise used. The Board decided that as "grammar expressions are not disclosed to have any 'rights expressions' associated with them", the applicant's claims did meet the novelty requirement.[8] Again the BPAI did not consider the issue of inventiveness, which given the identity of the processes in the two 'inventions' should surely have pointed to the difference being a matter of words not substance.

For an economic policy analyst, the way in which judges deal with only some of the requirements for patentability when considering grant of a patent monopoly is perplexing. From an economic policy perspective

– and surely from a legal perspective – *all* the conditions for grant should be met before a patent is granted. Yet legal appeal bodies seem quite willing to consider only one narrow issue (here novelty) without also considering the closely related issue of inventiveness. In this case the processes in the two 'inventions' were identical but one handled "grammar expressions" and the other "rights expressions" – effectively sub-phrases from a legal contract. There is no economic sense in granting a monopoly for this use of a known process for different subject matter.

Contentguard has two other 'inventions' among the selected cases. *Networked services licensing system and method* (AU2003219907, priority February 2002) uses "rights expressions" to switch control of licensing details to content owners. *System and method for specifying and processing legality expressions* (AU2003243179, priority April 2002) identifies a number of elements (a duty, a prohibition, an intent and a claim) to write a "legality expression" (licensing contract) for agreeing access to digitised material. Both cases have been appealed to the BPAI, but here the ground of rejection was obviousness not novelty. It will be interesting to see how the BPAI handles the two cases.

Distributed Transaction Event Matching (AU2003204278, priority May 2002) is a software system for tracking and coding "network events" (hits on a web site). It is for use by parties who have agreed a set of contractual obligations, including pricing and settlement rules, for such events. In other words it implements agreed commercial rules. The system monitors defined events (advertisements, electronic products, or information), and determines payment amounts. It calculates volumes and invoice amounts, a standard procedure in billing for decades if not centuries.

The Australian examiner rejected the application on novelty and inventiveness grounds, citing previous patents and common general knowledge about network gateways and bridges. The claim was amended and granted. Accenture argued that the amendments included features not in the cited existing knowledge: "identification of groups of network events representative of activities associated with contractually defined rules" and "network events within the subset . . . associated to identify a client session". This detail does not obscure the essence of the invention – computerisation of agreed charges to generate invoices – a kind of online parallel to counting groceries. It appears examiners can be daunted by over-articulation of elements in a combination and fail to recognise (or not be allowed to recognise) that this does not create inventiveness, merely difference. There is no contribution to knowledge in any field.

It was allowed by the USPTO in March 2009, after seven rejections and one appeal notice. The seventh rejection advised that *all claims were obvious* compared to three earlier patent documents. In their final amendments

Accenture argued that there would be no reasonable expectation that *combining* the three documents on existing knowledge would yield the *exact combination* claimed. Following a phone interview the examiner amended the first independent claim so that the contract is "between at least *two* of a plurality of service providers and an entity other . . .".[9] This change to the number of parties providing the service was therefore instrumental in creating the inventiveness that was previously lacking. The notice of allowance shows the examiner's amendments and simply cites the totality of the complex independent claims as not being taught in the prior art. The experience with this application shows the difficulty US examiners have in rejecting what appear to be complex processes. It is the nature of business processes that they involve many steps – steps that the patent system sees as separate elements. Yet unless the steps tie together into a seamless delivery to a customer, the business process will not work. Here complex language is used to suggest that the simple process of counting and invoicing for website hits is sufficiently complex to merit a patent monopoly.

This application has been refused by the EPO. The refusal was appealed and the appeal has been refused. The initial EPO rejection, in October 2004, was based on both excluded subject matter (Articles 52(2) and (3)) and lack of any inventive step. Back in 2004 EPO examiners were allowed to mention subject matter as a ground for exclusion. The applicant amended the claims "to bring out the technical nature" of the invention. A second rejection was again based on lack of inventiveness. The claims were further amended, but were refused. In making the appeal the applicant had argued that it "is the object of the invention to enhance efficiency of data transactions and/or exchange." In refusing the appeal the Board commented that the data exchange system "is a brute force approach rather than efficient network usage."[10] The appeal was refused not for this inefficiency, but because there was no technical inventiveness.

As demonstrated here, where the word obvious takes its ordinary meaning rather than the narrow meaning of patent law, simple computerisation 'inventions' are extremely obvious. They involve no contributions to knowledge or know-how. Other simple computerisation cases are discussed elsewhere to illustrate particular doctrines involved in the inventiveness standard.[11]

Australia is perhaps unique in accepting that simple computerisation is inventive. This policy was created by the courts in 1994 (*CCOMb*). In other jurisdictions claims to software have to be drafted to pretend they are not software. In the USA computer programs in themselves are non-patentable subject matter, and seven cases (including five of the pure computerisation cases) were initially rejected on these, among other grounds. Examiners often helpfully point out how re-drafting these claims to word them as "computer-readable medium" claims will usually overcome the objection. This is illustrated in two of the cases discussed in this chapter. Another patentability issue for business processes under US law is the requirement for a process to be tied to a specific machine or to involve a genuine transformation.[12] In seven of the pure computerisation cases such objections were raised (including one case where the issue was the lack of a tangible result). Again redrafting overcame these problems.

Under the EPC software as such is not patentable. The subterfuge of pretending that software is not software when the claims are drafted in specific word forms led Prescott J, in the UK patent court, to remark that "[y]ou are not allowed to get round the objection – that you are attempting to patent a computer program – by claiming it as a physical artefact, a mere change of form" (*CFPH* at 36). A useful guiding principle would be that used in Canada that "[a]n operation which is not patentable when carried out by an individual cannot be made patentable merely by having it carried out by a computer" (Sarginson and Langan 2001: 5).

6.3 TWO OR MORE OLD METHODS

The combination patents presented here simply take two or more known processes and combine them, usually in a computerised or networked environment. The six cases discussed show how very trivial these "new uses" of old processes are. There is a long-standing legal doctrine that workshop improvements should not be patentable, but clearly many of these cases are possibly workshop variations rather than even workshop improvements. The doctrine on workshop improvements is discussed further in Section 7.3.

System and method for conducting online auctions (AU2003206509, priority March 2002) combines selecting suppliers from pre-qualified panels and an auction process. Pre-qualification of suppliers is a standard process in Australia and I personally participated in such a process in the early 1990s. This particular combination depends on modern networks to operate effectively. As is normal with auctions, where a successful bid is not made, the controlling party can consider revising the reserve price. The claims are written as a general auction process where either the buyer or the seller can be the controlling party; they are also re-stated specifically for award of a supply contract to pre-qualified suppliers (claims 11–18). In the latter version, software is used to calculate a quality-weighted price that each supplier would need to bid to be successful. This "current bid to win" (CBTW) estimate is advised to each supplier (for their use in bidding). This last feature is possible due to the power of computers, but it just computerises the mental steps that the person making the final choice among bidders (tenderers) would undertake anyway. Sharing information on the distance to a winning bid is done to encourage acceptable price offers. Information sharing is a very old idea, and the way it is done in this context is a quality of networks, not of this 'invention'.

There is no contribution to knowledge or know-how, either in the business or software fields. The combination of two known methods within a network environment, including computerisation of the mental steps behind the CBTW estimate, create a combination that would be deemed inventive under the suggestion doctrine. But if the applicants had to point to the contribution to knowledge offered by the 'invention', they would find it difficult to do so.

No novelty or inventiveness objections were raised in Australia. In the USA the applicant was directed to select either the reverse or the normal auction system. The first examiner's report rejected the application based on subject matter concerns and lack of novelty and inventiveness. The applicant amended the claims arguing that the cited knowledge did not disclose a *reserve price negotiation phase*, though it did indicate an option to negotiate directly with one or more buyers (which is effectively a negotiation about the reserve price). The application was allowed following further amendments agreed in a telephone conversation between applicant and examiner. The key features specified in the notice of allowance were the quality weighting of bids, supply of current bid to win prices and the *interrelation* of the various features.[13] The examiner did not identify that the CBTW price arrangement was the technical equivalent of a reserve price negotiation phase. The application was actively withdrawn from the EPO before any exam report was issued (EP2003704110).

This case illustrates not only the importance of the suggestion doctrine in granting uninventive combination patents, but also confirms the narrowness of the patent view of an inventive concept. The requirement by the USPTO that the applicant select one of two identified 'inventions' indicates the ability of examiners to identify multiple inventions where many people would perceive none. In this case the selection process was initially set out as either a normal or a reverse auction. These two systems are closely related and should surely be considered to be workshop variations of each other. In patent law, however, these are two separate inventions – yet another signal of the very low quantum of inventiveness required for a patent.[14]

Automated receiving and delivery system and method (AU2003262357, priority November 1999) is a software system for scheduling deliveries into sections of a container with an electronic lock. Several well-known processes are combined to do this: traditional delivery systems, sending electronic signals and confirming that delivery has been made (see translated claims in Box 6.2).

BOX 6.2 AUTOMATED RECEIVING AND DELIVERY SYSTEM AND METHOD: SUMMARY OF CLAIMS AS GRANTED BY THE EPO (EP1250670 B1)

1 Method of delivering orders to multiple locked containers, each used by a customer and using a scheduler, with the steps of:
- ordering goods for a first customer (who has one of the locked containers);
- determining if their container is available at specified times;
- identifying a time for a first delivery;
- sending an access signal to the container allowing access at that time.

2 Method as in claim 1, with further steps:
- ordering goods for a second delivery to the first customer;
- determining if their container is available at specified times;
- identifying a time for a second delivery;
- sending an access signal to the container allowing access at that time.

3 Method as in claim 2, with further steps:
- ordering goods for a second customer (who has one of the locked containers);
- determining if their container is available at specified times;
- identifying a time for delivery;
- sending an access signal to the container allowing access at that time.

4 Method as in claim 2, with further steps:
- people delivering first and second orders to relevant containers, each opening the right container each using "an identifier".

5 Method as in claim 1 including steps:
- determining the size of the delivery;
- checking available room in the container.

6 Method as in claim 5 including reserving space if this is available.

7 Method as in claim 1 including charging the account after delivery (after the container has signalled that the delivery has been made).

8 Method as in claim 7 where first locked container signals the first delivery has been made.

9 System for delivering orders to multiple locked containers at multiple locations, each used by a customer; determiner to determine availability to containers at specified times; scheduler receiving availability information and identifying time for delivery and sending an access signal to the locked container at that time.

Note: The Australian version (AU2003262357, priority 9 November 1999) varies in that size, together with checking sufficiency of space in container, is included in claim 1 not claim 5. There is no reference to a second customer or a second order from the first customer, but the customer is asked if they prefer a single or multiple deliveries.

This case again demonstrates the capacity of patent offices to perceive multiple inventions where an ordinary person can see none. The Australian examiner expressed concern that there were two 'inventions' – checking for space and sending a delivery-made advice. As the file wrapper is missing for the US version, the issues raised by the USPTO examiner in the two rejection notices that preceded grant of a patent are unknown (09/708571). The EPO examiner also found two 'inventions' – scheduling a delivery time and managing delivery of different sized goods. Delivery systems have been around for centuries and some suppliers have learned to provide systems that work well for their customers. Most manage the delivery of different sized goods quite easily. The issue of the size of the goods illustrates how patent applicants set up a trivial 'problem' which does not merit the term. It is fascinating that the EPO would consider delivery of goods a technical invention, and it would be enlightening to see a justification of this patent grant.

The EPO considered claims 15 and 23 lacked novelty, but found that claim 1 was new as previous documents did not teach "identifying, using the scheduler, a first time interval during which the first delivery can be made and accessing the first locked storage container *only* during the first time interval. The skill [sic] man would not derive these features from the available prior art, nor would he combine these documents to arrive at the solution of the invention."[15] The scheduler is a software module. Quite how the EPO determined that there was a *technical* problem to overcome in scheduling a delivery and then accessing the locked container only at that time is unclear. Just what aspect of this straightforward programming of a known business process involves any technology is not evident from the examiner's report. Unusually for a business method application there was no discussion of the technical and non-technical elements. Perhaps the long-established business process of delivery became technical because the box had an electronic lock. But nothing in the claim is about the electronics of unlocking the box.

Payment card processing system and methods (AU2003262344, priority September 2003) is a system for reducing the number of plastic cards one carries by combining a normal credit card and a store-specific card. In responding to the examiner's rejection in the light of four US patent documents the attorney argued this existing knowledge *allow[ed] for multiple accounts* rather than a *single account* on a *multi-use card*; that none *specifically combined a store card and a credit card*, even though they loaded a range of functions and accounts onto a single card; and that *specific details were not 'taught' in the prior art*. These specific details were an upgrade process for converting current store cards to dual cards; migration of data; in-store issuance of a card; and activation on customer request. All these are, of course, very well-known processes. However because the examiner was unable to find written evidence of the exact combination, the patent monopoly was granted. This 'invention' has also been granted a patent in the USA and is pending at the EPO.[16]

Many of us have wished to carry fewer plastic cards around. But clearly the idea of offering such multi-use cards has occurred to many others: at least four US patents have been granted. While the specific combination of accounts on this card may differ from that on other cards, and there may be a different combination of back-room processing features compared to other patented multi-use cards, none of the applicant's arguments indicate any new knowledge or know-how.

Management Control of Pharmaceutical Substances (AU2004211006, priority February 2003) computerises the supply of pharmaceuticals from a distance and centres on checking patient identity and the prescription. A key feature in checking identity is that enough time elapses between sending and receiving secure ID. The ID includes biometric capture, but the 'invention' is not about the biometrics or their capture, simply their transmission and assessment. It simply links databases, using decision making rules. The applicant asked for expedited examination, due to concerns about possible infringement. In other words such an 'invention' was obvious to others working in the area. The Australian examiner raised novelty and obviousness objections and the claims were amended, principally by bringing the element "where the stored data records are logically separate from the biometric records" from dependent claim 3 into independent claim 1. The attorney argued that *the specific arrangement* was not previously disclosed and inclusion of such elements as the correct dose were "significant advantages over the cited prior art". It is rather surprising that providing the correct prescription dose could be seen as an inventive feature – this is a standard expectation of anyone seeking to have a prescription filled. The patent was granted.

While this is a mere combination of known processes, it was the amendments, with narrow semantic differences from closely similar combinations which achieved grant. To the industry policy analyst moving words from dependent to independent claim seems a poor substitute for the development of new technology.

The USPTO has rejected the application three times. Once the examiner had identified the relevant existing knowledge the applicant created specific variations from the identified knowledge to suggest inventiveness (as defined in patent law). The first response focused on earlier systems authorising supply of pharmaceuticals to medical staff rather than patients. The examiner clarified that the earlier systems also covered supply to patients. The second response focused on the difference of a process step whereby *the patient is first enrolled into a program* as a differentiating feature. The enrolling process involved the "management computer" receiving a request from the patient to commence the rest of the process. The examiner was unconvinced and responded that the cited documents had a process initiated by the patient using an identification key. The applicant did not reply to this third rejection and the application is deemed abandoned (10/508398).

The EPO examiner identified an earlier computerised ID matching system for pharmaceutical supply, incorporating biometric records, and argued the only difference was in *secure communication* between the biometric apparatus and the computer, which was disclosed in a second document. The applicant amended the claims to emphasise *that the stored data records are logically separate from the biometric records* and argued this made the 'invention' eligible for a patent. The EPO disagreed. In rejecting the three minor differences from existing knowledge as being inventive, the examiner noted that ". . . no combined *synergistic* effect is produced . . . Hence the combination of these three features amounts to a *mere aggregation* which is obvious . . ." (emphasis added).[17] This clearly sets out the marked difference between using the synergy and the suggestion doctrines.

The final two cases in this section both include an element in the combination where user definition became the distinguishing feature creating 'inventiveness'. In both cases user definition was added during the amendment process after the application was originally rejected for want of novelty.

Most finance products are services rather than goods. The key to good service delivery is effective processes. *A Security System* (AU2003201332, priority October 2000) is a method of reducing credit-card fraud by sending alerts to mobile devices. It is an excellent example of combining two known processes from closely related fields. Banks have been contacting customers when anomalous (that is, probably fraudulent) transactions occurred on their accounts for some time before 2000. I first experienced this myself in 1997. The examiner considered the claims lacked novelty and inventiveness compared to a Citibank system sending SMS messages. The applicant amended the claims to emphasise that *the user* could define the anomalous events, arguing that "the CitiAlert system does not teach or suggest this feature". This minor change in the specification overcame the objection and a patent was granted. The idea of users defining their preferences is ubiquitous and can be critical to high service quality, but this obvious idea is unlikely to exist in patent documents. Nor would it be written down in combination with the advising process used here. There are no contributions to knowledge. This is a child of a PCT application for a similar system sending notifications about defined stock market events. There were no overseas parallels.

Skills Dissemination Tool (AU2005234625, priority November 2005), is an online employment register including non-vocational data. It has a publicly searchable database of subscribing members, including their skills and geographic location. Searching uses statistical word association techniques, an approach originally reported in 1961 (Stiles 1961). Subsidiary claims relate to access, payment and the data items. Online job search systems have been available since at least the mid 1990s.

The examiner rejected the application as lacking inventiveness compared to common general knowledge and nine US patents. The claims were revised to include public searchability. The attorney also argued that inclusion of non-vocational data by members differentiated this system. He commented on each of the cited patents, arguing that each differed from the application. These arguments involved such design minutiae as earlier systems being limited to specific geographic areas (compared to selecting by geographic area) or selecting only one candidate (compared to a list of candidates). He even argued that the *absence* of an ability to search and apply for vacant positions created inventiveness compared to previously patented combinations. The examiner accepted these arguments in part, but maintained the application was uninventive compared to two documents.

The claims were amended again, by adding to claim 1 that the geographic indicator allowed *the subscriber* to a define a maximum availability distance. The attorney argued this was a key differentiating factor. He also argued that the use of statistical word association algorithms was not suggested by the earlier patents (despite the fact that the technique was over 40 years old), that potential candidates were listed rather than ranked, and that although other systems were limited to specific geographic areas they did not allow for selection by geographic area. The patent was granted.

The USPTO rejected six claims as non-functional descriptive material; all claims were considered obvious and there were various problems with indefiniteness (11/371325). The applicant did not respond and the application was abandoned.

Clearly this 'invention' involves no contributions to knowledge in any field. The differences compared to existing knowledge are trivial, and are matters of design rather than function. Yet the addition of user definition of distance to claim 1 was critical in the grant of the patent. This is another case where a narrowing in the scope of an 'invention' appears to be instrumental in creating inventiveness where it did not previously exist. A surreal outcome.

6.4 ISSUES IDENTIFIED

The cases presented in this chapter are all combination patents. Had the older synergy doctrine not been overturned in both Australia and the USA then examiners in those countries would have been able to reject many obvious combinations of old processes, and it is likely that many of the cases discussed above would not have been granted. The EPO clearly used this doctrine to reject the pharmaceutical dispensing case.

There does not seem to be a clear process for the economic evaluation of new patent policy doctrines. Nor does there seem to be any regular process for amending statute law when such economically questionable decisions change the basis of important innovation policy. The Australian case which changed the combinations doctrine dates from 1980. But the impact of this decision was not discussed in the major economic review of the patent system (IPAC 1984). A later review of whether 'intellectual property' legislation conformed to fundamental competition principles (that legislation not interfere with market competition unless there is a demonstrated national benefit) also ignored this issue (IPCRC 2000). Indeed the 2000 review *presumed,* citing no evidence, that the Australian inventive step was high enough to prevent the grant of any business method patents. While there is academic discussion of the suggestion doctrine in the USA, there does not appear to be any Congressional review of the matter and it has been only partially considered by the Supreme Court in *KSR*.

These cases also reinforce the role of amendment, discussed in Chapter 5, in creating minute differences from identified existing knowledge and thus achieving a monopoly grant. Both in the USA and in Australia applicants seem to have the right to endlessly amend their claims. Amendment was critical in achieving Australian grant in three of these cases. In the USA there are two cases where the prohibition on software patenting was circumvented by changes in wording and one case where the examiner redrafted the claims to assist the applicant to gain a monopoly. In contrast, EPO procedures generally limit the interaction between examiner and applicant to one report then a call to oral examination, reducing the opportunities for amendment compared to other jurisdictions.[18]

These cases illustrate a number of ways in which the patent law definition of inventiveness differs from the ordinary meaning of the term. Minute design and implementation features were important in the grant of a patent for the combined store and credit card. That applicant also argued that as their combination had fewer features than existing knowledge it was different and thus inventive – a kind of less is more argument. A similar argument was put forward in the online skills database system. Small variations also underlay the patent grant for automated pharmaceutical dispensing. As Australian examiners do not provide reasons for grant it is unclear how much weight the rather standard added feature of the correct dose had in that case – it may simply have been the movement of another design aspect from dependent to independent claims that created inventiveness.

The acceptance of a "current bid to win" procedure as being something other than a reserve price negotiation phase indicates how examiners' lack of familiarity with business processes can lead to a failure to identify workshop improvements and technical equivalents. These cases also demonstrate that many business methods have already been patented – in most cases examiners were able to find earlier patent documentation which already claims monopolies for closely related business processes. Perhaps the most surprising aspect of the above cases is the EPO's grant of a patent for a software process for delivering goods – clearly a business process. Despite the explicit exclusion of business methods and software from patentability the examiner's report presented no argument about why any aspect of this software program met the subject matter requirements of the EPC.

If the patentability test were contribution to new knowledge or know-how none of these trivial 'inventions' would have been eligible for a patent.

7. The quantum of inventiveness: other approaches and rules

7.1 INTRODUCTION

The cases considered here cover both the issue of different approaches under the EPC and a range of policy rules which were designed to ensure that patents were not granted for very trivial inventions. The cases considered in Section 7.2 are all ones where a patent has been granted under the EPC, often assumed to have a higher inventive step.

Patent policy includes a number of doctrines which are designed to ensure that patents are not granted for minor modifications and variations. The cases presented in Section 7.3 are ones where one might have expected the analogous use doctrine or doctrines about workshop variations and technical equivalents to apply. There are a variety of other doctrinal rules that affect the grant of patents and the cases discussed in Section 7.4 provide some insights into such doctrines as the problem/solution approach, the requirement for a tangible output and prohibitions against the patenting of ideas.

7.2 GRANTED UNDER THE EPC

The European Patent Convention (EPC) contrasts with patent law in both the USA and Australia in that there is a statutory exclusion of certain types of subject matter, including software and business methods. In the USA and Australia these exclusions had a traditional, common law basis. There is a widespread view that the specific exclusions in the EPC have been largely ineffective where there is an "as such" qualifier. But because the EPC operates with the synergy doctrine for combination inventions it can be expected to have a higher inventive step requirement than Australia or the USA.

The UK is a signatory to the EPC and its patent statute mirrors the EPC. There are differences in approach between the UK and the EPO, with the approach in the UK becoming much clearer in late 2006 when new guidelines (a four-step test) were introduced.[1] Step one involves construing the claim – identifying what the applicant is claiming. Step two involves identifying the actual contribution to the stock of human knowledge. If this contribution falls solely within excluded (unpatentable) subject matter, then the application is not patentable (step three). If part of the knowledge contribution goes beyond excluded subject matter then the examiner moves on to step four and considers whether the contribution to knowledge is technical in nature.

This contrasts with the EPO approach. For most business method applications the EPO starts by separating the claim into 'technical' and 'non-technical' elements. It then assesses whether the 'technical' elements meet the Article 56 inventiveness requirement. The EPO defines the meaning of technical very broadly. A general purpose computer is not only technical, but instantly confers technicality on excluded software. The EPO interprets the "as such" exclusion of Article 52(3) to mean that any software (or business method) with a 'technical' effect is not software or a business method "as such" and is therefore patentable. Effectively this means that software is always potentially patentable. The EPO has less difficulty with the business method exclusion. Although it refuses simply to reject such inventions as excluded subject matter, it regularly finds they fail to meet the inventiveness requirement.

The cases where there are EPO or UK grants or refusals allow further insights into the approaches used under the EPC. There are four cases where the EPO has granted a patent.[2] The UKIPO has granted patents in six further cases, one of which was rejected by the EPO Appeal Board. The EPO has also refused eight cases as being uninventive and the UK has refused at least three others as excluded subject matter. All cases of EPO grant are discussed here – two only briefly as they were discussed in detail in earlier chapters. Also discussed are three cases of UK grant (including the case refused by the EPO) and two cases of UK refusal.

In the first of the EPO grant cases, the EPO immediately perceived technical inventiveness in a system for delivering to an electronically locked box. In the three other cases the EPO initially could discern no technical inventiveness. However when words were moved from dependent claims to the independent claims the applications acquired technical inventiveness. Such word games are troublesome. They should have no place in a policy designed to promote technological innovation.

The case of delivering goods at an agreed time into a locked container was discussed in Section 6.3. The application was immediately assessed as technically inventive. The examiner's search of existing knowledge found no documents 'teaching' both identifying a time interval for delivery and delivering only at that time. The 'invention' as a whole is a simple software process combining the traditional mental steps of scheduling deliveries with the more modern process of opening an electronic lock. There is no identifiable contribution to knowledge. EPO examiners, unlike their USPTO counterparts, are not required to give reasons for granting a patent so it is impossible to understand just why the EPO considered this to have any technical inventiveness.

In the case of fingerprint authorisation for network access to financial systems (discussed in Section 5.3) the EPO initially found the 'invention' lacked any technically inventive features. When the applicant moved nine words from dependent claim 2 to independent claim 1 – "wherein the stored fingerprint is in an encrypted format" – this uninventive application instantly achieved technical inventiveness. Again the lack of reasons for grant prevent one from understanding why a minor rearrangement in claim wording created technical inventiveness at the EPO where previously there had been none.

The other two cases where amendment achieved technical inventiveness at the EPO have not been discussed earlier, so are presented in full here. One involves a software system for uploading and sharing data on the conditions experienced while goods are being shipped. The other involves communications between manned and unmanned equipment on outdoor worksites.

Logistics Chain Management System (AU2003262306, priority October 2000) is a computerised system for managing the transport of goods. It has also been granted in New Zealand and the USA. In the US it was identified as a broader recitation of the parent and, following rules against double patenting, a terminal disclaimer was filed (10/798573). No other objections were raised. The invention is a software system for monitoring the quality of goods during transport (temperature and shocks) according to agreed standards.

It does not claim a new or improved device for continuously maintaining or recording temperatures. Nor does it discuss how to monitor shocks. It simply provides a computerised system that collects data on temperature and shocks and provides these to sellers, transport providers, storage providers and buyers. The system includes a sensor device which collects and transmits data, but the claims are not about any aspect of this device (see summarised claims in Box 7.1). There is no contribution to any field of economic endeavour or any field of technology. The Australian search report identified seven relevant patent documents but no non-patent knowledge. No objections as to novelty or inventiveness were raised.

Initially the EPO considered that there was no technical solution to any technical problem. The examiner's report specifically noted four patent documents, two regarding data collection means. The examiner rejected the conclusion in the Australian IPER – that the claims were novel and

BOX 7.1 LOGISTICS CHAIN MANAGEMENT SYSTEM: SUMMARY OF CLAIMS AS GRANTED BY THE EPO (EP1342191 B1)

1 Logistics chain system for members (suppliers, transporters, customers etc.) complying with agreed conditions including:
- accessible communications network;
- data storage accessible over the network;
- means for providing consignment details;
- communication between members;
- means to collect data on condition of goods (including data logger that senses data on condition of goods and sends these data to the storage);
- means for recording and tracking these data over time (and including current location);
- reporting means.

2 System as in claim 1, including responsible manager.
3 System as in claim 1, where communications system is the internet.
4 System as in claim 1 or 2 where one of the agreed conditions is temperature range and the data logger senses and transmits temperature.
5 System as in claim 1 where one of the agreed conditions is avoiding shocks and the data logger includes a shock sensor to record and transmit shock events.
6 System as in claim 1, where storage includes suppliers' data, including a bulletin board for listing transport requirements; registering interest in providing transport and means for communication (users must agree to comply with conditions).
7 System as in claim 6, with a manager responsible for the network and the data logging system.

Note: In the Australian version (AU2003262306, priority 5 October 2000) the "data logger that periodically senses . . . and stores or transmits the data" is in claim 4 in respect of temperature and claim 5 in respect of shocks. There is also a claim 8 which repeats earlier elements in a method including agreed conditions, the data logger and review of data from the logger against the agreed conditions.

inventive, saying "in fact any data processing apparatus inherently and coercively implies data collection means as it could not process data unless it acquires i.e. collects them. . . . Any input device, keyboard, mouse, cameras, network etc. could be used to acquire such data."[3] The applicant amended the claims to emphasise "a data logger arranged to sense data corresponding to the predetermined condition of the goods and provide the sensed data to the data storage means." This is little different from the initial drafting – the quoted words were simply moved from dependent claim 4 to independent claim 1. One diagram implies the data logger could be a software module receiving data from radio frequency chips embedded in the consignment. Radio frequency identification (RFID) systems have been around since the late 1960s. In this system they could be a means of sending the data. But the 'invention' does not claim any RFID invention. Once these words had been moved the EPO granted a patent.

Comparing the amended claims to the original examiner's rejection, the EPO must have considered that the "data logger" is inventive compared to other data input devices. Why this should be so is not self-evident, particularly given their earlier strong comments about data input devices. This is another case of the movement of words magically creating technical inventiveness where previously there was none.

The next case was also granted both in the USA and by the EPO. *Method and apparatus for managing information exchanges between apparatus on a worksite* (AU2004307528, priority October 2003) lies in the field of information management. The system was developed in the context of road construction, but claim 1 generalises this to outdoor worksites. A hierarchical networked communication system links equipment (with or without human operators), each item having a unique address. The system can determine the position of mobile equipment. Each item can communicate directly with all others. A work plan is automatically executed sending information about tasks to relevant equipment. It is effectively a software system for communicating between hierarchically arranged networked addresses in a specific context.

The Australian examiner rejected the application for lack of inventiveness, on the basis that differences from the prior art (unique hierarchically structured addresses, and communication between each element) were "mere workshop improvements". The IPER, issued by European Patent Office, noted that the solution to the problem addressed in the application – activating a module to manage an item over a network – would be obvious, including the fact that URLs have by definition a hierarchical structure. In other words the initial EPO assessment was also a lack of inventiveness. Their examiner's first report identified the 'problem' addressed as how to activate, over a network, a module specific to a particular piece of apparatus. This was not considered inventive compared to previous patent documents (EP2004790711).

The claims were amended in similar ways in both Australia and at the EPO. In the EPO version words were moved from dependent claims 3 and 8 into the independent claims. Other minor detail from the specification was also added to claim 1, for example that the outdoor worksite now has an office, the equipment items are mobile or static and sometimes have human operators. A new claim 2 was added. Though these amendments are minor, and do not change the nature of this networked communications system, the patent was then granted in both countries. This 'invention' is an enhancement of the previous Osyris system funded as a European Union project. It is hard to specify any addition to human knowledge or know-how. The initial R&D investment was funded by the taxpayer, so this 'invention' was clearly not induced by the patent system. Interestingly, this application was terminated before grant in the UK, probably because of a subject matter refusal.[4]

The USPTO rejected the application five times before granting it. All rejection advices indicated lack of inventiveness, and in all nine US patent documents were cited. Across several sets of amendment and argument the applicant maintained that it was improper for the examiner to use as relevant existing knowledge a document from the field of networked communications as this had nothing to do with managing networks on a worksite. The examiner consistently replied that the cited document used simple network management protocol to gather information from network devices and that relevant existing knowledge outside the exact field of endeavour could be used if it was reasonably pertinent to the particular problem addressed – clearly so in this case. Just before the fifth rejection the examiner phoned the attorney to propose amendments "that would have moved the prosecution case forward". Another examiner who is very helpful in assisting applicants to gain monopolies. The final amendments introduced the qualifier "fixed and mobile" to the items of apparatus in claims 31 and 48 and added two complex sub-paragraphs to independent claims 29 and 52. These referred to the positions of the items in the network being changeable. The notice of allowance includes a final examiner amendment and simply cites in full the detailed one and a half page long first claim, saying this exact formulation is not 'taught' in the nearest existing knowledge.[5]

These four cases show how the EPO's elliptical approach to assessing eligibility fails to prevent the grant of patents to business method 'inventions' that make no contribution to human knowledge or know-how. So despite the statutory exclusion of business methods from patentability, the EPO grants such patents. These four cases are all software-implemented, but not one makes any contribution to software know-how nor do they introduce any new business process knowledge. It is hard to understand the basis on which the EPO separated these cases from others – equally lacking in new knowledge – which it refused.

The EPO has refused ten cases. Two were refused after appeal and two have appeals pending. The 'invention' computerising PCT application processes, where the application was withdrawn and a continuation lodged, has been counted as a refusal as the continuation was refused. Three other cases were actively withdrawn after two negative reports, indicating that refusal would otherwise have been recorded. In another nine cases applications were abandoned after one or more negative reports by the examiner. These data suggest as many as 19 refusals among the 38 EPO applications. These refusals are not on the simple grounds of non-patentable subject matter, but because of lack of 'technical' inventiveness.

The UK, operating under parallel law, granted patents to five other cases before the introduction of its four-step test in late 2006. Surprisingly it also granted a patent to a sixth case after the four-step test came into effect. But seven other cases were terminated before grant, three of which were definitely refused on subject matter grounds, one before the introduction of the four-step test. Three of the UK grant cases and two of the subject matter refusal cases are discussed here.

A tax refund system (AU2003219472, priority March 2002) deals with refunds of value added tax (VAT), and simply computerises a manual process – as noted in the EPO IPER, it is "straight forward automation". Effectively the bank issuer code embedded in a credit card is used to identify VAT refund eligibility. The system is designed as an add-on to the point-of-sales (POS) terminals used by retailers. A message prompts the retailer to question the cardholder about eligibility for a tax refund. "VAT refunds" has been widely used as a point-of-sales advertising message on the shopfronts of many European retailers since well before 2002. Indeed awareness of VAT refunds is so high that many retailers easily identify likely eligibility, based on accent and general conversation during the sales process, well before they swipe any credit card.[6] There is no contribution to knowledge of either business methods or software.

The Australian examiner rejected it as neither novel nor inventive. The applicant amended the claims and wrote at length arguing that cited prior art did not teach *all* the features of this 'invention'. It was then granted. The application has been granted in the UK and New Zealand.[7] It was refused by the EPO after an appeal. It will be interesting to see if the UK now reviews its grant.

In late 2003 the EPO provided a brief written opinion, citing two US patent documents, and advising no technical problem could be identified.

The examiner report, in mid 2006, acknowledged the 'invention' had technical character conferred by use of a computer in a network. However the steps in the method were seen as non-technical (business) processes and no specific documents were used in rejecting the application as uninventive. The claims were amended several more times (including during the oral hearing) but the EPO maintained that adding a tax recognition feature to a POS terminal was not technically inventive. The applicant appealed. Four versions of the claims were presented to the Appeal Board. The Appeal Board determined that the decision to use bank issuer codes in credit cards to determine VAT refund eligibility was a non-technical decision, whose implementation involved no inventive step. The application was refused.[8]

The case remains pending at the USPTO where so far two rejections have been issued. The first rejection notice was issued in March 2009 and so raised patentable subject matter objections citing *In re Bilski* among other cases. Other problems raised included obviousness and lack of novelty.[9] The applicant amended the claims to overcome the subject matter objection, showing it remains easy to use semantics to overcome subject matter exclusions despite the *In re Bilski* decision. Following a second rejection for want of novelty and inventiveness the applicant cancelled all claims and replaced them with new claims. No further examiner report is yet available.

Despite the use of the word 'device' in *Email Alert Device and Method* (AU2003236451, priority March 2000), there is no device in this software system alerting users to incoming email messages without incurring phone charges. The claims of the granted UK version (GB2403319) were used to achieve grant in Australia. The application as initially drafted was rejected in Australia on novelty and inventiveness grounds, and on the grounds that "[t]he claims are too broad and speculative, and go well beyond the enabling disclosure."[10]

The 74 claims basically repeat themselves four times: as claims for "an indicating device", a system, a method and a "computer program product". The claims are written in very general language, for example a telephone is referred to as a device. Claims are for such things as "an indicating device", "a signal input means", that the audible signal is distinctive, that the visual display depends on the signal received. The core concept is sending an alert message for such a short period of time that the receiving phone is not taken off the hook, avoiding call charges. It was granted in the UK before the four-step test was introduced, but it is hard to see the basis on which it was accepted. It is a simple software product and thus is excluded subject matter. The simple idea is couched in such general language that it probably precludes all other uses of the idea.

Even with a priority date of March 2000, the core idea does not show any particular ingenuity – it simply extends common telephone practices to an email environment. The implementation makes no contribution to knowledge. In fact the third and fourth USPTO rejections refer to a US patent,[11] filed in December 1997, for sending a signal through a communications system upon the occurrence of an event, without incurring charges, and so rejects this 'invention' for want of novelty. The US version has been abandoned after four rejection notices and various amendments. Given this earlier patent it seems probable the UK and Australian patents are invalid.

The next case was granted in the UK after the introduction of the four-step test. *A system for and method of monitoring an item* (AU2003302490) covers both RFID and non-RFID tags, and is designed to identify items along a supply chain from manufacturers, through distributors, to final consumers. At each stage identity information (including biometric information) is scanned and checked against databases for manufacturers, distributors and consumers. The ID is attached to the item (claim 9), possibly by the manufacturer (claim 10). Seller ID is included in the receipt for the product. Despite the biometrics and radio technologies that can be incorporated these are not the subject of the claims. The 74 claims simply cover a data analysis system for reading, storing and linking the three databases. Two of the claims specify how the system would work if the item were luggage, suggesting it was developed for tracking luggage, but has been generalised to claim a wider monopoly.

Comparing this 'invention' with processes in use in June 2003, one can identify core processes used by airlines, post offices and delivery services. While this particular invention uses biometrics, this is simply one data item within the linked databases. Nothing in the claims concerns any technical aspect of biometric use. The patent monopoly covers a system without RFID tags as well as one using RFID tags. Software to link databases was a very standard task by 2003. There is no new knowledge or know-how contributed in any field.

No novelty or inventiveness objections were raised in Australia. This is the sole case where a US patent was granted without any novelty or inventiveness objections being raised, though the examiner required a restriction to just one of the four inventive concepts he found in the claims. A patent was granted in the UK (GB2422035) shortly after the introduction of the four-step test requiring that the inventiveness not reside in the business method or software parts of the claims. At the time of the 'invention' scanning technology and RFID tags were both well-established. The idea of linking databases of product identity information between the manufacturing, distribution and consumption processes simply takes normal stocktaking processes one step further. Moreover it parallels processes used for some time in businesses which organize transport and delivery. It is hard to see where the UK patent office found an inventive contribution at all.

The EPO examiner's report of June 2008 accepts that technical means are used in implementing the system (networked computers, databases, RFID tags, GPS etc.) but could not find any technical problem solved by this combination of technical means. The applicant amended the claims arguing that associating each item with an ID device was a technical means of ensuring that "the data entered into the database is accurate for each stage in the supply chain."[12] Tag data are independently verified before data entry (this sounds like a manual process, or at least a process undertaken outside the scope of the patent claims). Data verification for input to computer programs is a very old concept.[13] However the applicant then failed to pay renewal fees and the application was effectively abandoned.

The next case was refused, on subject matter grounds, in the UK before the introduction of the four-step test. *Automatic Flight Management in an Online Marketplace* (AU2003200436, priority February 2002) is a software system for estimating the best way to spend an internet advertising budget. The objective is to spend the total budget, evenly over time. Key issues are where to advertise, how much to pay, and periodic assessment of the impact of the campaign. This is no different from the issues in a non-internet advertising campaign. The complex detail in the claim would never be attempted outside a computerised environment, but the programming is straightforward as is the advertising concept.

The Australian examiner initially rejected the application, principally on novelty grounds. The applicant amended the claims, replacing them with claims in US 7231358 (granted May 2007). He claimed that the 'invention' addressed the significant technical problem of how much to bid for different listings. He further argued that the cited knowledge failed to suggest the unique features in this 'invention', such as "receiving advertising flight parameters from an advertiser" (i.e. receiving input data) and "adjusting bid amounts of the specified advertiser search listings to achieve advertiser goals of the advertising flight parameters" (deciding to pay more or less, after judging the effectiveness of advertising to date). These seem to be fairly straightforward advertising matters. While Australian examiners do not give reasons for granting patent monopolies, it seems clear that the grant was automatic, given the use of the claims already patented in the USA. In four cases in the dataset the substitution of claims from successful overseas applications automatically led to grant in Australia.

The US parallel was initially rejected on a variety of grounds, including that three claims were written as computer program claims and all claims were obvious with respect to eBay and US patent 5835896. Four claims were deleted, one added and 21 amended, the amendments including rephrasing the computer program claims as a "computer readable data storage medium". Following a phone discussion, the claims were further amended. In the notice of allowance the words "on line" were replaced with "pay-for-placement" in many of the claims. The correspondence indicates that a "pay-for-placement" marketplace is a marketplace with a database of advertiser search listings. Depending on how this is read, this could be narrower or wider in scope than an online marketplace. The notice of allowance shows that the principal reason for grant was that the existing knowledge did not 'teach' using the approach in "a pay-for-placement marketplace".[14] This is another case where using known methods in an allegedly different environment overcomes lack of inventiveness. Other cases of this type are discussed in the next section, which covers analogous uses of known processes.

The application has been deemed withdrawn at the EPO. The examiner reported that the subject matter was excluded by EPC Articles 52(2) and (3), but that rejection on these grounds was not allowed because of (uncited) case law. The examiner found however that there was no inventive step as no technical solution was proposed, nor any surprising technical effect claimed.[15] Although a time extension was granted no substantive response was sent, and the application has been abandoned. The application was refused in the UK as unpatentable subject matter. In June 2003 the UK examiner wrote:

> The application concerns a computerised system for managing an advertising "flight" online i.e. the business activity of promoting a particular set of products over some specific time interval. Although the invention is carried out on a computer, the invention does not make a *technical contribution* to the art.[16]

The applicant, Overture, appears to be building a patent thicket around the technology of managing online advertising. The US version of this application has two parents, one of which has six children, and the other 17 children. In other words the granted US patent has 22 siblings. Some of these siblings have children. Esp@cenet's INPADOC system identifies 89 family members deriving from 69 applications.

The UK patent office refused as many as five of the cases as non-patentable subject matter after introduction of the four-step test (and two before). Because the UK has only recently begun providing accessible case data, subject matter refusals are inferred for four cases, based on the time lag between the request for substantive examination and the termination.[17] The two clear refusals that occurred after the new test was introduced are both owned by Cantor Index, a subsidiary of the global financial firm Cantor Fitzgerald. One of these was used to present evidence showing the reverse onus of proof (Section 5.4). The other is presented here.

Cantor Index appealed the UK refusal but the appeal was dismissed.[18] *System and method for betting on a subset of participants in an event* (AU2003252947, priority April 2003) was also refused by the EPO but granted in the USA. This 'invention' is basically for a negative bet – rather like short-selling on financial markets. Such bets are longstanding, and are called "betting against the field". The US grant came after one refusal and a simple amendment which emphasised that the bet on the field was only defined after betting had closed and before the race began. This was despite a strong negative first examiner's report which identified three patent documents and used the official notice procedure to identify that negative bets were very well known.[19] In contrast the EPO consistently maintained a view that a negative bet was simply a non-technical variation in betting rules which required no inventiveness in its implementation (EP2003816823). Cantor Index amended the claims arguing that the invention addressed a technical problem of reducing high betting volumes immediately prior to a race by allowing group bets rather than multiple single bets. The EPO considered that any increased betting efficiency was achieved through additional betting rules, a non-technical attribute. The application was refused.

7.3 DOCTRINES TO PREVENT TRIVIAL GRANT

Two longstanding doctrinal rules which were introduced by courts to prevent the grant of patents for trivial variations are discussed here. These are the analogous use doctrine and doctrines about workshop variations and technical equivalents. These doctrines should set a minimum floor to inventiveness – that is the scintilla of invention required in the UK and Australia should be some quantum that exceeds this floor.

7.3.1 Analogous Use

The very long-standing analogous use doctrine was introduced in 1838 in the UK. "The law on this subject is this: that you cannot have a patent for applying to a well-known thing, which might be applied to 50,000 different purposes, for applying it to an operation which is exactly analogous to what was done before."[20] By analogy, this reasoning should apply equally to processes. Surprisingly this seems not to occur either in the USA or in Australia. Examples of patents that seem obvious by analogy abound in the business method field. Particularly well-known examples are Amazon's 1-click paying process and priceline.com's online auction system (Brennan 2002).

There are several cases in this study where one would have expected a refusal based on the analogous use doctrine. One is the expert medical system discussed in Section 5.3. As expert systems were first commercially introduced in the 1980s any use of this approach in a new field should surely be deemed obvious using this doctrine – unless of course the applicant can show unusually challenging problems which generate new knowledge or know-how. Four other cases where the analogous use principle should have applied are discussed here.

Method and tool for assessing the sustainability of a development (AU2004200942, priority March 2003) gathers data on a range of sustainability indices, compares their values with benchmarks and targets and then derives as sustainability score. That's it. The examiner seems not to have been aware of the well-known benchmarking approach to assessing relative outcomes.[21] This case indicates two difficulties in the narrow legal interpretation of the current body of knowledge. The identified knowledge was a single document – the range of academic, government and business material on benchmarking was not located by the examiner. Secondly, the fact that the cited knowledge used benchmarking in a different environment seems to have been sufficient to sustain an argument of inventiveness.

A system for validation of chemical usage in the production of foodstuffs (AU2004233489, priority November 2004) uses standard audit methodology, and claims both manual and computerised versions (see summarised claims in Box 7.2). What is audited is the use of chemicals in agriculture. But the critical factor in the grant of this patent was the fact that previous publications did not specify an audit system extending as far through the supply chain as this one. What this case shows is that many patents have already been granted for the use of audit methodologies in this one narrow field of application. This is despite the fact that the analogous use doctrine should have prevented the grant of any patents for using audit for this clearly suitable purpose.

Audit, like benchmarking, is a broad enabling methodology, designed for use in a wide variety of contexts. To grant a patent for a particular audit process, simply because use for that process may not previously have been written down, does not contribute to the objectives of the patent system. Indeed it could better be seen as bringing the patent system into disrepute.

Korea refused to grant a patent for *Service points liquidation system* (AU2003280529, priority November 2002). This marketing 'invention' uses the old marketing concept of reward points in association with used

BOX 7.2 A SYSTEM FOR VALIDATION OF CHEMICAL USAGE IN THE PRODUCTION OF FOODSTUFFS (SUMMARY OF CLAIMS)

AU2004233489; priority 26 November 2004

1 Method to validate chemical use in producing foodstuffs from chemical supply to foods reseller with steps of: recording chemical sales and usage; and verifying these data through an on-site audit
   2 sales data includes technical details of the chemicals
      3 obtained by scanning containers
   4 sales data stored in database
   5 chemical usage includes details at claim 2 plus other items
   6 chemical usage data recorded by user or independent party
   7 on-site audit includes chemicals storage inspection
   8 on-site audit includes inspection of foodstuffs
   9 on-site audit includes inspection of equipment used
   10 on-site audit conducted by inspector independent of chemicals user
      11 auditor is an agronomist
         12 agronomist is engaged by the chemicals seller
13 certification that foods produced according to set chemical use criteria
14 certification that foods comply with set chemical residue levels
15 identification of benchmarking data on chemicals usage and foods production from a number of chemicals users
   16 compare chemical users to identify efficient practice
   17 data include foods and chemical use data
   18 data include foods yield and residue levels on foods

tickets. The claims cover converting various types of tickets to points and managing a database for storing the points for each customer (including accumulating and using points). The abstract points to a motivation to stimulate consumption, and is reminiscent of the 'stamps' used to this end in the UK through the 1960s and 1970s. Frequent flier points and other variations of this basic customer loyalty system have been used regularly over ensuing decades in a wide variety of environments. Its use for this particular product seems no different to its use for those previous varied product lines. It simply seems an analogous use, with no contributions to knowledge or know-how.

The application has been abandoned at both the EPO and the USPTO, following negative examiner reports. The EPO examiner accepted that independent claim 1 possessed technical character as "the subject-matter of the claim is directed to an information processing apparatus". The report went on to "note that none of the features of any information processing apparatus are disclosed [sic] the application".[22] No 'prior art' was cited. The examiner concluded that implementation of the business scheme would be a normal task. No response was received to the USPTO examiner's first report where half the claims were found to be not novel and the remainder obvious with respect to two US patent documents (10/489405). The Australian examiner raised no objections as to novelty or inventiveness.

The next case is based on usage of general ledger (GL) codes – a fundamental building block of all modern accounting systems. Indeed GL coding is so basic to accounting that its use within an accounting product is perhaps more accurately classified as standard operating procedure than analogous use.

Transaction accounting processing system and approach (AU2005255399, priority June 2004) is an accounting system that allocates GL codes to invoices ("transaction-based documents"), with the user able to define the codes. Most computerised accounting systems allow user classification of GL codes. The small difference in this system is that a single GL code can be classified differently depending of the time of day. This may be a useful feature, but surely should not lead to a government-granted monopoly? At best this is a design feature or workshop variation. The US International Preliminary Search Report (IPSR) relied heavily on an electronic document delivery patent and an accounting patent. The Australian examiner used only the document delivery patent in rejecting the application for lack of novelty and inventiveness. The applicant wrote a cogent response as to why the non-accounting patent was not relevant. The patent was granted.

The IPSR states that this 'invention' is simply a computer program. There was substantial negotiation between the applicant and the US examiner – four examiner reports were issued (11/121158). The initial rejection, based on novelty and inventiveness grounds, cited only two US patent documents. The second rejection argued that the claims were for a computer program *per se*. The third rejection accepted that the 'invention' was not a computer program *per se* (though outside the patent world it would still be defined as a computer program), but maintained the objection that it lacked any tangible result. At this point the applicant made some minimal amendments to the claims, for example removing the words "at least one" from the first claim. He renewed the argument that there was a tangible result. The examiner then asked the applicant to choose between two sub-sets of the claims, and once the applicant had done this, the application was allowed. The Notice of Allowance was uninformative simply noting "no teaching of the specific transacting processing system".[23]

This lengthy and substantial negotiation process did not include any discussion of the myriad real-world uses of computerised accounting systems. Because GL codes are so fundamental to accounting it would be hard to envisage that any of these many systems did not use GL codes. Nonetheless this 'invention' has been granted patents in Australia, New Zealand and the USA. At the EPO it was amended following receipt of the European search report, but then abandoned before examination (EP2005756525).

7.3.2 Workshop Variations

In theory the novelty requirement for grant of a patent should allow for rejecting technical equivalents of existing processes as not novel. Similarly the inventiveness requirement should also allow for rejection of applications where these are mechanical equivalents or mere workshop variations, even where these applications are combinations of known processes and features. In practice, although examiners raise such issues, these policy doctrines rarely seem to be maintained as grounds for rejecting uninventive inventions. While this seems particularly the case in Australia, such cases are also evident at the USPTO. There are no examples of this at the EPO, though there the simple movement of words from dependent to independent claims can create technical inventiveness (see Section 7.2).

Mobile report capture (AU2003246060, priority September 2003) uses a 'wireless handheld device' to capture images and generate reports on real estate. Standard templates and date/time stamping are used to overcome 'problems' of possible transcription delays, errors and fraud. The 12 claims of this extremely simple 'invention' are shown in full in the Appendix. Features such as date and time stamps are common with modern electronic technology, and were not new in late 2003.

The Australian examiner raised novelty and inventiveness objections. The claims were amended and the applicant argued that the cited documents did not involve generation of the report at the remote site, but rather generation of the report *on a server, following data collection at the remote site*. He also argued that the cited knowledge did not involve date and time stamping the written and image data, nor did it involve pre-configuration of the report format. Finally he argued that images were *optional* in the prior art, but *compulsory* in this invention. The patent was accepted within the month. This is a second case where a mere change in the location of an activity seems to make it inventive under patent law. The design detail of optional rather than compulsory features has also been used to argue inventiveness in other cases.

The USPTO twice rejected the application on novelty grounds, citing a new document after the claims had been amended to avoid anticipation. A third rejection raised subject matter issues (lack of transformation or connection to a specific apparatus) and identified two further patent documents to challenge inventiveness. The Australian applicant did not respond and the application was deemed abandoned. The application was terminated before grant in the UK.[24]

This case illustrates very clearly the trivial nature of elements which determine inventiveness – here pre-configuration of report formats and a different location for the activity. These seem to be simple workshop variations of well-known methods. They do not even seem to merit the term workshop improvements. These trivial differences were introduced through amendment. If the applicant had to demonstrate inventiveness beyond reasonable doubt this would surely be impossible.

Among the cases are two sibling patents, both titled *Performance evaluation tool and method* (AU2003268606 and AU2003268607, filed in December 2003). These are the oldest of the selected cases, claiming a May 1998 priority from their parent, a US PCT case with the same title. With such old priority dates, both were directed to request examination shortly after they were filed. The applicant, US-based etalk Corporation, took the longest possible time to accede to this direction in both cases. Neither has an overseas parallel, but the parent has had difficulty gaining a patent at either the USPTO or the EPO.[25]

The '606 case is a simple performance evaluation method which stores questions, guidelines and organisational unit identities to calculate performance indices. Subsidiary claims specify that the questions are weighted, that there are target scores, that answer types are pre-defined, and that there is an algorithm for calculating the productivity score. Such evaluation systems were in regular use in a variety of environments for at least a decade before the priority date, so this 'invention' could be classed as another case where the analogous use doctrine should have prevented grant. The Australian examiner raised no objections.

In the '607 case, the system establishes and stores an organisational structure based on user input, imports productivity data, and maps this to the organisational structure using a configuration table, all quite old techniques. The Australian examiner rejected all eight claims as neither novel nor inventive compared to a single US patent. The attorney responded amending the claims to emphasise that the productivity data were *third-party* data used in a *third-party* application and that the configuration table included *user-defined elements*. She then argued that these features were inventive compared to the cited US patent which analysed customer data and converted these to productivity data. The patent was accepted within three weeks. From an economic viewpoint these distinguishing elements are trivial design features not contributions to knowledge or know-how.

Financial products (AU2005265435, priority November 2004) is a process for delivering and maintaining a combined loan/investment product, where the loan is used partly to pay off the loan and partly to fund the investment. Despite the 62 detailed claims this process parallels many geared investment products available on financial markets for well over a decade before 2004. It is a very simple process, as shown in the flowchart from the PCT version.[26] This shows five steps: receive loan parameters, determine payments based on a repayment rule, determine an allocation for making repayments relating to the loan and acquiring an investment, receive payments and use payments based on allocation. The only feature that *might* be deemed unusual is the use of the loan to pay the loan, though this sounds rather like digging oneself deeper into debt. That ownership of the investment is acquired gradually as the loan is paid off is a simple tautology. Most home-owners consider they acquire increasingly large shares of their homes as they pay down their mortgages. In the case of this geared investment the proportion of the shares owned will increase automatically as the loan is paid off. Indeed this feature is strongly reminiscent of decades-old lay-by (pay-by-instalment) retail schemes. The use of the loan to pay off a loan is not a new idea and its use in this context does nothing to create a combination with a surprising or synergistic effect.

The 'invention' involves simple computerisation of known processes ('mental steps'). Despite this essential simplicity, and the availability on the market of a range of similar if not identical products, the Australian examiner raised no novelty or inventiveness objections. The search of existing knowledge identified five patent documents, and one 2000 web paper on investment loans. The paper came from the Cornell University archive arXiv.org, a website for maths and science disciplines. Why academic financial journals were not searched is unclear – perhaps such databases were not available to the examiner even in 2006. Lerner has shown, for the USA, that finance patent applications cite less in the way of relevant academic knowledge than other fields (Lerner 2002).

A patent was granted in the USA after four amendments and two rejections. The examiner then agreed in a phone conversation that amending the last two independent claims to include selling a portion of the investment at the end of the loan would overcome inventiveness objections.[27] This feature seems a trivial variation – indeed simply a design feature. Where an asset is associated with a loan, the owner may very well need to sell part or all of the asset if s/he wants to repay the loan. This has been understood for centuries rather than decades. But this standard element generated inventiveness in the USA. This seems more like a workshop variation than even a workshop improvement.

The response of the patent attorney to the examiner's objections to the next application provides further insights into how trivial is the quantum of difference defined as 'inventive' in patent law. *Spare part procurement method* (AU2004202060, priority May 2004) is a method for a broker to negotiate with a manufacturer to sell spare parts from inventory. The potential seller answers a set of multiple-choice questions, and the answers are scored to reveal whether the part is excess to manufacturing needs. If it is, a means is provided for the buyer and seller to negotiate purchase and transfer. The method can operate over the internet, and includes a facility for the buyer to continuously monitor the broker's progress in obtaining the part. The claims are shown in full in the Appendix.

The Australian examiner rejected the eight claims as lacking any inventive step, being the mere technical equivalent of a previously patented invention. The attorney replied with an amendment bringing the words of dependent claim 4 into independent claim 1. These words covered the question-asking process. The attorney disagreed strongly with the view that ". . . the step of asking the specific questions required in the claimed method is a technical equivalent to the practice in the [prior art] document of assessing a potential seller's spare parts surplus by directly examining the potential seller's inventory and product planning databases." He argued that asking questions elicited "higher value information" than inspecting data (an arguable point), and thus

> . . provides a more refined understanding of whether a particular spare part is excess to the foreseeable needs of the potential seller than would be achieved by simply examining the potential seller's inventory and product planning databases, which does not involve a score based system for determining relative importance of a part.[28]

The patent was accepted within a week of this response being received by the examiner.

So in Australia patent inventiveness encompasses the minute difference between examination of data to obtain an answer and achieving the same answer by posing a set of questions to an individual. One might ask whether the earlier invention was not superior, as the manufacturer was not required to spend time answering a series of questions. Certainly the examiner's initial judgement that this is a mere workshop variation seems sound and one wonders why the response led to a change in this judgement. Does an applicant in Australia simply need to argue for the Australian patent office to withdraw a legitimate objection to the grant of a patent monopoly? This 'invention' contributes no knowledge to any field.

The US version remains pending. Following a first rejection on patentable subject matter and inventiveness grounds all eight claims were cancelled and four new claims filed. These were again rejected on inventiveness grounds. The applicant then cancelled two of the four claims and added six new ones. The supporting argument is interesting in its recitation of the CAFC's post-*Bilski* view of the exclusion of abstract ideas from patentable processes. Citing *Research Corporation* the applicant argues "the Federal Circuit took a very narrow view of what constitutes an abstract idea."[29] The applicant also argued that the identified existing knowledge was not properly applicable to the field of its invention, that there was no reason to combine the two documents and that the possible unwillingness of potential suppliers to sell any parts was a distinguishing feature of the 'invention'. The application remains pending.

Stargames' jackpot 'invention' (AU2005200984, priority March 2004) was initially rejected as a mere workshop improvement compared to three US patents. The applicant amended the claims and argued that these earlier patents covered linked progressive jackpot systems rather than communal games systems. The patent was granted within a month of receipt of this argument. This contrasts with the failure of identical argument both at the EPO and the USPTO. The EPO examination occurred first and the examiner was completely unconvinced by Stargames' argument that there was a technical difference between the elements in this communal games 'invention' and those in earlier "linked progressive" systems. Stargames actively withdrew the application from the EPO in December 2007 (EP2005251278). The USPTO initially rejected the application as being a computer program and on novelty grounds (in September 2007). Amendment took care of these two problems but the revised claims were rejected as obvious. Stargames repeated similar arguments about its 'invention' but the examiner rejected the application for a third time, again as being obvious. The claim was deemed abandoned in August 2009 (11/071427). In this case in both Europe and the USA the use of known elements in a marginally different environment was insufficient to achieve inventiveness. In Australia, however, the examiner immediately accepted minor amendments as trumping his view that this was simply a workshop improvement.

7.4 OTHER DOCTRINAL (POLICY) ISSUES

There are a vast number of detailed rules in patent examiner manuals. These build up over time, sometimes in response to legal decisions and sometimes in response to discussions with key stakeholders.[30] Only a small number of these rules are considered here.

As has been evident from the cases already discussed the 'problems' that many of these 'inventions' solve are trivial in the extreme. The 'problem/solution' approach is frequently used in examination and thoroughly diverts attention from the more important question of what is the contribution to human knowledge. An extreme example of how this rule operates is provided here. Other examples – such as the 'problem' of updating internet bookmarks – were discussed earlier.

The old rule against patenting ideas was discussed in Chapter 4. As has been seen several of these cases seem to involve no more than business concepts, with claims specified at a very high level of generality. This allows for the possibility that these patents, if enforced, would have a particularly negative impact on competition. Two examples of 'inventions' that seem little more than ideas are also discussed in this section.

Another doctrinal rule developed to assist in determining whether an 'invention' is patentable is whether it produces a tangible useful output. This rule derives from the search to operationalise the old concept of a manner of new manufacture. The rule is closely associated with the move away from requiring a technology base for something to be patentable. Given the subject matter of the cases studied here – business methods – the outputs are generally completely intangible. Claims generally spell out a software process for delivering a customer service. One case is discussed here.

Since 2000 the World Intellectual Property Organization (WIPO) has been working on a Substantive Patent Law Treaty. This initiative is very controversial. Industrialised countries are keen to advance the proposal to reduce the costs incurred by their major global companies in obtaining worldwide patent royalties. Others see it as further widening claims for patent monopolies. The proposal seems to have stalled, but still remains as a report item in one of WIPO's major committees.[31] There are already a number of harmonised procedures to reduce costs for patent applicants, though it is unclear what public benefits are provided by reducing the cost of acquiring monopolies. Among the cases is one where the applicant asked for modified examination, where Australia simply accepted patent grant in the USA as meeting all the requirements for grant in Australia. In other cases the issue of accepting the version of claims granted overseas arose during the examination process. Two such cases are discussed here.

7.4.1 The Problem/Solution Approach

One of the doctrines that has developed within the patent system is the use of a problem/solution approach to assessing whether there is inventiveness. The way this operates is by identifying the problem proposed, without reference to the solution in the application, then assessing whether existing knowledge solves the problem in a manner similar to the proposed claims. Kahin (2003b) has suggested that this approach characterises many business method patents and it certainly applies in many of the cases here. It is the applicants who set up the alleged 'problem' in the specification. The approach is widely evident during examination and examiners frequently refer to 'the problem'. Like other doctrines developed to assess inventiveness, the problem/solution approach avoids the critical question of what new knowledge or know-how is contributed. The approach *assumes* there is a problem. But as the cases discussed above show, the 'problems' identified do not really merit the term problem.

This is well illustrated in the next case. *Means to facilitate delivery of electronic documents into a postal network* (AU2003254402, priority October 2002) was granted in New Zealand but did not enter national phase in Europe. It was abandoned in the USA after two rejections on obviousness grounds. Modern electronic networks are used to arrange for the physical production of electronic documents closer to the point of receipt prior to mailing. This is clearly a useful service, as it reduces unnecessary travel for postal items. But the whole process for doing this simply involves computerisation of known 'mental steps' of printing for mailing, with the addition of a step to determine where to print the document. The *idea* of printing closer to the destination may be novel, though globally distributed newspapers have been printing at the reader destination for decades. The application of this idea to individual documents is made possible by the creation of global electronic networks. There are no knowledge or know-how contributions. Indeed there would appear to be substantial first-mover and network advantages, making a government monopoly unnecessary.

An interesting aspect of this patent is that the trivial problems identified and solved are largely based on the company's earlier PCT application (WO99/21330), which was not granted in any jurisdiction. The disadvantages of the parent system are: failure to verify correct address positioning for the envelope window, no ability to reposition portions of the document, no forwarding rules or quarantine processes, no software for managing documents, etc. Unspecified other systems are criticised for deficiencies such as not handling billing. This discussion of deficiencies in the existing systems demonstrates very clearly the focus on not merely incremental, but minute, changes in basic design aspects of a business process. The 'problems' lie outside any field of technology and appear to be normal issues in running a business effectively rather than genuine problems.

The Australian IPER found all 80 claims for system, method and computer readable medium to be novel and inventive. The search report shows three X documents which should have led to some concerns.[32] But the examiner considered these did not cover *all* the combined elements of this detailed claim. The documents identified in the Australian search did not include the two documents cited by the US examiner in the 15 pages of detailed analysis demonstrating a lack of inventiveness.[33]

This case also demonstrates how the patent system allows multiple patent grants for closely related 'inventions', however trivial the 'problem' addressed. This company has generated five patent applications around the concept of printing close to the delivery point (excluding the original ungranted WO version). There is a child (2005244517, sealed August 2006), which in turn has a child (2006201479, sealed December 2006). The grandchild has a child, a patent of addition (2006203578, sealed August 2007). It centres on a user's single-click (reminding one of the famous Amazon patent) to send a graphic image file (perhaps a pdf document) to a remote printing facility. The patent of addition has a child (2007201506, sealed September 2007). Australia has granted five patent monopolies around this business process idea.

7.4.2 Ideas and their Implementation

There is a longstanding agreement that patents provide a limited period of market monopoly for new artefacts and processes. It has never been the intent to allow the monopolisation of new ideas – there is a strong argument that new ideas need to remain in the public domain to maximise economic well-being. However specific proprietary embodiments of new ideas may require considerable research and development to achieve a commercial stage, and this is the underlying economic rationale for the grant of patent monopolies. In the fields of software and business methods claims are often so broadly specified that they can amount to the patenting of ideas if examiners are not vigilant. As Kahin has pointed out, "[b]usiness methods . . . are broad concepts that can be implemented in hundreds of different ways. . . . the barriers to simply thinking up methods and models for conducting business can be very low, but patents at this level can preempt a wide swath of competitive alternatives" (Kahin 2003a).

In one case in the dataset the US examiner considered that the application amounted to the patenting of an idea. The applicant appealed to the BPAI. The BPAI upheld the examiner's view, referring to the machine-or-transformation test as the governing test for process patentability. The BPAI noted that "[t]he purpose of this test *is to prevent the pre-emption of the use of fundamental principles*".[34]

This case, *Interactive Wagering Systems and Methods with Parimutuel Pool Features* (AU2004202762, priority April 2000) provides gamblers with information on how their planned bet will affect the total bet pool and hence any winnings. It received four final rejections and three non-final rejections from the USPTO. The US examiner put the view that, given the problem posed, there was only one method of determining the odds, thus making it obvious. The applicant was invited to present evidence on any other method. Instead they appealed.[35] The BPAI considered two issues – whether the 'invention' was patentable subject matter and whether it was inventive. In dealing with the subject matter issue the BPAI referred to *In re Bilski* and concluded that the claimed method was neither tied to a particular machine or apparatus nor did it transform a particular article into a different state/thing. In considering the obviousness issue the BPAI referred to the recent *KSR* decision, that a person of ordinary skills in the art has ordinary creativity. The BPAI concluded that it would be obvious to use the known calculation method for a projected bet as well as for an actual bet. The examiner in Australia raised no novelty or inventiveness objections.

The EPO has also rejected this application. In an unusually clear wording on excluded business method subject matter, the examiner advised that the "claims of the application are considered to relate to subject matter excluded from patentability under Art. 52(2) and (3) EPC and formulated to merely specify commonplace features relating to a technological implementation of such matter without inventive step (Article 56 EPC)."[36] In the summons to attend an oral hearing the examiner commented that modifying a well-known interactive wagering system to simulate the placing of a bet required no inventive skills. The application was refused.

There are six betting patents among the selected cases. Probability theory underlies all betting patents, and is a very well understood branch of mathematics. While clear thinking is required, given a type of betting system there is a single defined outcome, given the particular problem posed. There may be more than one method of calculating this outcome, but such alternative methods are well-known, and will produce identical outcomes. This logic underlies the USPTO rejection of the ODS application. So in regard to betting patents it is hard to see how there could ever be any contribution to knowledge – or indeed any inventiveness. Some of the betting patent applicants are developing quite large patent thickets. The case discussed above is owned by ODS Properties Inc, a US company. A search of the Canadian, US and New Zealand databases to attempt to identify parallel applications identified 22 applications in Canada, 24 in New Zealand and 27 in the USA (of which 13 had been granted).[37] With very low inventiveness standards it is not surprising that a single company can come up with a large number of patentable ideas.

Betting patents challenge several traditional areas of patent policy. Their subject matter was traditionally excluded from patentability, their ability to produce a tangible output is dubious,[38] they appear to be based on specifying a problem (after which the solution is obvious) and so seem to patent ideas rather than artefacts. Some of these ideas are well known. There is no identifiable new knowledge, so the grant of betting patents produces no spillover benefits to offset their costs. These issues are, of course, aside from the larger issue of whether a society wants to encourage gambling.

There are several other examples in the dataset of patents which are so generally specified that they seem to amount to the patenting of business ideas. The ideas are set down in flow charts and legalese. But they do not have any technical challenges in implementation nor do they contribute to knowledge. The printing close to the delivery case discussed above is one example.[39] Few of the ideas in these cases provide any advances in systems and methods of doing business. They are simply ideas. Another example is presented here.

Method for managing printed medium activated revenue sharing domain name system schemas (AU2004201637, priority April 1999) was rejected in Norway in September 2005. It was withdrawn in Europe six months after receipt of the first examiner's report, which rejected the application as not novel. It has been granted in the USA but little information is available as the file wrapper (and hence all supporting documentation) is missing. The allowance occurred less than a month after the first examiner's report suggesting the report raised only formalities.[40]

This US-owned e-commerce patent has a very large family: INPADOC shows 65 applications. The 1999 priority date is claimed from an earlier Australian patent, but it is actually a continuation of granted US 6314457, which itself has three children. The US version of AU2004201637 has itself eight children, two granted and six abandoned. With such large and complex families, where titles, abstracts and subsidiary claims are frequently identical, tracing specific parallel applications is challenging. However as the applicant requested modified examination in Australia, allowable where a patent has been granted in a prescribed country and the description and claims are the same, one of the granted US patents must be virtually identical. This is one of the oldest cases considered, with a 1999 priority date. The application was published a month after filing. Although the gap between priority date and acceptance was five years, the lag between filing and acceptance was a mere six months.

Does a very significant invention underlie such a large patenting effort? The 'invention' provides a service where scanned bar codes (or ISBN numbers) are linked to their websites. The claims are drafted at a very high level of generality (see full claim wording in the Appendix) and identify an "end-user device" (a scanner) capable of reading "machine-readable code" (bar codes). A link table associates codes with their websites. Subsidiary claims cover steps for charging sign-up and usage fees, a credit-card module, a transaction tracking module and a module to underpin loyalty/reward programs. A critical question from a policy perspective is whether the manner in which the claims are drafted allows other businesses to use other variants of this business idea. If there is no difference between the idea and the patent claims this would give the owner rights of exclusion over a wide range of means of linking bar codes to web pages.

The idea that scanning barcodes could link to product information rather than an inventory record or cash register was not new at the time, as evidenced by the EPO's rejection of the application against the very low standard of patent novelty. That is, compared to a single previous patent document all features of claim 1 were disclosed. The examiner also found dependent claims 2, 8 and 10 to lack novelty and the remaining dependent claims to lack inventiveness.[41] The application was abandoned. There is no knowledge contribution to any field of technology.

7.4.3 Subject Matter: Tangible Useful Output

Method and processing arrangement for providing various financing options (AU2006202244, priority May 2005) is a reverse mortgage system. This application has 55 claims for a system where the early repayment amount on a home equity loan depends on the current value of the asset if the value has increased, but not if it has decreased. Essentially the lender wins either way. Reverse mortgages typically involve a single repayment of capital and interest at the end of the loan period. A variety of such products have appeared on the market over the last decade, in response to changing demographics. This 'invention' uses a loan-to-value pricing model to calculate repayment values.

The underlying model is very straightforward. Like other finance patent claims, the maths involved is well known and any competent student faced with the problem would be able to identify the appropriate mathematical approach and put forward options for solutions. As different students would come up with different variations on the theme, there would be no *single* obvious combination of features, so the Australian examiners would not, under current rules, be allowed to argue that any specific combination was obvious. There is no contribution to financial product or process knowledge or know-how. The examiner raised no concerns about novelty or inventiveness.

Given the overall competitiveness and innovativeness of financial markets, such products have been entering the market in a continuous stream for decades. With the advent of patenting additional commercial advantages can be perceived by some parties. The applicant asked for expedited examination as negotiations with a potential partner were underway. The applicant was also "concerned with the activities of a potential infringer". In other words the development was obvious within the field.

In the event Greenway Capital Limited (an Australian residential real estate finance specialist) opposed the application, paying the $550 opposition fee. The three individual applicants chose not to pay the $140 acceptance fee by the due date and the application lapsed. Because it lapsed so soon after opposition was notified, no papers specifying the grounds of opposition were lodged. Given the business of the opposing party, and the simplicity of the 'invention' it seems likely that Greenway would have argued that the 'invention' was neither novel nor inventive. Because the Australian examiner considered the original application had more than one 'invention' (the other two being different types of repayment value estimates) two divisional applications were also lodged. Each was granted and each was opposed by Greenway.[42]

In Europe the application lapsed before entering national phase. As in Australia, the USPTO identified more than one inventive concept. Following restriction to one sub-set of claims, the application was rejected as being neither novel nor inventive in relation to one US patent document (with one inventor in common with the current application). The applicant amended the claims and argued that the earlier application did not cover each and every element of the current application, and that, notwithstanding the *KSR* decision, this new combination was clearly inventive. In the examiner's third rejection new grounds for rejection were raised – that the subject matter was not patentable in light of the 2008 *In re Bilski* decision. In particular the examiner referred to the transformation being "insignificant post solution activity" such as data gathering or outputting. The examiner went on to provide a detailed argument that the revised claims were obvious compared to the earlier application and also raised double patenting issues.[43] The applicant did not reply to this third report and the application was deemed abandoned.

The claimed process outputs "the repayment amount determined for the loan". This 'tangible, useful output' meets Australia's manner of manufacture test and thus makes a non-patentable algorithm patentable. Australia has had a very wide eligibility for patentable subject matter, developed through a series of judgements drawing on the High Court *NRDC* decision in 1959. The Advisory Council on Intellectual Property (ACIP) completed a two-year study into patentable subject matter. After considering the TRIPS objectives, which focus very much on technological innovation, ACIP opted to recommend a definition of "an artificially created state of affairs in the field of economic endeavour" (ACIP 2010: 13). This is an extremely low threshold, avoiding any focus on technology.[44] It merely reflects current case law that, with the exception of fine arts and legal processes, if you can earn a dollar from it anything is patentable subject matter in Australia. It remains to be seen whether semantics will be allowed to evade the re-affirmed US doctrine that "insignificant post-solution activity" does not confer patentability on a process. Certainly this doctrine appears to be reaffirmed, in a slightly different context, in the Supreme Court's *Mayo* decision. But patent systems are not robust to semantic abuse.

7.4.4 Harmonisation: Using Overseas Grants to get Domestic Grant

Companies owning large numbers of patents regularly push for the democratic governments of sovereign nations to harmonise their patent laws to make it easier to extract rents from a larger number of consumers. Their argument of regulatory rationalisation is superficially attractive until one remembers that what is being harmonised here is a monopoly-granting system rather than a best practice process for ensuring a competitive economy. One aspect of harmonisation is where a country agrees to grant a patent monopoly without examining the patent. Among the 72 cases considered here is one where the applicant asked for modified examination based on its granted US patent (6314457). This case – a system for scanning barcodes to link to websites – was discussed above.

But going beyond formal processes, there are another four cases where, in response to Australian examiner objections of lack of inventiveness, the applicants offered alternative claim wordings that had been granted in the US or the UK. In all four of these cases the examiner immediately granted the patent. Two of these cases were discussed earlier in this chapter (email warning 'device' and internet advertising campaign). A third is a software system whereby a passenger can swipe her boarding card to select which luggage belt her suitcase will arrive on (*Luggage collection installation*, AU2005247009, priority July 2001). This case had applications only in the USA and Australia. In Australia, in response to the examiner's lack of inventiveness objections the applicant withdrew all 55 claims replacing these with the 14 claims granted in the USA. The US application had been rejected twice before grant.[45] The final distinguishing feature that led to grant in the USA was user selection.

In the fourth case where an overseas grant was used to gain an Australian grant it was the examiner who suggested use of the overseas version to the applicant. *Automated Price Improvement Protocol Processor* (AU2004222811, priority December 1998) is owned by Cantor Fitzgerald, a globally recognised name in financial services. It has been granted in the USA and Israel as well as Australia and New Zealand. This financial patent is an auction trading system for fixed interest security instruments and similar financial products. It allows bids to be revised and provides time-limited opportunities for high bidding buyers or low bidding sellers to complete transactions. The claim was initially rejected as lacking inventiveness. The examiner drew the applicant's attention to the narrower claims of their granted US 6963856. The original claims were withdrawn and replaced with these narrower claims. This is not the only case where examiners go out of their way to help their clients to gain patent monopolies.

The US version was rejected three times prior to grant, so clearly inventiveness issues were raised by the USPTO examiner too.[46] The family members were fairly hard to track down,[47] and in fact there are two closely related families. The EPO examiner was unimpressed that the applicant had fully amended the 128 claims and 47 pages of description without providing any marked-up copy showing the changes. Nonetheless he went on to say that all claims failed the inventiveness requirement – the nearest pre-existing knowledge was a data processing system with a central serving and multiple workstations. The examiner pointed out that "input keys having changeable indicia . . . so-called 'soft keys' were also generally known in the art".[48]

The applicant responded by replacing the 128 claims with two, arguing this highlighted the technical feature of increasing computer efficiency by allowing high-volume trading. The examiner agreed the revised claims were technical as they involved interconnected computers, but beyond this the claims "relate solely to a computer program as such which implements a business method as such" and therefore lacked novelty.[49] The application was refused by the EPO and the applicant advised in June 2012 that an appeal would be lodged.

The claims offer a simple auction system with a fixed time period where those who are closest in price can negotiate without participation by others (standard procedure in incomplete auction events). It is unsurprising that objections would have been raised, even given the narrow constraints within which patent examiners operate. At best this is a combination of old ideas; it might better be classified as a very trivial variation on pre-existing systems. There are no contributions to knowledge. The priority date on this patent is just 4 months after grant of the priceline.com patent (US 5794207). That patent grant quickly generated substantial controversy and public comment.

7.5 SUMMARY

While the EPO has rejected at least eight cases (and more likely 19) for want of inventiveness and the UK has rejected between three and seven cases as non-patentable subject matter, both offices have granted patents to some of these cases. The cases which have achieved EPO or UK patent grant are similar to all the other cases studied in that they contain no contributions to knowledge or know-how. It is unclear how they passed the inventiveness test, particularly at the EPO where the inventiveness is further required to be 'technical'. Certainly the EPO used the synergy doctrine to refuse a number of these trivial 'inventions', but the fact that some were allowed does seem to confirm the view presented by Bakels and Hugenholtz (2002) that the inventive step is also very low at the EPO.

Other cases presented in this chapter indicate that doctrines designed to set a floor to how trivial a patented invention is do not appear to be operating, at least in this technology field. This could be due to a narrow reading of the analogous use doctrine – that it applies to things not processes. Certainly in Australia the patent advisory body takes the view that the analogous use doctrine does not apply to combinations (ACIP 2008: 18). It was considered but rejected by Justice Heerey when confirming a patent for the use of dynamic storage in a consumer loyalty environment (*Welcome*).

But other doctrines also seem not to be operating as intended. In particular the doctrines that should prevent workshop variations or differences in design features from achieving a patent do not appear to be operating. Features such as adding user definition to an already known process have made the difference to patent grant in both Australia and the USA. Particularly surprising is that a difference in location of an activity creates inventiveness for patent purposes (fingerprint authentication and property report cases). Where examiners raise issues of technical equivalence, as in the spare parts case, they seem to back away from this view when challenged. In the USA very trivial amendments achieve patent grant, for example the difference between an online and pay-for-placement marketplace or paying off part of a loan. The worksite case reinforces earlier evidence about the helpfulness of US examiners. They assist applicants to redraft their claims to overcome objections. Changing the order of words in a claim can generate technical inventiveness at the EPO and in Australia.

The failure of traditional doctrines to play their role in eliminating trivial patents has shifted the point of balance in patent systems. The cases presented here and in previous chapters add to the earlier evidence that patent systems have extremely low quality standards, particularly as regards the height of the inventive step. This low standard does nothing to increase the level of technological innovation, but may well have a negative impact on innovating firms generally. The essence of the patent privilege is negative: the right granted is the right to prevent other innovating firms from a particular area of activity.

The cases presented indicate other issues that are problematic when the government is granting monopolies. Patent systems cause difficult tensions between public and private interests. Allowing applicants to lodge closely similar divisionals then withdraw the parent just before refusal reinforces the questions that have been raised elsewhere about allowing applicants to lodge endless divisionals and continuations (Lemley and Moore 2003). In particular it calls into question whether any divisional should be allowed an 18-month period hidden from the public. There is also a conflict in perspectives between the patent world's very narrow definition of an 'invention' and the business perspective whereby any process to deliver services tends to be complex and multi-faceted. In this environment requiring applicants to split their 'invention' into multiple applications (as in the reverse mortgage case) simply increases costs for firms wishing to oppose grant of such monopoly rights.

8. Rebalancing the patent system

8.1 THE EVIDENCE ON PATENT POLICY

Earlier chapters have presented evidence on inventiveness from a scientifically selected sample of granted business method cases. If inventiveness is defined as a contribution to new knowledge or know-how, none was found in any of these cases. There were two possible new ideas, though they did not contribute knowledge in themselves or in their implementation. These results suggest that the patent law definition of inventiveness has become irrelevant to the purpose of patent policy – encouraging innovation to the benefit of society.

The reasons for the grant of so many obvious patents are to be found in the detailed prescriptive rules that have developed through case law in Australia, the UK and the USA and through administrative practice at the EPO. These rules seek to objectify what is essentially a subjective judgement. The objectification completely disregards the goals of the patent system and the economic reasons why such monopolies might provide a national benefit. This disconnect has resulted in both examiners and courts asking the wrong question. They do not ask if there is a genuine contribution to knowledge which might create spillover benefits and justify a monopoly grant. Instead they ask whether they are justified in refusing a monopoly on the basis of a sub-set of documented knowledge and a definition of inventive as narrow difference. Older doctrines (policies) which attempted to set a minimum standard for the grant of a patent seem to have evaporated.

The doctrines which lead to the grant of very obvious business method patents are the same doctrines as those that apply in genuine fields of technology. This – and other independent evidence – suggests that the inventiveness standard is low across the board. What is required for grant of a patent is not inventiveness but a minute difference. Such minute differences contribute nothing in exchange for the patent privilege. The overall conclusion is that the patent system is *inefficient*. It is granting many patents where there is no benefit, but where there could well be costs.

There is a substantial body of other evidence questioning the *effectiveness* of current patent policy. Major empirical studies of industrial innovation demonstrate that most firms rely on market mechanisms to obtain a return to their investment in innovation. Their use of the patent system is mainly forced by its existence. Given the strength of the monopoly provided by the patent system – the right to stop others innovating – where there is a 'strong' patent system innovating firms must obtain their own patents to cross-challenge in litigation situations or to cross-negotiate for access to complementary and overlapping technology. The research evidence substantiates the view that in general patents are not needed to stimulate innovation; indeed "successful innovation depends on the *absence* of patents owned by others affecting the innovation" (Quillen 2006: 209, emphasis added).

There are exceptions. Where a technology is highly codified it can be copied more readily. In situations where a useable substitute product can in practice reach the market quickly and cheaply, patents may be needed if the innovation is to occur. These features characterise the modern pharmaceutical industry but few others. Some commentators have argued that patent policy is precisely designed for this type of industry (Mandeville 1996; Macdonald 2004). For these highly codified and easy to copy technologies, patent policy may generate more benefits than costs. In other situations it does not (Bessen and Meurer 2008).

Direct evidence from patent data on the effectiveness of patent policy is weaker. Patent offices do not produce data in a form that is useful for policy analysis. They collect no data on how the monopolies they grant are used, despite having administrative renewal systems which could be used to collect such data. The databases they produce are entirely oriented to the needs of applicants for patents – indeed in Europe it does not seem possible for an innovating firm to interrogate the official patent databases to obtain a list of what patents are in force in a particular field of technology.[1] Some calls for the independent collection of data to study the use and impact of patents seem to have been deliberately undermined (Kahin 2003a). FTC recommendation 10, about increased evidence based analysis of the patent system, was strongly rejected by the Intellectual Property Owners Association.

Despite this absence of systematic data, a number of researchers have undertaken detailed studies of patent outcomes, identifying that the quantum of inventiveness required for validity is extremely low. There is substantial evidence from validity cases heard by US courts showing that the proportion of cases held to be invalid has fallen since 1982, suggesting a fall in the inventiveness threshold (Lunney 2004; Quillen 2006). In 2007 the Supreme Court reassessed the test used for the inventive step and confirmed that the bar had been set at too low a level (Dreyfuss 2008). IP Australia publicly recognises that the inventiveness standard in Australia is lower than in other jurisdictions (IP Australia 2009a: 10). Some researchers consider the inventive step is also very low under the EPC (Bakels and Hugenholtz 2002).

Inventiveness is, of course, the key variable determining the overall impact of a patent system. If the standard is set too high, useful innovations may not occur. If it is set too low there will be many obvious patents, imposing costs on other innovating firms and on consumers. Studying the height of the inventive step empirically is challenging. Inventiveness is a continuum and identifying the quantum of inventiveness needed to create balance in a patent system is very much a qualitative judgement. There are no good proxies for measuring inventiveness – it is the distance between an invention and what was previously known. None of the proxies generally used in larger scale studies really measure this underlying variable. The one previous in-depth study of the quality of granted patents reviewed 50 of the 'best' software patents granted by the USPTO against USPTO standards. Two were found to be obvious and the remainder involved only incremental levels of innovation (Campbell-Kelly and Valduriez 2005).

In-depth analysis of patents is expensive and time-consuming. The case material presented here appears to be the first systematic review of a scientifically selected sample of patents to determine the actual quantum of inventiveness against an economically relevant yardstick. It confirms the more anecdotal evidence provided in earlier studies. If inventiveness is defined as a contribution to knowledge or know-how then none of these cases show any such contribution. If inventiveness is defined as some form of ingenuity, then two of these cases *may* contain a new idea. But neither of these possible new ideas involves substantial R&D costs and their implementation creates no new knowledge or know-how. Grant of a patent monopoly in these circumstances reduces competition with no offsetting gains to society.

In democratic nations it is not the intent of elected governments to implement or maintain policies which make the nation worse off. Ideally patents would only be granted where they are needed to induce socially valuable innovation. Unfortunately this first-best policy approach would be very difficult to implement. A second-best alternative needs to be considered. If patents are granted only where there is a benefit to the nation – spillover benefits exceeding the costs of reduced competition – then the patent system will be well-balanced and produce a net benefit. The critical element in grant of a patent should be at least the possibility of such spillover benefits. A minimum condition for this to occur is that there actually is new knowledge or know-how embodied in the patented invention. This study shows clearly that the current rules do not require this.

While the cases presented in this study are drawn entirely from the business method field, the data show that they are granted because of a range of prescriptive policy rules which are unrelated to the goals of the patent system. Neither the examination process nor litigation about validity raises the question of what new knowledge or know-how is contributed by the invention. It seems likely legislators had this intent – requiring that inventiveness be assessed in relation to existing knowledge. But in practice a different question is asked and answered – can we legitimately reject this application as being obvious to a skilled person in that technology field? This leads to quite different outcomes.

A range of legal doctrines (policy rules) have led to the reduction of the inventiveness/obviousness test to a simple requirement for a very marginal difference. There are doctrinal rules which should provide a floor to this 'marginal difference' outcome, but they do not seem to operate effectively. These rules include technical and mechanical equivalence, workshop improvements and analogous use. In the case of combinations the standard operating rule was actively lowered, by courts, in both Australia and the USA from the synergy to the suggestion test. Under this rule extraordinarily obvious 'inventions' can be patented, provided there is a minute difference in the combination. This minute difference can take the form of a different location, the exact field of application, a marginally longer supply chain, user-definition of elements, the roles of different actors or different software modules or they can be inessential design features.

The impact of using very minimal difference as the inventiveness standard is compounded by allowing applicants to continuously amend their claims, seeking wording changes that evade the documented current knowledge. In Australia the statutory change allowing continual amendment was introduced in 1953 and has never been evaluated. Such an evaluation is clearly overdue. The presumption in patent statutes or patent manuals that it is the patent office that must demonstrate lack of inventiveness rather than the applicant demonstrating a genuine new contribution reinforces the low patent quality standards. The so-called problem/solution approach used in examination also allows a reframing of the qualifications for a patent away from the requirement for a net benefit to the nation.

These doctrinal rules operate across all fields of technology. They apply as much to the grant of pharmaceutical patents – where there may be a real need for the patent incentive – as to the grant of business method patents. The European Commission found that a single new chemical entity could have nearly 100 product-specific patent families and that for major new chemical entities there was "a steady rise in patent applications throughout the life cycle of a product" (European Commission 2009: 10). Such outcomes can only be possible if the inventiveness requirement is very low. There are special challenges in applying the current concept of the inventive step to pharmaceuticals (Correa 2008: 40–43). The recent development and spread of additional market intervention for pharmaceuticals, test data exclusivity, raises interesting issues about patents.[2] Quillen suggests that these data exclusivity provisions mean that "higher standards for patentability, which are decidedly in the interest of other innovators, will not diminish pharmaceutical innovation" (Quillen 2008: 62).

8.2 IMPLICATIONS OF RAISING THE INVENTIVE STEP

The courts have gradually built the current system with its very low threshold for monopoly grant. When case law has been adopted into statute law there has been a lack of economic evaluation. Clearly for the system to be improved executive governments and parliaments need to recognise that important economic policies cannot be left to the courts to administer. What would happen if the test to meet the inventive step requirement was amended to become a test for a reasonable contribution to knowledge or know-how?

First, the number of patent grants (and applications) would fall dramatically – by thousands in smaller countries such as Australia and by tens of thousands in Europe and the USA. In 2010 Australia granted 14,557 patents, the UK 5,594, the EPO 58,108 and the USA 219,614.[3] If the proposed change in standard eliminated even half the current grants this would clean out nearly 150,000 grants a year across these four granting offices. If the change in standards cut out 75 per cent of grants then the volume of granted monopolies would drop from nearly 300,000 to around 75,000. This is still a remarkable number of monopolies for these four offices to be handing out each year. Indeed if one stops to think about inventiveness such very large volumes of patents directly imply a very low inventive step, even given the vast growth in major economies over the past three decades.

Falls of these magnitudes would substantially reduce noise in the system, making patent search a far cheaper and more efficient process. As others have noted, fewer higher quality patents would have more positive effect on innovation and fewer negative impacts on competition (Freedman 2000). A change to the inventive step definition would also be TRIPS compliant.

Who would benefit? The major beneficiaries would be innovating firms, particularly in those industries where "truckloads of patents" need to be exchanged for firms to use each other's complementary and overlapping technologies, effectively allowing these firms to proceed as if the patent system did not exist. In 2011 in the US alone IBM was granted 6,148 patents, Samsung 4,868, Canon 2,818, Panasonic 2,533, Toshiba 2,451, Microsoft 2,309 and Sony 2,265.[4] A further 266 organisations, mostly companies, obtained 100 or more US patents during 2011. Most of these were in industries where electronics is core technology.

The proposed change in the test for inventiveness would have no effect on genuine inventions – these would have no trouble passing the test and gaining patents. There should therefore be no impact on the overall level of innovation. The associated cost should fall, at least by the amount incurred in obtaining techno-legal advice in drafting and applying for all the trivial patents no longer needed. While this would be a small proportion of costs in the very large companies who take out so many patents, it might make a significant contribution to competitiveness for smaller companies. In particular it would free managers from spending time thinking about regulatory impediments to innovation. Overall one can anticipate some fall in costs and no change in benefits. This would improve the net economic outcome.

The cost-saving to innovative companies also points to the identity of the main losers from such a policy change – the patent attorney profession. The ratio between the number of patent attorneys and expenditure on R&D, which grew exponentially from the mid-1980s (Barton 2000) would fall back to its historic norm. The largest part of the cost of patenting is the drafting advice from patent attorneys. In addition of course fewer patent examiners would be needed.

The greatest objections to this proposal would therefore come from the well-organised patent attorney profession. Such organisations as the International Intellectual Property Institute (IIPI), the American Intellectual Property Law Association (AIPLA), the European Patent Lawyers Association (EPLA) and the Institute of Patent and Trade Mark Attorneys of Australia (IPTA) are active and well-resourced lobbyists. IP Australia's advisory committee is chaired by a past president of the IPTA, for example. These intermediaries play a role similar to that of tariff consultants in regimes with high barriers to free trade. Whenever there is regulation such groups of intermediaries develop to exploit opportunities to take advantage of the regulatory intervention in the market.

The pharmaceutical industry, well-recognised as a major beneficiary of the patent system (Bessen and Meurer 2008: 109), would also protest. The pharmaceutical industry has been a strong supporter of the requirement that patent systems not 'discriminate' between technologies – yet it is the one industry where there is some evidence of a need for market intervention. As indicated by the recent European Commission competition enquiry it relies on the very low standards of inventiveness to extend the patent life of its products (European Commission 2009). The pharmaceutical industry has a demonstrated record of gathering partners from other industries so that it does not stand alone in arguing for global monopolies. Because of its use of very low inventiveness standards, and pure semantics such as Swiss medical claims, it could be expected to strongly resist any move to create a genuine inventive step in any patent system. It has been a strong advocate of a range of patent practices which allow patents on small variations in chemical compositions, particularly new uses and formulations, putting pressure on countries like Brazil and India who have tried to require at least some therapeutic benefit in exchange for a monopoly grant.[5]

Larger companies might therefore be persuaded to join the pharmaceutical industry in resisting such an improvement in policy. They might in particular be joined by companies which employ in-house patent attorneys. In such companies providing advice on the impact of patent policy on the company is often devolved to the senior patent attorney. The overall position adopted by such companies may therefore be based on faith rather than evidence.[6] Others have noted the self-reinforcing expansionist views held by members of the patent community (Thambisetty 2009). Even governments have tended to devolve the role of advising on patent law to the most interested party – the patent office.[7] There are exceptions but these are rare. In New Zealand advice on patent policy is provided by the Ministry of Economic Development. Discussions with New Zealand officials indicate a healthy scepticism about the unsubstantiated mantra that 'stronger' patent policy will encourage innovation.

8.3 A WELL-BALANCED PATENT ACT

The history of patent law confirms that this is a very active area of judicial law-making. In this form of law-making there is no prior enquiry into the facts, the need or the economic impact. In many jurisdictions, including the quasi-courts of the EPO, there is no attention to the impact of these decisions on the shape of public law, nor any consideration of the impact on the economic goals of patent policy. This characterises all the jurisdictions considered here but is perhaps most clearly expressed in Australia. The Full Federal Court took the view that it was not for them to ask the question of whether a patent would provide a net benefit to Australia, although the definition of a patentable invention in Australia is that of the Statute of Monopolies 1623, which was drafted to ensure a benefit to the nation.

As patent statutes do not clearly spell out the objectives of patent law it is perhaps not surprising that judges so often fail to consider these objectives.

Patent law has similarities with tax law and competition law. In each of these systems well-resourced individuals and organisations can gain great benefits if they are able to shape and bend the rules. Considerable effort goes into finding ways around the rules. In all these important areas of economic policy it has become clear that policy development cannot simply be delegated to courts. Governments must actively monitor how courts interpret and change economic policy and intervene where specific decisions begin to change the overall direction of the underlying policy. The lack of government oversight of the patent system over the past several decades has allowed the system to move further and further away from delivering on its economic objectives.

Governments have learned how to manage complex economic policies delivered through the courts, in relation to both competition policy and tax policy. A number of successful approaches have been developed in the tax policy arena and these have been demonstrated to be effective in reducing at least some of the strategic games which otherwise undermine the overall objectives. These lessons can usefully be applied in reforming patent law.

The most important lesson is that in more dynamic complex domains simple rules are ineffective (Braithwaite 2005: 144–55). Over-arching principles must be spelled out and must trump detailed rules where there is any conflict. This lesson reinforces the need to include in patent statutes a clear statement of objectives and principles.

This would include the objective of encouraging a higher level of investment in innovation than would otherwise occur. But equally it must include the condition that a patent monopoly be granted only where it is likely there will be a net benefit to the nation. There should be a recognition that patents impose costs, not only on consumers but also on other innovating companies.

In regard to raising the height of the inventive step useful reforms include removal of the statutory presumption in favour of applicants and statutory and case law limitations on existing knowledge. The inventive step should be applied from a positive not a negative perspective – as a contribution to new knowledge or know-how that is sufficient to offset the costs imposed on the nation by grant of the patent monopoly. This condition could replace the current novelty and inventiveness tests.

The resistance of the patent community to modernising archaic language is also interesting. One can speculate that if technology were referred to as technology rather than as 'art' then judges might have hesitated more before extending the system beyond the scope of what is normally understood as technology. Similarly if existing knowledge were referred to as existing knowledge and not as 'prior art' then perhaps the focus might have remained on knowledge. The patent community seems to dislike limiting the patent system to genuine fields of technology and the use of the word 'art' for technology assists in ducking this issue. After a two-year review of patentable subject matter ACIP has recommended a very expansionary definition of patentable subject matter ("an artificially created state of affairs in the field of economic endeavour"). After considering the *NRDC* view that "inventions belong to the useful rather than the fine arts" ACIP considered but rejected using the language of the TRIPS Agreement's "field of technology" definition, seeing this as "dangerous" (ACIP 2010: 55).

Another set of reforms should be introduced to reduce (or preferably eliminate) the games playing behaviour of applicants and their advisors. One component would be a much more limited right to amendment. Any rearrangement in the wording of claims to achieve grant of a patent should be accompanied by a clear statement of how this demonstrates the contributed new knowledge or know-how. Indeed it would be useful for all patent grants to be accompanied by a clear statement from the examiner of the exact new knowledge or know-how contributed. Such a statement must not be a mere recitation of complex claims, but rather a clearly-worded statement which should be included in the final abstract in a section identifying the contribution made by the patent. This enhanced role for examiners would offset to some degree the reduced time needed to examine fewer patent applications.

Another element in reducing games playing would be to institute penalties on both applicants and their advisors if semantics are used to attempt to undermine the purpose of patent law. It is widely known within the patent community that simple wording can be used to avoid statutory prohibitions on patenting. Perhaps the worst example of this is "Swiss medical claims", designed to avoid the prohibition under the EPC on patenting second medical uses of known substances. They were designed by the Swiss Patent Office to get round the prohibition (Thambisetty 2009: 16–17). These actions directly undermine the law and it is astonishing that patent offices not only accept them but actively design them. They parallel the design of financial products such as tax shelters to evade tax liabilities. Such anti-social activities in the tax field can now be tackled through the general anti-avoidance provisions of tax law (Braithwaite 2005: 151–4).

Similar provisions and associated financial (and possibly criminal) penalties are clearly needed in patent law.

In this regard it is interesting to reflect that there are very poor penalties to recoup the losses to society where an invalid patent has been used. In the case of the Amazon 1-click patent, the scope was significantly reduced due to an opposition lodged by a disinterested party. In such situations there is no ready avenue for companies who have paid royalties for the invalid monopoly to seek compensation. There can be adjustments where there is a dispute between two parties. When it became evident that their patent was very weak, Amazon settled out-of-court with barnesandnoble.com, presumably reimbursing them for their losses. But the incentive to challenge an invalid patent is weak and introducing a right to recoup the excess profits achieved through a patent found to be invalid – perhaps payable to the challenging party to recompense them for the cost and risk – would encourage greater vigilance by all parties. A payment in respect of consumer losses could be used to fund agencies charged with protecting consumer interests. These penalties would not only encourage those badly affected by weak patents to seek to overturn these, but it would also encourage the owners of weak patents to extract lower rents from dubious 'inventions'.

These reforms could be consolidated by ensuring that patent administration and patent policy comes under the overview of government agencies charged with promoting competition policy. It is competition which is the major driver of innovation. Patent policy is merely a tool which can assist in limited circumstances and for specific types of technologies. Placing patent policy within the competition portfolio would ensure that the closed patent community is opened to a wider range of views on a more balanced role for patent regulation. This administrative change would assist in ensuring regular monitoring and evaluation of specific legal decisions and active reporting to government when the law needed further clarification to those administering it. Such an administrative re-arrangement could also encourage review of the multiple overlapping sources of government assistance to innovators and creators. At present some types of innovators can enjoy the multiple benefits of R&D grants and/or tax assistance, patent monopolies, encryption and copyright 'protection'. This seems an excessive impost on society.

All the above proposals are TRIPS-compliant.

A challenge to implementing these reforms is of course that the beneficiaries are widely dispersed and the losers are well organised and experienced lobbyists. As noted above some of the winners may, at first consideration, think they would be losers. It is clear that large innovating firms would benefit from a higher inventive step, but in many such companies views on patent policy are determined by their patent advisors rather than their senior executives. The deliberate complexity of patent policy is used to encourage devolution of thinking about company policy on patents to 'experts'. But these experts have built well-paid careers from the patent system and tend to have a whole-hearted faith in the unsubstantiated mantra that 'stronger' patent policy promotes innovation. It simply promotes patenting.[8]

Those who advocate 'strong' patent policy have spent several decades supporting the idea that no-one will innovate without a patent incentive. While the evidence shows that this is clearly a myth, Macdonald notes that myths, like faith, can be impervious to evidence (Macdonald 2004). As noted in the preface, the field of 'intellectual property' is rife with words which over-claim and present a slanted view of the world. For example patents are said to 'protect' innovation rather than stifle competition. Those who use knowledge developed by others are said to be 'free-riders' rather than seen as spreading the diffusion of new technologies and so lifting overall productivity levels (Lemley 2005).

But patent policy is a massive government intervention into the market. As such it needs to be based on substantial independent evidence that the intervention is both effective and efficient and provides maximum benefits for minimum costs. Concerns about government intervention in markets are well based – they can too readily be manipulated by sectional interests whose goal is to slope the economic playing field in their own favour. This is particularly so when self-interested pleading from these players replaces solid empirical data. It is past time that governments in democracies looked to the evidence and re-shaped this important public policy to reflect the public interest.

This book has been a small contribution to the weight of evidence in favour of re-introducing a genuine inventive step into the patent system.

Notes

CHAPTER 1

1. There is a vast literature on this but for overviews see Jaffe and Lerner (2004), Boldrin and Levine (2008), Bessen and Meurer (2008) and Drahos (2010).
2. The Australian Patent Office is part of a wider body currently known as IP Australia and previously known as the Australian Industrial Property Office.
3. Hall discusses a 2002 CAFC ruling that examiners may not reject applications on the basis of general knowledge unless that knowledge is articulated and placed on the record. A then deputy commissioner of patents commented that the ruling meant "we can't reject something just because it's stupid" (quoted in the *Los Angeles Times*, 7 February 2003) (Hall 2009: 16).
4. There are nine refusals from the EPO including two cases waiting appeal. The UKIPO has definitely refused three cases and may have refused four others. One case refused by the EPO was granted by the UKIPO and one case granted by the EPO was probably refused by the UKIPO. One betting case was clearly refused by both offices. Overall between 10 and 16 cases have been refused in at least one of these offices.

CHAPTER 2

1. These assumptions are more reasonable in commodity markets, particularly agricultural commodities. In such markets there is little differentiation between goods and the incentive structures for innovators and followers are different. But in markets for manufactured products there is substantial segmentation and differentiation so products can gain market share on the basis of quality as well as price. Such differentiated markets typically involve imperfect rather than perfect competition.
2. However, these are very compromised by the questionable proxies available. In particular most use the Ginarte and Park index to measure patent system "strength" (Ginarte and Park 1997). But as van Pottelsberghe has shown this is a measure of patent friendliness not patent "strength" (van Pottelsberghe 2011). Boldrin and Levine (2008: 192–8) identify 23 such studies and summarise their results as showing weak or no evidence that stronger patent regimes increase innovation.
3. JSTOR yielded 61 citations of Mansfield's 1981 study and Google Scholar yielded 1,047 (but displayed only 1,000 of these). None referred to any subsequent empirical work on the cost of imitation. A search for citations of Cohen and Levinthal's 1989 study on the importance of R&D for imitation and learning yielded 105 citations in JSTOR. This included one theoretical

piece assuming imitation took time, but no empirical studies on imitation costs or time.

4. The interesting literature on the role of labour movement in the diffusion of innovation and on barriers to such diffusion through anti-competitive laws is a diversion from the theme of this book. But this line of research provides very useful material that innovation policy makers might well review. A starting point is Boldrin and Levine's report of research by Gibson finding that the differential success of Silicon Valley compared to Route 128 is likely due to differences in labour laws. Post-employment non-compete covenants are unlawful in California but not in Massachusetts (Boldrin and Levine 2008: 198–200).
5. Mandeville (1996) discusses the conditions which will encourage such sharing, while Sena (2004) provides a review of recent literature on R&D cooperation.
6. Though this argument (advanced by Schäffle, who called it head-start profits) was rejected during the nineteenth century Great Patent Debate, because at that time perfect markets were thought to be pervasive (Machlup and Penrose 1950).
7. 'Strengthening' usually means extended patent coverage, either through reduced inventiveness standards or broader subject matter coverage. It can also incorporate more powerful regimes for enforcing patents. In contrast a 'weak' patent system is once which protects the public interest through a high inventive step and a narrower range of patentable subject matter.
8. This does not mean that secrecy is a good alternative to patenting in a world with patents. As Quillen (2008) points out, secrecy often needs to be reinforced by patents, especially since the creation of the CAFC.
9. In Japan imitation lags are shorter than in the USA, but lead-time is still reported as a significant means for obtaining a return for innovation (Cohen et al 2002).
10. This review does not include any data from Australian innovation surveys. Data from the 2003 survey indicate that over half of new to the world innovators do not use patents (Australian Bureau of Statistics 2005), again confirming their relative lack of importance to innovating firms.
11. An excellent exposition of this is the review article by Dempster (1994). This study is hard to obtain, though the library at the Australian Commonwealth Department of Industry, Innovation, Science, Research and Tertiary Education has a copy. There are even broader definitions of spillovers from new technology (all benefits not captured by the originator of the new technology). Baumol considers Romer's view that if all externalities from new technology were captured by the innovator, there would have been no increase in the standard of living over the past several centuries (Baumol 2000: 124).
12. Recent Canadian research indicates that 32 per cent of innovations occur in firms which neither fund nor undertake any formal R&D (Hanel 2008: 294). Pavitt (1984) has pointed to the importance of production engineering departments and undifferentiated design and development inputs in small specialised firms.
13. Oppenheim (2000) reports that while 97 per cent of a sample of UK SMEs say one reason for patenting is to stop copying, only 40 per cent report this as the *sole* reason for patenting.
14. It uses the patent right of prevention to exclude firms from alternative

products and processes thus extending the scope of the monopoly on the actually produced innovation. In earlier times this would have been considered an anti-competitive use of the patent system.

15. 2003 OECD survey by the Committee for Scientific and Technological Policy (Blind et al 2006: 658).
16. As noted above this also explains why firms that emphasise secrecy also take out patents (Quillen 2008: 73).
17. Fabricated metal products followed with 12 per cent, then electrical equipment at 11 per cent, primary metals 1 per cent, and instruments at 1 per cent. For four industries the figure was zero (Mansfield 1986: 175).
18. This result is supported by the evidence on pharmaceuticals assembled by Boldrin and Levine (2008: 212–42).
19. In fact the proportion not taken out for defensive purposes cannot be calculated directly from these data as firms reported multiple reasons for patenting. But as these estimates still exceed the direct estimates of the proportion that would not occur provided by Mansfield, they provide a reasonable upper estimate of induced patents.
20. For a summary of the real world experience see Boldrin and Levine (2008: Chapter 9).
21. Where "rent" is used in the classical economic sense of above-normal returns (excess profit).
22. Using GDP as a measure of market size and 2009 data (the most recent year available) from the OECD.
23. While Canada is also a member of the G7, its proximity to the USA and its membership of NAFTA create a different dynamic. It is assumed here that Canadian firms consider the joint Canada/USA market when making investment decisions. They are thus treated in the same manner as US firms.
24. Of course, patent data are not available by industry classification. The two classes selected (see Table 2.1) seem to come closest to covering the drugs and fine chemicals industries, though it is clear from the classification descriptions that these are in fact quite heterogeneous classes. To that extent, use of these classes as approximations will over-estimate induced innovation.
25. As the relevant Australian data are no longer provided on IP Australia's website and therefore cannot be updated, my original US estimates have also not been updated. Given the 'back-of-the-envelope' nature of the estimates the results are illustrative only.
26. Firestone's study of the economic utility and disutility of patents in Canada is one of very few studies of patent use. The focus was on whether patents were worked (used in production). Only 15 per cent were worked in Canada, though 50 per cent were worked in at least one country (Firestone 1971: 347).
27. Including the subsidiaries of overseas companies, where these subsidiaries give Australia as their address.
28. Patent renewal data are mostly used to calculate the private value of patents. There are marked inter-country differences in renewals, but these largely disappear once industry is controlled. There are also differences in renewal rates by patent cohort and by residence, with renewal rates being much lower for domestic than for foreign patent owners. There are no single effective summary measures of renewal rates, and they are usually shown graphically. Neither Schankerman and Pakes (1986) nor Pakes and colleagues (Pakes et al 1989) give summary measures of renewal rates.

29. There is a very extensive literature on US patent 5729594, both academic and popular (Lesavich 2001; Stern 2001, http://en.wikipedia.org/wiki/1-Click). Although it simply computerises the well-known process of running a customer account and despite the public outcry about obviousness, nothing happened until mid 2006 when the USPTO agreed to New Zealander Peter Calveley's request for re-examination based on lack of novelty. Amazon lodged 167 documents (weighing 7 kg) in defence of their monopoly.
30. Though Arrow considered that direct R&D subsidies would be more efficient for such large projects.
31. The USPTO website provides data on major users of their patent system annually since 1963. For patents filed in the years 1990 to 2001 there were 1,713,605 grants, of which 1,468,408 (86 per cent) were granted to organisations. Of these 45 per cent (656,974) are owned by just 300 companies who each owned 1,000 or more patents granted between 1963 and 2006. The 100 most prolific patenters held 513,228 patents in aggregate, or 35 per cent of patents granted to organisations. In Australia 161,404 patents were granted from 1990 to 2001 applications, of which 141,584 (88 per cent) were to organisations. The 100 companies holding most patents held 34 per cent of patents granted to organisations (Moir 2009c: Table 2).
32. Though Bonatti and Comino's (2011) theoretical work suggests it is very poor policy.

CHAPTER 3

1. In 2005 the majority of the US *Board of Patent Appeals and Interferences* (BPAI) reversed an examiner's decision to reject a process which was not tied to any known science or technology, finding it introduced a new test for patentability. Smith J dissented, finding it reasonable to interpret the term 'useful arts' in the Constitution as 'technological arts' (*Lundgren*).
2. *Stare decisis et non quieta movere* (*stare decisis* for short) literally means "[t]o stand by things decided, and not to disturb settled points", *Black's Law Dictionary*, 1443 (8th ed. 2004).
3. From a policy perspective, the phrase "which others at the time of making such letters patent and grants shall not use" emphasises the quality of newness in the phrase "manner of new manufacture" by repeating that monopolies are only for what others are not already using. But the modern legal interpretation can be quite different: the phrase is interpreted by some lawyers as *conferring* the monopoly exclusion right. Walterscheid (1995a: 877) explains this as a shift in language usage and cites Coke's 1628 exposition on the validity of patents to provide an authoritative view from the time that this was in fact a re-emphasis of the novelty requirement.
4. When it was dropped as being ineffective (as the Swan Committee had noted the ease with which the provisions of this section of the UK Patent Act could be evaded by drafting) (Palombi 2009b: 396).
5. This lowest-common-denominator outcome of the negotiations which led to the adoption of the EPC is one of the public policy problems with international harmonisation in response to lobbying rather than sound economic analysis.

6. See Frankel (2008) for a discussion of a key New Zealand decision on this traditional exclusion, particularly whether changing such exclusions should be a matter for judges or parliaments.
7. The District Court of the Southern District of New York made a summary judgment invalidating Myriad's claims to isolated DNA sequences for breast cancer genes (*AMP 2010*). The CAFC reversed this decision on a 2–1 basis in July 2011 (*AMP 2011*) and the matter was appealed to the Supreme Court. The Supreme Court remanded the case back to the CAFC to reconsider in this light of its *Mayo* decision. The CAFC heard oral argument on 20 July 2012 and a decision is yet to issue.
8. One case has recently (2010) been filed in the Federal Court (*Cancer Voices*).
9. Others have covered this issue well. See, for example, Palombi (2009a).
10. The dissenting judges noted that, "[i]n *Parker v. Flook*, we further held that such a computer program could not be transformed into a patentable process by the addition of post-solution activity that was not claimed to be novel" (*Diehr* at 216).
11. *Mirabella.* For a discussion of this case see Brennan and Christie (1997). This decision has caused concern in the patent community, who consider it introduces a new requirement for patentability – that an invention be an invention! Their preference is that all aspects of inventiveness be considered under the inventive step criterion. For a fascinating discussion of this patent community perspective see ACIP (2010).
12. In 1980 in the USA and 1984 in Australia. Indeed the USA put considerable pressure on Japan to follow suit (Samuelson et al 1994).
13. For further details on the changes over time in 'protection' for computer software in the USA, see the excellent expositions in Samuelson et al (1994), Graham and Mowery (2003) and Smith and Mann (2004).
14. This and other ground-breaking software patent decisions have an adverse impact on the stock market value of firms which are likely to have experienced increased costs as a result (Hall and MacGarvie 2006).
15. The *Vicom* invention centres on a mathematical algorithm for filtering digital images. The Appeal Board agreed this in itself was not patentable. In this landmark decision the Board considered the 'invention' contributed to the performance of a general purpose computer and as this was "a claim directed to a technical process" it could not be regarded as a computer program *as such*. Palombi summarised this decision as "the mere application of the algorithm in a computer was enough to side step the prohibition [on software]." (Palombi 2004: 62)
16. At no point in the judgement was the question "what has the inventor added to human knowledge?" actually applied to the analysis of the validity of the *Aerotel* patent.
17. In a subsequent (2008) case the UK Patent Court held that if a process was patentable then its computer program version was also patentable, bringing the UK more closely into line with the EPO position (*Astron*).
18. Similar difficulties were raised in the report to the European Parliament on the proposed (but defeated) European Software Directive (Bakels and Hugenholtz 2002).
19. See the discussion paper on a proposed Trans-Tasman Patent Attorney regulatory system http://www.ipaustralia.gov.au/46106/FINAL_Discussion_Paper_-_SEM_Attorney_Framework.pdf: 43).

20. Hall (2009) provides data on granted US business methods and summarises the literature making policy recommendations with respect to such patents. Hunter (2004) provides a useful categorisation of 33 articles while Merges (2003) provides background on the antecedent legal changes. Some attempt to measure the 'quality' of business method patents can be found in Allison and Tiller (2003) and Hunter (2004).
21. By 18 July 2012 Australia had granted 1,633 patents for business methods filed in the period 2000–2006 (calculated from AusPat data). For the cohort of 284 business method applications filed in 2000, 75 per cent were granted, a reduction from the 82 per cent granted for 1997 filings. The grant rate fell to 55 per cent for the 2001 cohort before rising to 56 per cent in 2002 and 61 per cent for 2003 filings. It then fell again to 52 and 52 per cent for 2004 and 2005 filings. The 2006 cohort is not yet completely processed – 14 per cent of applications remain pending.
22. Though 27 per cent were withdrawn. If withdrawal occurred after a negative examiner report it can also be taken as an effective refusal.
23. In the USA the abbreviation is PHOSITA: person having ordinary skills in the art.
24. The cited text is Frost, *Letters Patent for Inventions*, 1912 (no publisher named).
25. Harris identifies seven secondary indicators used by the CAFC as at August 1988. These include commercial success, "long felt need in the industry" and success in licensing the patent (Harris 1989: 191–2).
26. Lunney (2004: 21) considers that a critical judgment was *ACS* (at 1577).
27. The most cited of which is *Aktiebolaget*.
28. The elevation of secondary (mainly commercial) criteria for determining obviousness; the relaxation of the need to demonstrate that any commercial success is due to the inventiveness of the patented item; and the elimination of the requirement to show that a combination of known elements produces an outcome greater than the sum of the parts.
29. The claim was for a wheel for use in railway carriages (Brennan and Christie 1997: 239, citing *Losh*).
30. *Hamilton* at 1499 (emphasis added).
31. Article 8 (1) (http://keionline.org/sites/default/files/tpp-10feb2011-us-text-ipr-chapter.pdf, emphasis added). The wording may be directed at India's requirement that a new pharmaceutical product provide an improved health outcome as a condition of patent grant. There are a range of other pressures on India to encourage India to limit use of the flexibilities in TRIPS (Sampat et al 2012).
32. An example is a top-selling product for the treatment of depression – venlafaxine – where the mirror compound, desvenlafaxine, was patented around the time that venlafaxine went off patent. Wyeth announced Food and Drug Administration approval of desvenlafaxine on 23 January 2007. Venlafaxine was first marketed in 1993 and the first generic version became available in the USA in August 2006 (see http://en.wikipedia.org/wiki/Desvenlafaxine and http://en.wikipedia.org/wiki/Venlafaxine).
33. This issue was considered in Australia by a committee charged with assessing whether the Patent Act met good competition principles. The committee recommended increasing the judgement standard from *benefit of the doubt* to *balance of probabilities*. It dismissed the *beyond all reasonable doubt* standard

as appropriate only in criminal cases without considering its close alignment to the stated competition principles under which the committee was established (IPCRC 2000: 166). Framing patent policy in a legal context allows the ready adoption of rules that are sub-optimal with regard to economic objectives.

34. The Full Court rejected the patent application on the three grounds: no physical effect; new legal findings are discoveries not inventions; and it was "a mere collocation of known parts" rather than a new combination. Tyacke and Webb (2007) provide a full discussion of the four decisions in this case.

CHAPTER 4

1. Though the four Supreme Court judges who dissented with the reasoning in the *Bilski* decision review evidence on the history of the term "useful arts" including that many commentators consider this to be what is now called technology.
2. See http://eupat.ffii.org/papers/bgh-dispo76/ (accessed 2 August 2012). Cited in Pilch (2003: 293).
3. See http://en.wikipedia.org/wiki/Mathematics#Definitions_of_mathematics (accessed 2 August 2012).
4. In photos shapes with identical colour attributes, such as sky, grass or solid-colour clothing, are broken into blocks and a matching pattern from a catalogue is assigned to each block, rather than to each pixel. "For example, the string AAADDDDDEE can be reduced to 3A5D2E"; see http://www.ischool.utexas.edu/~l38613dw/website_fall_02/readings/Compression.html (accessed 18 July 2012). For data, variable record length techniques, first introduced in the early 1970s, aggregate sequences with similar values into the two dimensions of quantity and value.
5. There are a number of technical suggestions for differentiating 'obvious' from inventive software – for example the concept of computational complexity (Chin 1998; Krause 2000).
6. This is a moot point. The Supreme Court argument was that the mathematical formula in question had "no substantial practical application except in connection with a digital computer, which means that if the judgment below is affirmed the patent would wholly pre-empt the mathematical formula and in practical effect would be a patent on the algorithm itself" (*Benson* at 71). In the case of the Nymeyer patent considered in *IBM Corp*, the novel idea was ranking buyers and sellers by the price they offered to determine the successful sale. The use of this idea on a computer (apart from its questionable novelty even in 1980) does of course fully pre-empt others from use of this algorithm.
7. There are excellent detailed discussions of the *State Street* decision, including the content of the Signature patent, and its progress through the lower court (Stern 1999; Thomas 1999a; Krause 2000). Stern (1999: Appendix A) provides a side-by-side comparison of Patent 5193056 and the relevant tax law. He reports that "claim 1 thoroughly foreclosed compliance with tax law requirements for avoiding multiple taxation of pooled-fund partnerships" (Stern 1999: 132). Drennan (2007) notes that the underlying maths is

multiplication of a matrix by a vector, which raises further questions about its inventiveness.

8. The *Rubber-Tip Pencil* case involved "implementation of an idea that was so simple that the idea and the embodiment merged" (Gladstone 2001).
9. See story at http://inventors.about.com/library/weekly/aa091297.htm (accessed 25 August 2012).
10. An extraordinary feature of the TRIPS Agreement is that, if someone is accused of infringing a patent for a chemical process patent, it is that person who must prove their innocence rather than the accuser proving guilt (Article 34). It is shocking that democratic nations have agreed to a reversal of one of the most fundamental of human rights: innocent until proven guilty.
11. Because of the diversity of business methods, compiling a useful set of key words is difficult, and in fact key words are often absent from patent titles (Murphy 2002). Chin (2009) finds keyword searches to be unreliable for locating patents.
12. Since the 2006 IPC update, revisions have become more frequent than the previous five-year intervals and are now referenced by year see http://www.wipo.int/export/sites/www/classifications/ipc/en/guide/guide_ipc.pdf.
13. That is, all G06Q sub-groups except G06Q/20/00.
14. A patent of addition is restricted to a single improvement or modification of an invention in a parent patent. Fees paid for the parent also cover the patent of addition. This case was converted to a patent of addition following the examiner's second rejection on inventiveness grounds. Its great-grandparent is also among the selected cases, so it is also not an independent case.
15. Personal discussion with a Silverbrook patent attorney at a workshop on commercialising inventions (Melbourne, February 2009). Silverbrook Research Pty Ltd started filing patent applications in both the USA and Australia in 1998. For further information on the Silverbrook business method applications excluded from the study see Moir (2009a: Appendix 6). Silverbrook has recently parted company with its previous partner, and its high-speed injek printing business, and the associated patents, were taken over by Memjet in May 2012 (http://www.memjet.com/technology/). Silverbrook continues to advise substantial patent ownership on its website (http://silverbrookresearch.com/index.html). Sites accessed 6 August 2012.
16. The set of 72 cases includes two where the application was accepted, but the grant was opposed. In one the opposition was withdrawn. But in the other the applicants did not pay the $140 acceptance fee so the application lapsed before sealing. It is included with the other cases as it was accepted by 30 June 2007.
17. The last sealed patent from the 2003 cohort is owned by Google Inc (AU2003286841 *Method and system for dynamic textual ad distribution via email*). Google asked for deferred sealing, and there was a 22-month delay between acceptance publication and sealing. The only explanation is strategic.
18. Jensen and colleagues show quite high proportions of patent filings still pending after six years in both the European and Japanese Patent Offices (Jensen et al 2006).
19. Twenty-three per cent of US patent applications and 52 per cent of litigated patents are continuations (Lemley and Moore 2003).
20. Of the 14 cases with priority dates in 2001 or earlier, one requested modified examination. There is clear evidence on file that eight of the others were

directed to request examination very shortly after filing. Seven took most of the allowed six months to comply with this request.

21. Details of overseas application numbers are provided, generally in footnotes. US cases can be accessed through the Public PAIR database at http://portal.uspto.gov/external/portal/pair) (accessed 2 August 2012). European cases can be accessed through the European Patent Register at https://register.epo.org/espacenet/regviewer?lng=en (accessed 2 August 2012). UK case numbers are publication not application numbers. Some UK data are provided on http://www.ipo.gov.uk/p-ipsum.
22. Because of the time-consuming nature of reading claims, researchers have generally used the number of claims and forward and backward citations as proxies for the novelty and inventiveness of the claimed invention, but no solid case has yet been made that they are good proxies for inventiveness.
23. Lerner (2002) also found a very low standard for patentability in an initial review of financial patents. In particular he found very limited citation of relevant academic knowledge. He investigated two patents in considerable depth demonstrating that the knowledge claimed was known.
24. See http://www.wipo.int/pct/en/seminar/basic_1/timeline.pdf for a useful diagrammatic illustration of these timelines (accessed 16 July 2012). In Australia the application must be accepted within 21 months of the examiner's first report or it lapses (*Patents Act 1990* s142(2)(e)).
25. Around 2010–11 the UK, Canada and Australia developed an information sharing project for their patent examiners. This means some further documents are provided publicly from this time, but does not provide back information for cases examined earlier. Some data on the parallel 13 UK cases are included here, but none for the Canadian cases.
26. Includes one case where the applicant, faced with the likelihood of a refusal at the oral hearing, lodged a divisional then actively withdrew the original application. The divisional has now progressed through the system and was refused at the oral hearing. It is counted as a refusal not a withdrawal. This case is discussed in Section 5.3.
27. Concentration in the ownership of business method patents has been noted by Lerner (2002), Wagner (2008) and Hall (2009).
28. There were no examiner objections in Australia. The US examiner rejected 34 of the 36 claims as not novel and the remaining two as obvious (application 10/516036). The application was abandoned.
29. It must surely be the *unusual* child who has *not* independently come up with the idea of getting an advance on their pocket money, which is what this element of the claim teaches.
30. But the response to the adverse first report is not on the file, and the original claims (the 'A' document) are not available online, so the extent of revision is unknown, as are the arguments put to the examiner. It seems likely the applicant placed the onus on the examiner to demonstrate that every feature of the probably revised claims existed in earlier documented knowledge. There were no overseas applications for this 'invention'.
31. http and html were introduced in the early 1990s and the first easy-to-use web browser, Mosaic, in 1993 (Brödner 2003: 153).
32. Airlines were well placed to take advantage of the network power of the web. They had already discovered the competitive advantage of effective electronic

reservation systems such as *Sabre* (introduced in the 1960s), *Amadeus* (quality-certified in 2000), *Galileo* and *Apollo* (now owned by Galileo).

33. 10/562672, non-final rejection of 30 October 2008, p. 9.
34. EP2005700144, annex to examination report, 26 October 2007, para 1.1.
35. EP2003723336 Annex of 27 March 2009, paras 2 and 3.
36. I myself own an electronic organiser, purchased in 1994 and going well, that does Gregorian and lunar event forecasts and enters them as diary appointments. The addition of a Julian calendar seems a design feature or a workshop improvement.
37. As the Microsoft patent has the term "recurring events" in the abstract it is surprising the Australian examiner did not find it. It seems likely that this patent is invalid in Australia.
38. This approach has just become well known in Australia due to a highly public dispute between the Australian Tax Office and one individual over 10 years of back taxes on the earnings from the reduced operator take on his high-volume betting; see Australian Financial Review, 11 February 2012 at http://afr.com/p/national/the_gambler_GwoSmf5IXaVFjmpyYXNu9J (accessed 2 August 2012). This indicates that the 'invention' has been in operation in Australia since at least 2002 and probably earlier.

CHAPTER 5

1. This presumption that applications are novel and inventive should not be confused with the further presumption in the USA that granted patents are valid. Other jurisdictions do not have this presumption about granted patents.
2. These allowable knowledge deficiencies were addressed in the *Intellectual Property Laws Amendment (Raising the Bar) Act 2012*. The Act does nothing to address the doctrines about the low quantum of inventiveness required.
3. The other two cases are AU2003268606 (*Performance evaluation tool and method*) and AU2003302490 (*System for and method of monitoring an item*), both discussed in Chapter 7.
4. 10/528755, examiner's fifth (final) rejection of 25 March 2011, pp. 4–11. This case was terminated before grant in the UK in March 2007, after a request for examination in April 2005 (GB2409554). This suggests an adverse examiner report, probably on grounds of non-patentable subject matter. It has been granted in the Philippines.
5. Australian IPER of 13 October 2003.
6. This is a typical EPO examiner response and indicates the difficulty EPO examiners have in providing clear advice, given the inconsistent Board of Appeal decisions on as such subject matter exclusions. The examiner advised that "[a]lthough T931/95 noted that the mere mention of a computer environment is not considered enough to lend technical character to a method claim as a whole, other decisions have concluded otherwise (T38/86 and T769/92)" (EP2003742467, annex to 27 March 2009 report, p. 2, para 2.1).
7. The UK grant (GB2404067) was before the introduction of the four-step test for patentable subject matter.

8. Indeed in the 1950s, and probably much earlier, schoolchildren often had their name tags sewn into removable items of clothing.
9. It is of some concern if costs to oppose grant of a monopoly are greater than the costs of obtaining them, at least in respect of official fees. In fact IP Australia has reduced the re-examination fee to $800 (as at 1 July 2012). This compares with fees of between $600 and $1,000 for opposition and $1,160 for a standard application (preceded by a provisional and including examination and acceptance fees).
10. 10/475155, applicant arguments of 6 June 2006, pp. 3 and 4 and Notice of Allowance of 6 July 2006, p. 2.
11. For the 2011 financial year 30 per cent of all USPTO patent filings were "requests for continued examination", that is, cases where applicants asked that the process continue after a final rejection; see http://www.bustpatents.com/RefilingStatsFY2011.pdf (accessed 27 July 2012).
12. 10/399880, claims as amended on 1 January 2009 and 15 March 2010.
13. EP2001980051, annex to examiner's report of 5 October 2007, para k, p. 4 (emphasis in original).
14. EP2001980051, annex to summons to oral, 1 July 2008, para d, p. 2.
15. EP2008169756, filed on 24 November 2008 a few hours before its parent was withdrawn.
16. *Method and apparatus for storing and retrieving items* (AU2003212105, priority March 2002) computerises another type of expert system. It focuses on efficient collection of orders in wholesale or mail-order centres. This type of problem has been bread-and-butter to operations research experts for many decades. Knowledge of the storage facility, the range of products, and the ordering pattern of customers is required both to determine where to store the items, and how best to retrieve them. This expert knowledge can then be written into detailed software specifications. Of course any such expert might come up with a marginally different system, and herein lies the difficulty for the examiner. No objections were raised in Australia and the patent was also granted in New Zealand. It was abandoned at the USPTO after one rejection which provided nearly 30 pages of detailed analysis on the lack of inventiveness (10/507154 non-final rejection of 24 August 2009, pp. 5–34).
17. The Korean *Patent Act 1961* defines inventiveness as a "highly advanced creation of technical idea utilizing the law of nature" (Section 2:1) (Lanteigne, 2003: 44). Lanteigne argues this is a much higher standard than required in either US or Australian patent law Korea has refused another five and granted four of the patents in this dataset. One of these grants followed an initial refusal.
18. Perhaps the best-known example is US 4528643, the Freeny patent. Filed in 1983 and granted in 1985 – well before the advent of e-commerce – this invention produces digital audio tapes in retail stores. The principal claim was written as a "method for reproducing information in material objects utilizing information manufacturing machines located at point of sale locations". The patent was acquired by E-Data in 1994. E-Data interpreted their claim as covering e-commerce sales and sued a number of companies. The District Court interpreted the claims narrowly, but on appeal the CAFC interpreted the claims widely, for example that points of sale included all locations with an internet connection (Bessen and Meurer 2008: 1–10). This extended the

monopoly far beyond the initial invention, imposing unnecessary costs on many e-commerce businesses. In contrast the UK Patent Court revoked the Freeny Patent in 2005; see http://www.theregister.co.uk/2005/06/09/court_rules_vs_edata/ (accessed 3 August 2012).

19. Ferris Research Bulletin, Report #418, February 2004. This report is no longer available directly but can be accessed via http://email-museum.com/ (accessed 27 July 2012).
20. No marked-up version of the amended claims is available on the file, and the A documents are missing from IP Australia's database; see http://pericles.ipaustralia.gov.au/aub/aub_pages_1.intro. The attorney's letter suggests the amendments were instrumental in overcoming the novelty/inventiveness objections.
21. EP2004250122, reply to communication from the Examining Division, 13 February 2006, p. 1.
22. T1937/09 – 3 May 2006. This appeal shows the generosity of patent system rules in attempting to accommodate requests for patent monopolies – the formal statement of appeal requests grant of the original rejected documents, marginally amended to clarify that monitoring is an ongoing process (truly), and also asks that each of three alternative specifications of the monopoly be considered for grant if the original is rejected (EP2004250122, 10 August 2009 Statement of Grounds of Appeal, p. 1).
23. The parent has been granted in the USA (2002), the UK (2004) and Europe (2007) as well as Australia.
24. And in the UK (GB2375637) where it was granted a patent in August 2004 before the four-step test.
25. GB2403571 was granted in 2005, before the four-step test.
26. The "such elements include . . ." wording on p. 3 of the specification is misleading as the listed data items are sufficient to place a trade on most online trading systems.
27. 10/125894, first rejection 23 March 2007, p. 12. This patent is from a very large family – 81 members from 65 applications. In the USA it is a continuation of a US PCT application and there are 15 closely related US applications, all with the same title.
28. EP2003726366 examiner's report of 29 July 2011, para 1.
29. Response of 20 March 2007 to second examination report.
30. 10/887454. The applicant, Forge Research Pty Ltd, a small Australian consultancy company, paid a US$525 fee for an extension of time to respond to the US examiner's report, but in the end did not respond.
31. The specific patent in the dataset is the child of a US PCT application and an exact parallel exists only in the USA where a terminal disclaimer was required. The details in the text for the EPO version are for the closely identical parent (EP2000947053).
32. US 09/610772, Notice of Allowance, 23 March 2005, p. 4 and 11/097491, Notice of Allowance 2, May 2007, p. 9 (emphasis as in original). Identical wording was used for both parent and child.
33. See http://www.coag.gov.au/node/52 (accessed 6 August 2012).
34. For example the Australian *Patent Act 1990* states, ". . . an invention is to be taken to involve an inventive step when compared with the prior art base unless . . ." (Section 7(2)) and Section 7(1) contain similar presumptions about novelty. Similar provisions are found in Articles 2 (novelty) and 3

(inventiveness) of the UK Patents Act, which of course reflects the provisions of the EPC.

35. The US Act (35 U.S.C.) does not spell out a similar presumption, but it is implied in the Manual of Patent Examining Procedure, Section 706 (Rejection of claims); see http://www.uspto.gov/web/offices/pac/mpep/mpep_e8r6_0700.pdf (accessed 6 August 2012).
36. In Australia this decision-making rule was changed from *benefit of the doubt* to *balance of probabilities* in 2001, moving to reflect UK practice. But in the 72 cases studied here, attorneys regularly argue that the examiner has not demonstrated lack of inventiveness and examiners do not refer to the balance of probabilities rule.
37. Attorney's letter of 14 July 2005.
38. 10/379574, non-final rejection notice of 20 March 2008, para 4, p. 2.
39. 10/429494, response of February 2010, p. 10, para 2. I attended a project management course in October 1997 and can assure the applicant that software-based project planning was a well-developed field then – some five years before this application was filed.
40. 10/429494, rejection of March 2010, p. 4, para 2.
41. Examination was requested in November 2004, and the application terminated in November 2006 (GB2405011). The time gap suggests a refusal as excluded subject matter.
42. 10/434276, pre-brief conference request of 29 April 2008, p. 2.
43. I clearly recollect being offered both date and fare options by Easyjet in an internet café in Thessaloniki in February 2001. Naturally I determined the number of passengers, and was given a booking reference number. This is over three years before the priority date of this 'invention'.
44. Attorney response of 28 October 2004, emphasis added.
45. Attorney response of 9 December 2004 to examiner's first report.
46. Cantor Index offers "spread bets on a wide range of [financial] markets" and is based in London. This type of betting is not available in the USA; see http://www.cantor.com/portfolio/cantor_index_uk (accessed 18 July 2012). Cantor Index is a subsidiary of Cantor Fitzgerald, a global bond trading firm. Cantor Fitzgerald also has one patent among the cases studied here.
47. Response of 11 April 2007 to examiner's second report, p. 2.
48. GB2403564 was determined in October 2007 after the four-step test was introduced. The refusal states that the invention falls solely within excluded (non-patentable) subject matter.
49. 10/687302, Notice of Allowance, 21 February 2012, p. 9.

CHAPTER 6

1. 10/180400, second (final) rejection of 31 May 2007, pp. 4–15.
2. The applicant, Accenture, has had a leading position in the business consulting market since its initial formation as a division of Arthur Andersen. It was established as a separate company in 2000/2001 and changed its name to Accenture – a change apparently planned before the Enron scandal; see http://en.wikipedia.org/wiki/Accenture (accessed 27 July 2012).

3. EP2002013603, paragraph 2.2 of annex to examination report, 28 February 2008.
4. 10/913645, applicant remarks made in an amendment, 28 January 2009, p. 12.
5. Contentguard has four patents in the dataset, all about digital rights management. All are simple computerisations of the mental steps involved in agreeing sales contract details. The simultaneous use of expedition and postponement shows Contentguard to be experienced in maximising private returns and minimising public convenience from the patent system.
6. 10/452928, BPAI decision on appeal 2010-006357, 1 April 2011.
7. No examiner objections were raised in Australia. The EPO rejected the application (EP2003783515) as not new in regard to two patent documents and Contentguard's own user manual. Amendments were filed but did not convince the EPO and the application was refused at an oral hearing in July 2012.
8. 10/712268, BPAI decision on appeal 2009-005613, 18 February 2010.
9. 10/152890, Notice of Allowance of 20 March 2009, p. 2.
10. T0634/08-3501 (EP2003253075) Notification of Board decision 23 May 2012, p. 8.
11. Filing a PCT application (AU2003244578) and an expert medical system (AU2003281184) were both discussed in Section 5.3 (amendment). A further expert system for use in mail order centres (AU2003212105) is described in a footnote in Section 5.3 but not discussed in the text. Updating website bookmarks (AU2003200819), a workflow management system (AU2003204420) and a system to coordinate electronic diaries (AU2003204139) are discussed in Section 5.4 (reverse onus of proof). A system for delivering to a locked box (AU2003262357) is discussed in Section 6.3 (general combinations). Using credit card identifiers for possible VAT refunds (AU2003219472), analysing website hits to estimate the value of web advertising (AU2003200436) and betting against winners (AU 2003252947) are discussed in Section 7.2 (EPO or UK grant). Using general ledger codes to define accounting categories (AU2005255399) and performance evaluation (AU2003268606 with its sibling AU2003268607) are discussed in Section 7.3 (doctrines to prevent obvious grant). A system for printing documents near the point of delivery (AU2003254402) is discussed in Section 7.4.
12. In advising of this problem USPTO examiners cite *Diehr*, *Flook* and *Benson*. Later reports also cite *In re Bilski*.
13. 10/506902, Notice of Allowance, 17 February 2010, pp. 8–9.
14. A 'child', containing the normal auction variant of this 'invention' was filed at the USPTO on 12 July 2010 (12/834889). A different examiner has been assigned but the one non-final rejection (to date) cites the same prior art and rejects the application on novelty grounds.
15. Emphasis added. EP 2000977142, report of 11 July 2005, p. 3. The 'prior art' identified two documents and the examiner advised that the elements of delivering to multiple locked containers, delivering goods to customers, delivering to locked containers and sending delivery made signals were not novel.
16. The file wrapper is missing for 09/593199, so it is not possible to see the content of the single non-final rejection issued by the USPTO prior to grant. In January 2010 the EPO advised problems of clarity, novelty and inventive step, citing ten patent documents. The applicant had replacing the original 37 claims with ten following the ISR; in July 2010 these ten claims were replaced with four very lengthy claims (EP2003749468).

17. EP2004709953, annex to summons to attend oral proceedings, 7 May 2010, para 3.1.6.
18. Though EPC applicants do amend their claims prior to examination, and at oral and appeal hearings applicants often put forward a number of alternative claims specifications for consideration.

CHAPTER 7

1. On 2 November 2006, following the *Aerotel* appeal decision, the UKIPO announced this new test, for use where there might be excluded subject matter; see http://www.ipo.gov.uk/pro-types/pro-patent/p-law/p-pn/p-pn-subjectmatter.htm (accessed 29 July 2012).
2. This includes one case where the EPO granted a patent to the closely similar parent.
3. EP2001971512, annex to examiner's report of 9 May 2007, para 2, p. 1.
4. Examination was requested in October 2003 and the application was terminated two years later. This time gap suggests a negative examination report (GB2407450).
5. 10/595439, Notice of Allowance, 5 May 2011, pp. 4–5.
6. Certainly this has been my own experience when visiting Europe in 2000–01.
7. GB2387929 was granted before the introduction of the four-step test.
8. EP2003715284, appeal decision of 18 May 2011 (T 0469/08).
9. 10/221929. The Australian examiner appears not to have used the main reference given by the US examiner.
10. First examiner's report of 12 July 2004.
11. US 6243739, *Reducing perceived latency in servicing user requests on low-bandwidth communication channels* (see 10/221929, non-final rejection of 27 June 2006, p. 3). Neither the two Australian searches nor the UKIPO search identified this novelty-destroying patent.
12. EP2004736030, applicant response of 23 December 2008, pp. 2–3.
13. The author was taught procedures for this at Brown University in 1972.
14. 10/072220 (Patent 7,231,358), Notice of Allowance, 27 October 2004, para 5, p. 2.
15. EP2003250822, attachment to examiner's report, paragraphs 2 and 2.1.
16. Emphasis is as in the original. Consistent with the then legislative requirement that details of overseas search reports be provided to the Australian Patent Office, the applicant provided a copy of the UK examiner's report, which is on the Australian file. The new Ipsum database confirms the case (GB2381896) was refused as excluded subject matter, but does not provide the document.
17. Based on the 13 cases here, the UKIPO processes cases quickly, usually granting a patent within a year of the exam request. In the terminated cases there is a gap of two or more years between examination request and termination. It seems likely that the UKIPO has issued an advice which subsequently led to the termination. The cases where subject matter refusal is not clearly stated are AU2003204420 (workflow prediction system), AU2003271414 (visual budgeting system), AU2003246060 (real estate pre-formatted reporting) and AU2004307528 (managing worksite apparatus).
18. GB2400202 was appealed; the appeal was dismissed (by consent) on

20 February 2008 (email advice from the Manager of the High Court Appeals Office, 24 June 2008).
19. 11/022394, examiner's report of 22 March 2007.
20. Brennan and Christie (1997: 29), citing (1838) 3 Hayward's Patent Cases 125 at 141.
21. Benchmarking was very popular during the Australian micro-economic reform period of the late 1980s and early 1990s and the BIE produced a series of reports on benchmarking reforms in the transport and communications industries. Australian government reports using this technique and dating back as far as 1995 can now be found at www.pc.gov.au (accessed 6 August 2012).
22. EP2003788705, examiner's report of 27 June 2006, paragraph 3.2 (a).
23. 11/121158, Notice of Allowance, 30 April 2008, p. 2.
24. Based on the time lag between the exam request and the termination, it is likely that the application was refused on subject matter grounds (GB2405970).
25. In this case the parent is quite different to the children. It focuses on updating user access privileges when organisational units change. The EPO found few technical elements and compared to common general knowledge considered these "obvious in the light of the straightforward implementation triggered by the non-technical concepts" (EP1999921812, annex to the summons to attend oral proceedings, 18 March 2008, p. 4., para 2). The application was refused and the applicant has appealed. In the USA amendments to the parent during examination included such highly specific details as a telephony switch or a third-party role (09/110103). The parent was abandoned after eight rejections.
26. See WO2006053387 at http://patentscope.wipo.int/search/en/search.jsf (accessed 6 August 2012).
27. 11/667964, Notice of Allowance of 17 February 2011, p. 12.
28. Applicant response of 26 July 2006, p. 2.
29. 11/569078, applicant arguments/remarks of 2 February 2011, p. 9.
30. Thambisetty, for example, discloses that the change to procedures changing the prohibition on patenting second uses of known medical products under the EPC was a response to pressure from the pharmaceutical industry (Thambisetty 2009: 17).
31. For example, Standing Committee on the Law of Patents, Twelfth Session, 2008; see http://www.wipo.int/edocs/mdocs/scp/en/scp_12/scp_12_3_rev_2.pdf (paras 167–72) (accessed 6 August 2012).
32. PCT search reports use X to identify documents which, if used alone, raise inventiveness objections; Y documents are those which when used in combination would raise such objections.
33. 11/099205, non-final rejection of 4 February 2009, pp. 2–16. The claims were amended but the examiner repeated his lengthy obviousness rejection and the application was abandoned.
34. 09/827509, BPAI decision of November 18, 2009, p. 6 (emphasis added).
35. This is another case indicating the strong entitlement attitude among patent applicants. During the examination process the applicant argued to the examiner that "it would not have occurred to one of ordinary skill in the art [betting methods] to implement a method that answers the question, 'What would be the odds if I wagered X?'" (09/827509, interview summary record, 6 December 2007).

36. EP2011928405, annex to examiner's report of 9 November 2006, para 2, pp. 1–2.
37. This is quite a small thicket compared to those found in electronics (for example Silverbrook's 3666 US patents) or some of the pharmaceutical thickets.
38. Examples include "simultaneously displaying the current odds and the projected odds" and "determining an amount of a win bet payout".
39. Examples discussed in other chapters are AU2003244552, where unwanted emails are not downloaded onto the server and AU2003302490 where items are tracked between manufacturers, retailers and consumers.
40. This can be determined from the data transaction history (09/951361).
41. EP2000923230, annex to examiner's report, 29 March 2005.
42. The allegedly multiple inventive concepts in the two divisionals (AU2007201104 and AU2007201087) are that repayment amounts are dependent on a proportion of the change in property value, and that repayments are based on the elapsed time and later valuation.
43. 11/139841, rejection of 7 December 2009, p. 3.
44. ACIP advises IP Australia. Advertisements for members indicate a strong preference for beneficiaries of the patents and trade marks systems, and membership reflects this preference.
45. Both rejections included novelty or obviousness problems. The claims were amended twice, including the introduction of the user selection feature, which became the key feature achieving a patent (11/268427).
46. Unfortunately the usual file wrapper is not available for this patent, so the examiner's reports cannot be accessed (10/251717). From the transaction history, three rejections can be identified: one a final. It is likely that amendments were made during the examination process.
47. The initial INPADOC search on the case produced no family members, despite the claims being identical to US 6963856 granted on 8 November 2005. A search for "automated" in the title and "Cantor Fitzgerald" as the applicant found nine family members, but within these nine the application lodged in China produced 34 family members. Such are the vagaries of patent databases.
48. EP1999973501, annex to examiner's report, 18 October 2006, para 3.4, p. 3.
49. EP1999973501, annex to summons to oral proceedings, 12 January 2012, paras 2.2, 4.2 and 5.10.

CHAPTER 8

1. A search on 30 July 2012 for the IPC class G06Q10/00 on esp@cenet finds approximately 10,206 items in the EP database but displays only 500 of them. The data displayed do not include grant status or designated countries. A similar query on the European Patent Register displays all 7,539 cases found, but again does not include grant status or designated countries. Finding these essential data items would require looking up each case individually – a massive cost.
2. This new government intervention in the market makes it harder for generic companies to use critical knowledge from the most expensive part of the R&D process – Phase III clinical trials.

3. See http://www.wipo.int/ipstats/en/statistics/patents/, patent grants by patent office (accessed 30 July 2012).
4. See http://www.uspto.gov/web/offices/ac/ido/oeip/taf/topo_11.htm, Patenting by Organizations 2011, Part B (accessed 30 July 2012).
5. A particularly vehement critic is Pharmaceutical Research and Manufacturers of America (PhRMA) (Shadlen 2011: 112). Shadlen also provides a general discussion of the effort to exclude trivial pharmaceutical inventions from patents in Brazil. See Sampat et al (2012) for how this issue is currently developing in India.
6. Quillen also noted this is relation to lobbying for the establishment of the CAFC (Quillen 2006: 227). Patent Attorneys can identify as much with the interests of their profession as with the interests of the company which currently employs them. Many also believe whole-heartedly in the mantra that no-one will innovate without a patent incentive and most are completely unaware that there is substantial empirical evidence refuting this position.
7. In Australia, for example, the Department of Industry, Innovation, Science, Research and Tertiary Education (DIISRT) is theoretically responsible for advising on patent policy. In practice this advice is provided by IP Australia, which is a unit within DIISRT. IP Australia's advisory body is almost entirely composed of beneficiaries of the patent and trade mark systems – there are no representatives of consumer bodies. The alternative source of advice from within DIISRT is the Innovation Policy branch, many of whose staff are ex patent examiners. In the USA policy advice is provided by the USPTO but there is also substantial input from interested parties (see, for example, Lehman 2001).
8. And of course greater income for patent attorneys.

Appendix. Original claims: selected patents

This appendix provides the exact wording of the claims for seven of the cases. This is to allow the reader to check the conclusions drawn in the analysis, at least for a sub-set of cases. Cases were selected on a non-random basis. The two criteria were that the claim length be relatively short, and that an electronic version relatively close to the Australian version be available. The seven patents included here have claim length of between five and 24 compared to the dataset range of four to 115. Average claims in the seven patents presented here is 12, compared to 30 for the full dataset. The seven patents presented here are all cases with multiple overseas applications, five using the PCT.

Much is made in the patent literature of the number of claims as a proxy for inventiveness, but this is not evident from these cases. Longer patent claims are often duplicated, as method, system, computer-readable medium, etc. claims. The underlying 'invention' is not more complex. The attorney has simply phrased the claims in alternative forms to maximise the chance that the patent will survive any legal challenge. One of the cases in this appendix (AU 2003271414, *A Financial Management System*) shows this approach: claims 1–11 are for a system. The substance of these claims is repeated in claims 12–22, for a method. The final two claims are "omnibus" claims and are a standard feature in Australian patents.

Another reason for lengthier claims is where the applicant includes a large amount of detail. This can tend to limit the scope of the claimed monopoly. But, based on these cases, it does not indicate greater inventiveness. These subsidiary claims often include remarkably everyday items.

Although these seven cases are unrepresentative in their brevity, they do provide a reasonably diverse insight into the types of claims and the actual claim language. None of them is among the most complex in terms of comprehensibility.

AU2003250595 INTERACTIVE PROPERTY TOUR

Granted in New Zealand; abandoned at EPO and USPTO

CLAIMS:

1. A system for creating a web based tour for an item of interest characterized in that it includes the steps of:
   - establishing a tour identity;
   - associating one or more reference images with the tour identity;
   - positioning one or more reference icons on one or more of said reference images, each of said reference icons being associated with a further reference image;
   - and wherein a position of each of said reference icons is selected to provide information relating to said further reference image.
2. A system for creating a web based tour according to claim 1, characterized in that said tour identity optionally has associated therewith a tour description.
3. A system for creating a web based tour according to claim 1, characterized in that each of said reference images optionally has an associated image description.
4. A system for creating a web based tour according to claim 3, characterized in that a reference image and a respective associated image description collectively form page and wherein said tour consists of a plurality of pages collected together as a list of pages.
5. A system for creating a web based tour according to claim 4, characterized in that each page is prepared according to a template selected from a number of predetermined template styles.
6. A system for creating a web based tour according to claim 1, characterized in that said reference images are stored on one or more remote host servers.
7. A system for creating a web based tour according to claim 1, characterized in that at least one of said reference images is a map.
8. A system for creating a web based tour according to claim 1, characterized in that in that at least one of said reference images is a plan.
9. A system for creating a web based tour according to claim 1, characterized in that each of said reference icons serve to provide information regarding said further reference image associated therewith.
10. A system for creating a web based tour according to claim 1, characterized in that said item of interest is real estate.
11. A system for creating a web based tour according to any one of claims 1 to 10, further including the step of:

- receiving user input indicating the position of the one or more icons on the one or more reference images and indicating an association between each icon and the further reference image, and wherein each reference icon is positioned in response to the user input.

12. A system for creating a web based tour according to claim 11, further including the step of:
    - displaying to the user the one or more reference images, allowing the user to subsequently provide the user input whilst viewing the one or more reference images.
13. A system for creating a web based tour according to claim 11 or 12, wherein the user input indicating the position of an icon is provided by clicking on a part of a displayed image.
14. A system for creating a web based tour according to claim 7, wherein the one or more reference icons are positioned on the map, at least one of the associated further images relates to the item of interest, and the position of the reference icon indicates the position of the item of interest on the map.

AU2003271414 A FINANCIAL MANAGEMENT SYSTEM

Pending at USPTO (5 rejections to date)

CLAIMS:

1. A financial management system including:
    - presentation means for presenting financial information to a user wherein the financial information includes a planned value in respect of a pre-determined period of time, a target value being a proportion of the planned value at a pre-determined point during the period of time, and an actual value as at the pre-determined point during the period of time, each of the planned value, the target value and the actual value being represented by a graphic;

    the graphics are associated with one another so that the variance between the target value and the actual value is visually apparent to the user;
    - the system further including manipulation means for manipulating at least one of the graphics in response to an action of a user; and
    - modifying means for modifying the financial information based on the manipulation of the at least one graphic.

2. A financial management system according to claim 1 wherein the financial information that the at least one graphic represents is proportional to a dimension of the graphic and the graphic may be manipulated by being resized.
3. A financial management system according to either claim 1 or claim 2 wherein the financial information that the at least one graphic represents corresponds to the position of the graphic and the graphic may be manipulated by being moved.
4. A financial management system according to any one of the preceding claim further including creation means for creating a graphic and the financial information represented by that graphic.
5. A financial management system according to any preceding claim further including means for generating icons indicative of positive and negative financial status.
6. A financial management system according to any preceding claim further including means for storing the financial information.
7. A financial management system according to any preceding claim further including means for substituting the at least one graphic with an alternative graphic.
8. A financial management system according to any preceding claim wherein the means for presenting the financial information can represent the financial information wholly numerically.
9. A financial management system according to any preceding claim wherein the planed value is a budget and the system further includes means for generating icons representative of budget items within the budget.
10. A financial management system according to claim 9 further including means for associating a graphic with each icon whereby that budget item can be modified by manipulating the graphic.
11. A financial management system according to either claim 9 or claim 10 further including means for generating icons representing the time period over which a budget is to extend.
12. A method of managing financial information including the steps of:
    - presenting financial information to a user wherein the financial information includes a planned value in respect of a predetermined period of time, a target value being a proportion of the planned value at a pre-determined point during the period of time, and an actual value as at the pre-determined point during the period of time, each of the planned value, the target value and the actual value being represented by a graphic;
    - associating the graphics with another so that the variance

between the target value and the actual value is visually apparent to the user;
- manipulating at least one of the graphics in response to an action of a user; and
- modifying the financial information based on the manipulation of the at least one graphic.

13. A method according to claim 12 wherein the financial information that the at least one graphic represents is proportional to a dimension of the graphic and the step of manipulating the graphic includes the step of resizing the graphic.
14. A method according to either claim 12 or claim 13 wherein the financial information that the at least one graphic represents corresponds to the position of the graphic and the step of manipulating the graphic includes the step of moving the graphic.
15. A method according to any one of claims 12 to 14 further including the step of creating a graphic and the financial information represented by that graphic.
16. A method according to any one of claims 12 to 15 further including the step of generating icons indicative of positive and negative financial status.
17. A method according to any one of claims 12 to 16 further including the step of storing the financial information.
18. A method according to any one of claims 12 to 17 further including the step of substituting the at least one graphic with an alternative graphic.
19. A method according to any one of claims 12 to 18 further including the step of representing the financial information wholly numerically.
20. A method according to any one of claims 12 to 19 wherein the planned value is a budget and further including the step of generating icons representative of budget items within the budget.
21. A method according to claim 20 further including the step of associating a graphic with each icon whereby that budget item can be modified by manipulating the graphic.
22. A method according to either claim 20 or claim 21 further including the step of generating icons representing a time period over which the budget is to extend.
23. A computer program arranged to instruct a computing system to implement a system according to any one of claims 1 to 11.
24. A computer readable medium carrying a computer program according to claim 23.

AU2003281184 MEDICAL WARNING SYSTEM

Refused in Korea; abandoned in the USA and actively withdrawn from the EPO

CLAIMS:

1. A medical data warning notifying system in which a patient terminal used by the patient, a server that controls data that is exchanged between the patient terminal and a hospital terminal, and the hospital terminal used by a doctor are connected via a network,
   wherein the server includes:
   - a medical data receiving portion for receiving medical data input at the patient terminal;
   - a medical data storage portion for storing the received medical data;
   - a judging portion for judging whether or not the received medical data include abnormal data;
   - a warning notifying portion for sending a warning signal to the hospital terminal if it is judged that the medical data include abnormal data; and
   - a message transceiver portion for receiving a message generated by the hospital terminal and sending the message to the patient terminal,
   - wherein the judging portion is provided with respective threshold values for the medical data for each patient for determining whether the received medical data includes abnormal data, and compares the received medical data with the respective threshold value, judging that the medical data includes abnormal data when a medical data out of the threshold value is detected, and
   - when the judging portion has judged that the medical data includes abnormal data, the server operates the warning notifying portion so as to send the warning signal to the hospital terminal and at the same time sends the medical data judged to be abnormal data to the hospital terminal, and then the server assumes a standby mode until a message is received from the hospital terminal, and when the message transceiver portion has received a message from the hospital terminal, the message is sent to the patient terminal from the message transceiver portion.
2. The medical data warning notifying system according to claim 1, wherein the judging portion determines that there is an abnormality if given medical data exceeds a predetermined threshold value.

3. The medical data warning notifying system according to claim 1, wherein received records are stored by type of the medical data, an average value is calculated, and the judging portion determines that there is an abnormality if the difference between the average value and the stored medical data exceeds a predetermined percentage of the average value.
4. The medical data warning notifying system according to claim 3, wherein the received records are records for a predetermined period of time and the average value is an average value for a specified period of time during the predetermined period of time.
5. The medical data warning notifying system according to any one of claims 1 to 4, wherein the warning signal is a signal that changes a display specification of the notified message.
6. The medical data warning notifying system according to any one of claims 1 to 3, wherein the warning signal is a signal that controls a sound output of the hospital terminal receiving the warning signal.
7. A medical data warning notifying method provided in an environment in which a patient terminal used by a patient, a server that controls data that is exchanged between the patient terminal and a hospital terminal, and the hospital terminal used by a doctor are connected via a network, wherein the server is operated so as to perform the steps of:
   - receiving medical data input at the patient terminal;
   - storing the received medical data;
   - judging whether or not the received medical data include abnormal data;
   - sending a warning signal to the hospital terminal if it is judged that the medical data include abnormal data;
   - receiving a message generated by the hospital terminal and sending the message to the patient terminal; and
   - wherein in the judging step, the received medical data is compared with respective threshold values for each patient for determining whether or not the received medical data includes abnormal data, and it is judged that the medical data includes abnormal data when a medical data out of threshold value is detected; and
   - when it has been judged that the medical data includes abnormal data, the server sends the warning signal to the hospital terminal and at the same time sends the medical data judged to be abnormal data to the hospital terminal, and then the server assumes a standby mode until a message is received from the hospital terminal, and when a message from the hospital

terminal has been received, the message is sent to the patient terminal from the message transceiver portion.

8. A recording medium storing a computer executable program in a server for implementing a medical data warning notifying method provided in an environment in which a patient terminal used by the patient, a server that controls data that is exchanged between the patient terminal and a hospital terminal, and the hospital terminal used by a doctor are connected via a network, the computer program being executable by the server to perform the steps of:
   - receiving medical data input at the patient terminal;
   - storing the received medical data in the server;
   - judging whether or not the received medical data includes abnormal data;
   - sending a warning signal to the hospital terminal if it is judged that the medical data includes abnormal data; and
   - receiving a message generated by the hospital terminal and sending the message to the patient terminal; and
   - wherein in the judging step, the received medical data is compared with respective threshold values for each patient for determining whether or not the received medical data includes abnormal data, and it is judged that the medical data includes abnormal data when a medical data out of the threshold value is detected, and
   - when it has been judged that the medical data includes abnormal data, the server sends the warning signal to the hospital terminal and at the same time sends the medical data judged to be abnormal data to the hospital terminal, and then the server assumes a standby mode until a message is received from the hospital terminal, and when a message from the hospital terminal has been received, the message is sent to the patient terminal from the message transceiver portion.
9. A medical data warning notifying system according to claim 1 substantially as hereinbefore described with reference to the accompanying drawings.
10. A medical data warning notifying method according to claim 7 substantially as hereinbefore described with reference to Figure 5 of the accompanying drawings.

AU2003204139 SYSTEM FOR CONFIRMING THE PRESENCE AT HOME

Abandoned at the USPTO

CLAIMS:

1. A system for offering a delivery service to a delivery destination, said system including:
   - at least one subscriber's terminal accessible to a communication network; and
   - at least one deliverer's terminal accessible to said communication network,
   - wherein said at least one subscriber's terminal includes a first function unit for allowing a subscriber to set, in said at least one subscriber's terminal, a presence-at-destination information which identifies whether said subscriber is present or absent at said delivery destination, and
   - wherein said at least one deliverer's terminal includes a second function unit for recognizing whether said subscriber is present or absent at said delivery destination, based on said presence-at-destination information.
2. The system as claimed in claim 1,
   - wherein said at least one deliverer's terminal further includes a third function unit for sending an inquiry for inquiring about said presence-at-destination information to said subscriber's terminal, and
   - wherein said subscriber's terminal further includes a fourth function unit for sending said presence-at-destination information as set by said first function unit to said deliverer's terminal in response to said inquiry from said deliverer's terminal.
3. The system as claimed in claim 2, further including:
   - a delivery information processor accessible to said communication network, wherein said deliverer's terminal further includes a fifth function unit for sending a notice of outstanding of a requested delivery service to said delivery destination and said delivery information processor.
4. The system as claimed in claim 3, wherein said subscriber's terminal further includes a sixth function unit for sending, to said delivery information processor, a request for offering a requested but outstanding delivery service to said delivery destination, in response to said notice from said deliverer's terminal.
5. The system as claimed in claim 4, wherein said delivery information processor includes a seventh function unit for collating said request

with said notice, to confirm a correspondence between said request and said notice.

6. The system as claimed in claim 5, wherein said delivery information processor includes an eighth function unit for sending, to said subscriber's terminal, a delivery schedule which notify when said deliverer plans to offer said outstanding delivery service at said delivery destination.
7. The system as claimed in claim 6, wherein the delivery information processor includes a ninth function unit for sending delivery-destination-related data to said deliverer's terminal, to enable said deliverer's terminal to send said inquiry to said subscriber's terminal based on said delivery-destination-related data.
8. A system for offering a delivery service to a delivery destination substantially as herein described with reference to an embodiment shown in Figs. 1 and 2 of the accompanying drawings.
9. A method for confirming presence at a delivery destination, said method substantially as herein described with reference to an embodiment shown in Figs. 1 and 2 of the accompanying drawings.

AU2003246060 MOBILE REPORT CAPTURE

Accepted in New Zealand; abandoned at the USPTO after three rejections

CLAIMS:

1. A method of generating and managing property reports, in which a report is generated using a remote device at the place of inspection or occurrence, said device including an image capture function, said report including both written and image data wherein the date and time of creation of both said data are recorded and related to each other.
2. A method according to claim 1, wherein the report is generated such that after a predetermined step the data cannot be revised by a user.
3. A method according to claim 1 or claim 2, wherein the report is generated using a predetermined format.
4. A system according to claim 3, wherein said predetermined format includes multiple fields, said fields specifying a data type, wherein said fields include at least data types being written data and image data, so that multiple fields may specify the same data type.
5. A method according to claim 4, wherein the fields also specify other data types.
6. A method according to claim 5, wherein said other data types include

one or more of audio, images, numbers, signatures and pre-loaded images.

7. A method for generating a property report, including at least the steps of:
   a) providing a handheld computing device including a predetermined report format accessible to the user;
   b) the user taking said device to a required location;
   c) the user commencing the preparation of a report using said predetermined format, said report preparation including taking a digital image with said device;
   d) the device retaining text and image data integrated into a report document together with an indication of the time and date said data was entered; and
   e) collating said data in a form suitable for an upload to a control device.
8. A method according to claim 7, wherein the report is generated using a predetermined format.
9. A method according to claim 8, wherein said predetermined format includes multiple fields, said fields specifying a data type, wherein said fields include at least data types being written data and image data, so that multiple fields may specify the same data type.
10. A method according to claim 9, wherein the fields also specify other data types.
11. A method according to claim 10, wherein said other data types include one or more of audio, images, numbers, signatures and pre-loaded images.
12. A method according to any one of claims 7 to 11, wherein after a predetermined step the data cannot be altered by the user.

AU2004202060 SPARE PART PROCUREMENT METHOD

Granted in New Zealand

CLAIMS:

1. A method of facilitating broker mediated matching of a potential buyer of a spare part with a potential seller of the spare part, the potential seller having an inventory of spare parts for use in a manufacturing process run by the potential seller, the method comprising the following steps undertaken by the broker:
   (a) receiving a request for the spare part from a potential buyer,

(b) enquiring with a potential seller as to the presence of the spare part in its inventory,

(c) if the spare part is present, assessing whether or not the spare part is excess to the foreseeable needs of the potential seller in running the manufacturing process efficiently by the application of software that presents a series of questions for answering by the potential seller, the answers to which will reveal whether or not the spare part is excess to said needs, and wherein the software further presents a plurality of possible answers to the potential seller for each question presented for answering by the potential seller, each possible answer for any one question having a predetermined score, the score for giving any one answer to a question being different to the score for giving any other answer to the question, whereby a cumulative score is achieved by answering the series of questions that will reveal whether or not the spare part is excess to said needs, and

(d) if the spare part is excess to said needs, providing means by which the potential seller and potential buyer will communicate with each other, whereby they may finalise details for securing the sale and transfer of the spare part.

2. The method of claim 1 wherein the series of questions are presented over the internet.
3. The method of claim 1 wherein the step of assessing whether or not the spare part is excess to the foreseeable needs of the potential seller includes asking questions to determine how critical is that spare part to the efficient running of the manufacturing process.
4. The method of claim 1 and including the steps of providing a rolling activity report on a dedicated portion of a website of the broker for continuously updating the potential buyer on steps the broker has taken in response to step (a), and logging and recording on the rolling activity report the steps taken by the broker.
5. The method of claim 1 wherein the request for the spare part is received via the internet from the potential buyer.
6. The method of claim 5 wherein the request for the spare part is received at a website of the broker.
7. The method of claim 6 wherein the request for the spare part is undertaken by completing an on-line request form appearing on the broker's website.

AU2004201637 METHOD FOR MANAGING PRINTED MEDIUM ACTIVATED REVENUE SHARING DOMAIN NAME SYSTEM SCHEMAS

Rejected Norway; granted USA; abandoned at the EPO

CLAIMS:

1. In a system that includes a plurality of end-user device systems each of which automatically reads machine-readable codes affixed to objects, sends code information representative of scanned machine-readable codes to a portal server, and receives provider information associated with at least one of the machine-readable codes from one or more remote servers coupled to the portal server over a communications network, wherein the portal server includes a link table that associates machine-readable codes recognized by the portal server with corresponding addresses of remote servers coupled to the portal server over the communications network, and each of a plurality of the remote servers corresponds to a different provider and has provider information associated with at least one of the machine-readable codes stored thereon, a method for operating the portal server comprising the steps of:
   (a) charging each provider a sign-up fee for including an entry in the link table that links each of a plurality of the end-user device systems to a remote server associated with the provider in response to scanning of a machine-readable code associated with the provider by an end-user device system; and
   (b) charging each provider a usage fee based on a frequency at which the link table links one of the plurality of end-user device systems to a remote server associated with the provider in response to scanning of a machine-readable code associated with the provider by an end-user device system.
2. The method according to claim 1 wherein the machine-readable codes are [universal product codes] UPC codes.
3. The method according to claim 1 wherein the portal server further comprises a credit card module in communication with one of the scanner, the receiver, or the portal server, the credit card module being capable of at least one of the steps of
   - tracking transactions and corresponding referrals,
   - accessing electronically credit limits for the transactions,
   - tracking the size and frequency of purchases and corresponding purchasers,
   - communicating in a two-way manner,

- obtaining credit and balance information and
- maintaining transactions.

4. The method according to claim 1 wherein the portal server further comprises a transaction tracking module in communications with one of the scanner or the receiver, the transaction tracking module being capable of tracking purchasers based on transaction size and frequency and matching the size and frequency to a scanner device such that the device cost is subsidized based on the size and frequency of the transaction.
5. The method according to claim 1 wherein the portal server further comprises an affinity information tracking module, the module maintaining at least one of benefit redemption, frequent flyer, or affinity information.

References

(Unless otherwise stated, all websites accessed July 2012.)

ACIP (2008), *Patentable Subject Matter: Issues Paper*, Canberra: Advisory Council on Intellectual Property.

ACIP (2010), *Patentable Subject Matter*, Canberra: Advisory Council on Intellectual Property.

Allison, J.R. and E.H. Tiller (2003), "Internet business method patents", pp. 259–84 in W.M. Cohen and S.A. Merrill (eds), *Patents in the Knowledge-Based Economy*, Washington, D.C.: The National Academies Press.

Andersen, B. (2003), "The rationales for intellectual property rights in the electronic age", pp. 985–1024 in D.C. Jones (ed.), *New Economy Handbook*, Amsterdam: Elsevier/Academic Press.

Archontopoulos, E. (2011), "Spot the differences: a computer-implemented invention or a software patent?", paper presented at *European Policy for Intellectual Property 6th Annual Conference*, Brussels.

Arrow, K.J. (1962), "Economic welfare and the allocation of resources for invention", pp. 609–25 in NBER (ed.), *The Rate and Direction of Inventive Activity: Economic and Social Factors*, Princeton: NBER.

Australian Bureau of Statistics (2005), *Innovation in Australian Business*, Canberra: Australian Bureau of Statistics, Cat. No. 8158.0.

Bagley, M. (2001), "Internet business model patents: obvious by analogy", *Michigan Telecommunications Technology Law Review* **7**: 253–88.

Bakels, R.B. and P.B. Hugenholtz (2002), *The Patentability of Computer Programs: Discussion of European-Level Legislation in the Field of Patents for Software*, Study commissioned by the European Parliament.

Barton, J.H. (2000), "Reforming the patent system", *Science* **287** (5460): 1933–4.

Bates, M. (2003), "Smaller developed nations: the cash cows for royalty milking?", *Australian Intellectual Property Law Bulletin* **16** (4): 54–6.

Bauerle, J.F. (2002), "'Beam me up, Scotty': business method patents as a transformational device in financial services", *The Banking Law Journal* **119** (4): 376–86.

Baumol, W J. (2000), *The Free Market Innovation Machine: Analyzing the*

Growth Miracle of Capitalism, Princeton, N.J.: Princeton University Press.

Beggs, J. (1981), "On the evaluation of the Australian patent system", pp. 39–44 in T.D. Mandeville, D.M. Lamberton, and E.J. Bishop (eds), *The Economic Implications of Patents in Australia*, Canberra: Australian Patent Office.

Beier, F.-K. (1986), "The inventive step in its historical development", *International Review of Industrial Property and Copyright Law* **17** (3): 301–23.

Bernstein, J.I. and M.I. Nadiri (1991), "Product Demand, Cost of Production, Spillovers and the Social Rate of Return to R&D", *NBER Working Paper 3625*, National Bureau of Economic Research.

Bessen, J.E. (2006), "Estimates of Firms' Patent Rents from Firm Market Value", *School of Law Working Paper No. 06-14*, Boston University.

Bessen, J.E. and M.J. Meurer (2007), "The Private Costs of Patent Litigation", *School of Law Working Paper, No. 07-08*, Boston University.

Bessen, J.E. and M.J. Meurer (2008), *Patent Failure: How Judges, Bureaucrats, and Lawyers Put Innovators at Risk*, Princeton and Oxford: Princeton University Press.

BIE (1994), *Beyond the Innovator: Spillovers from Australian Industrial R&D*, Canberra: Bureau of Industry Economics Occasional Paper 16.

Blind, K., J. Edler, R. Frietsch and U. Schmoch (2003), "Scope and nature of the patent surge: a view from Germany", paper presented at *OECD Intellectual Property Rights (IPR), Innovation and Economic Performance Conference*, Paris: OECD.

Blind, K., J. Edler, R. Frietsch and U. Schmoch (2006), "Motives to patent: empirical evidence from Germany", *Research Policy* **35** (5): 655–72.

Blonder, G. (2005), "Cutting through the patent thicket", *Business Week*, 19 December.

Bochnovic, J. (1982), *The Inventive Step: its Evolution in Canada, the United Kingdom and the United States*, Munich: Max Planck Institute for Foreign and International Patent, Copyright and Competition Law.

Boldrin, M. and D.K. Levine (2004), "The case against intellectual monopoly", *International Economic Review* **45** (2): 327–50.

Boldrin, M. and D.K. Levine (2008), *Against Intellectual Monopoly*, Cambridge: Cambridge University Press.

Bonatti, L. and S. Comino (2011), "The inefficiency of patents when R&D projects are imperfectly correlated and imitation takes time", *Journal of Institutional and Theoretical Economics* **167** (2): 327–42.

Bosworth, D., D. Filiou and M. Longlans (2003), *Measuring the "Quality" of Patents*, Manchester and Oxford: UMIST and Oxford Intellectual Property Centre.

Braithwaite, J. (2005), *Markets in Vice, Markets in Virtue*, Sydney: The Federation Press.

Brennan, D.J. (2002), "An essay on the eligibility of business methods for Australian patent protection", *Journal of Law and Information Science* **13** (1): 8–33.

Brennan, D.J. and A.F. Christie (1997), "Patent claims for analogous use and the threshold requirement of inventiveness", *Federal Law Review* **25** (2): 237–62.

Brödner, P. (2003), "The internet: universal information infrastructure for the emerging knowledge society", pp. 147–69 in E. Helmstädter (ed.), *The Economics of Knowledge Sharing: A New Institutional Approach*, Cheltenham, UK and Northampton, MA, US: Edward Elgar.

Campbell-Kelly, M. and P.A. Valduriez (2005), "A technical critique of fifty software patents", *Marquette Intellectual Property Law Review* **9** (2): 249–305.

CBO (Congressional Budget Office US) (2005), *R&D and Productivity Growth: A Background Paper* Washington, DC.

Cheung, S. (1986), "Property rights and invention", *Research in Law and Economics* **8**: 5–18.

Chin, A. (1998), "Computational complexity and the scope of software patents", *Jurimetrics* **39** (1): 17–28.

Chin, A. (2009), "Search for tomorrow: some side effects of patent office automation", *North Carolina Law Review* **87**: 1617–56.

Christie, A.F. (2000), "Some observations on the requirement of inherent patentability in the context of business method patents", *Intellectual Property Forum* **43**: 16–22.

Cockburn, I.M. and M.J. MacGarvie (2006), "Entry, exit and patenting in the software industry", *NBER Working Paper 12563*, Cambridge, Mass.: National Bureau of Economic Research.

Cohen, J.E. and M.A. Lemley (2001), "Patent scope and innovation in the software industry", *California Law Review* **89** (1): 1–57.

Cohen, W.M. (2005), "Patents and appropriation: concerns and evidence", *Journal of Technology Transfer* **30** (1–2): 57–71.

Cohen, W.M., R.R. Nelson and J.P. Walsh (2000), "Protecting their intellectual assets: appropriability conditions and why U.S. manufacturing firms patent (or not)", *NBER Working Paper 7552*, Cambridge, MA: National Bureau of Economic Research

Cohen, W.M., A. Goto, A. Nagata, R.R. Nelson and J.P. Walsh (2002), "R&D spillovers, patents and the incentives to innovate in Japan and the United States", *Research Policy* **31** (8–9): 1349–67.

Cohen, W.M. and D.A. Levinthal (1989), "Innovation and learning: the two faces of R&D", *The Economic Journal* **99** (397): 569–96.

Cole, J.H. (2001), "Patents and copyrights: do the benefits exceed the costs?", *Journal of Libertarian Studies* **15** (4): 79–105.

Correa, C.M. (2008), *A Guide to Pharmaceutical Patents, Volume 1*, Geneva: South Centre.

Curtis, L.J. and R.T.G. Lahey (1954), "Subject-matter for letters patent", paper presented at *ANZAAS General Meeting.*

Dahlin, K.B. and D.M. Behrens (2005), "When is an invention really radical? Defining and measuring technological radicalness", *Research Policy* **34** (5): 717–37.

David, P.A. (1993), "Intellectual property institutions and the panda's thumb: patents, copyrights, and trade secrets in economic theory and history", pp. 19–62 in M.B. Wallerstein, M.E. Mogee and R.A. Schoen (eds), *Global Dimensions of Intellectual Property Rights in Science and Technology*, Washington, D.C.: National Research Council.

Deardorff, A.V. (1992), "Welfare effects of global patent protection", *Economica, New Series* **59** (233, Feb): 35–51.

Dempster, P. (1994), "Empirical estimates of external returns to business expenditure on R&D: an introduction to the literature", *BIE Working Paper No. 91*, Canberra: Bureau of Industry Economics.

Desrochers, P. (1998), "On the abuse of patents as economic indicators", *Quarterly Journal of Austrian Economics* **1** (4): 51–74.

Diallo, B. (2003), "Historical perspectives on IP protection for software in selected countries worldwide", *World Patent Information* **25** (1): 19–25.

Drahos, P. (2002), *Information Feudalism: Who Owns the Knowledge Economy*, London: Earthscan.

Drahos, P. (2010), *The Global Governance of Knowledge: Patent Offices and Their Clients*, Cambridge: Cambridge University Press.

Drennan, W.A. (2007), "The patented loophole: how should Congress respond to this judicial invention?", *Florida Law Review* **59** (2): 229–331.

Dreyfuss, R.C. (2000), "Are business method patents bad for business?", *Santa Clara Computer & High Technology Law Journal* **16** (2): 263–80.

Dreyfuss, R.C (2008), "Nonobviousness: a comment on three learned papers", *Lewis & Clark Law Review* **12** (2): 431–41.

Dutfield, G. (2003), *Intellectual Property Rights and the Life Science Industries: A 20th Century History*, Burlington: Ashgate.

Dutton, H.I. (1984), *The Patent System and Inventive Activity during the Industrial Revolution, 1750–1852*, Manchester: Manchester University Press.

Edwards, C.D. (1949), *Maintaining Competition: Requisites of a Governmental Policy*, New York: McGraw-Hill.

Encaoua, D., D. Guellec and C. Martínez (2006), "Patent systems for

encouraging innovation: lessons from economic analysis", *Research Policy* **35** (9): 1423–40.
European Commission (2009), *Final Report: Competition Inquiry into the Pharmaceutical Sector*, Brussels: European Commission.
European Union (2000), "Enforcing small firms' patent rights", *CORDIS/Innovation Policy Studies*, Brussels: available at ftp://ftp.cordis.europa.eu/pub/innovation-policy/studies/studies_enforcing_firms_patent_rights.pdf, (accessed 6 August 2012).
Evensen, A.L. (2004), "Don't let the sun go down on me: an in-depth look at opportunistic business method patent licensing and a proposed solution to allow small-defendant business method users to sing a happier tune", *John Marshall Law Review* **37** (4): 1359–92.
Firestone, O.J. (1971), *Economic Implications of Patents*, Ottawa: University of Ottawa Press.
Frankel, S. (2008), "Lord Cooke and patents: the scope of 'invention'", *Victoria University of Wellington Law Review* **39**: 73–98.
Freedman, C.D. (2000), "Software and computer-related business-method inventions: must Europe adopt American patent culture?", *International Journal of Law and Information Technology* **8** (3): 285.
FTC (Federal Trade Commission US) (2003), *To Promote Innovation: The Proper Balance of Competition and Patent Law and Policy*, Washington, D.C.: Federal Trade Commission.
Gallini, N.T. and S. Scotchmer (2002), "Intellectual property: when is it the best incentive system?", pp. 51–78 in A.B. Jaffe, J. Lerner and S. Stern (eds), *Innovation Policy and the Economy, Volume 2*, Cambridge Mass.: MIT Press.
Gandal, N. (2002), "A first look at internet business method patents", *Science, Technology and the Economy Program (STE), Working Paper Series STE-WP-12*, Israel Institute of Technology, Samuel Neaman Institute.
Gans, J.S., P.L. Williams and D. Briggs (2004), "Intellectual property rights: a grant of monopoly or an aid to competition?", *The Australian Economic Review* **37** (4): 436–45.
Ghosh, S. (2004), "Patents and the regulatory state: rethinking the patent bargain metaphor after Eldred", *Berkeley Technology Law Journal* **19** (4): 1315–88.
Ginarte, J.C. and W.G. Park (1997), "Determinants of patent rights: a cross-national study", *Research Policy* **26** (3): 283–301.
Gladstone, J.A. (2001), "An argument against business method patents demonstrating that algorithms are abstract and business methods are obvious", *Journal of Law and Information Science* **12** (1): 8–23
Gladstone, J.A. (2002), "Why patenting information technology and

business methods is not sound policy: lessons from history and prophecies for the future", *Hamline Law Review* **25**: 217–33.

Graham, S. and D. Somaya (2003), "The use of patents, copyrights and trademarks in software: evidence from litigation", paper presented at *OECD Intellectual Property Rights (IPR), Innovation and Economic Performance Conference*, Paris: OECD.

Graham, S.J.H. and D.C. Mowery (2003), "Intellectual property protection in the U.S. software industry", pp. 219–58 in W.M. Cohen and S.A. Merrill (eds), *Patents in the Knowledge-Based Economy*, Washington, D.C.: The National Academies Press.

Granstrand, O. (1999), *The Economics and Management of Intellectual Property – Towards Intellectual Capitalism*, Cheltenham, UK and Northampton, MA, US: Edward Elgar.

Griliches, Z. (1990), "Patent statistics as economic indicators: a survey", *Journal of Economic Literature* **28** (4): 1661–707.

Gruen, N., I. Bruce and G. Prior (1996), *Extending Patent Life: Is It in Australia's Economic Interests?* Canberra: Industry Commission.

Hall, B.H. (2005), "Exploring the patent explosion", *Journal of Technology Transfer* **30** (1–2): 35–48.

Hall, B.H. (2009), "Business and financial method patents, innovation, and policy", *NBER Working Paper 14868*, Cambridge: National Bureau of Economic Research.

Hall, B.H. and M. MacGarvie (2006), "The private value of software patents", *NBER Working Paper No. 12195*, Cambridge, Mass.: NBER.

Hanel, P. (2008), "The use of intellectual property rights and innovation by manufacturing firms in Canada", *Economics of Invention and New Technology* **17** (4): 285–309.

Harris, R.W. (1986), "Prospects for Supreme Court review of the Federal Circuit standards for obviousness of inventions combining old elements", *Journal of the Patent and Trademark Office Society* **68** (2): 66–82.

Harris, R.W. (1989), "The emerging primacy of 'secondary considerations' as validity ammunition: has the Federal Circuit gone too far?", *Journal of the Patent and Trademark Office Society* **71** (3): 185–201.

Hirschey, M. and V.J. Richardson (2001), "Valuation effects of patent quality: a comparison for Japanese and U.S. firms", *Pacific-Basin Finance Journal* **9**: 65–82.

Hirschman, A.O. (1977), *The Passions and the Interests: Political Arguments for Capitalism before its Triumph*, Princeton: Princeton University Press.

Hunt, R.M. (1999), *Nonobviousness and the Incentive to Innovate: An Economic Analysis of Intellectual Property Reform*, Philadelphia: Federal Reserve Bank of Philadelphia.

Hunter, S.D. (2004), "Have business method patents gotten a bum rap? some empirical evidence", *The Journal of Information Technology Theory and Application* **6** (1): 1–24.

IP Australia (2009a), "Getting the Balance Right: Toward a Stronger and More Efficient IP Rights System", *Consultation Paper, March 2009*, Canberra: IP Australia.

IP Australia (2009b), *Toward a Stronger and More Efficient IP Rights System: Proposed Reforms*, Canberra: IP Australia.

IPAC (1984), *Patents, Innovation and Competition in Australia*, Canberra: Industrial Property Advisory Committee (now available at http://www.acip.gov.au/reviews_other.html).

IPCRC (2000), *Review of Intellectual Property Legislation Under the Competition Principles Agreement: Final Report*, Canberra: Attorney-General's Department (Intellectual Property and Competition Review Committee).

Jaffe, A.B. (1986), "Technological opportunity and spillovers of R&D: evidence form firms' patents, profits and market value", *American Economic Review* **76** (5): 984–1001.

Jaffe, A.B. (1988), "Demand and supply influences in R&D intensity and productivity growth", *The Review of Economics and Statistics* **70** (3): 431–7.

Jaffe, A.B. (2000), "The US patent system in transition: policy innovation and the innovation process", *Research Policy* **29** (4–5): 531–57.

Jaffe, A.B. and J. Lerner (2004), *Innovation and its Discontents: How Our Broken Patents System is Endangering Innovation and Progress, and What to Do About It*, Princeton: Princeton University Press.

Jensen, P.H., A. Palangkaraya and E.M. Webster (2006), "Disharmony in international patent office decisions", *The Federal Circuit Bar Journal* **15** (4): 679–712.

Jensen, P.H. and E.M. Webster (2004), "Achieving the optimal power of patent rights", *The Australian Economic Review* **37** (4): 419–26.

Kahin, B. (2003a), "Information process patents in the US and Europe: policy avoidance and policy divergence", *First Monday* **8** (3).

Kahin, B (2003b), "Through the lens of intangibles: what patents on software and services reveal about the system", paper presented at *OECD Intellectual Property Rights (IPR), Innovation and Economic Performance Conference*, Paris: OECD.

Khan, B. (2010), "An economic history of patent institutions", in R. Whaples (ed.) *The EH Encyclopedia*, http://eh.net/encyclopedia/article/khan.patents (accessed 7 October 2012).

Kitch, E.W. (1966), "Graham v. John Deere Co.: new standard for patents", *Supreme Court Review*: 293–346.

Kitch, E.W. (1977), "The nature and function of the patent system", *Journal of Law and Economics* **20**: 265–90.

Koenig, G.K. (1980), *Patent Invalidity: A Statistical and Substantive Analysis*, New York: Clark Boardman.

Kortum, S. and J. Lerner (1999), "What is behind the recent surge in patenting?", *Research Policy* **28** (1): 1–22.

Krause, W. (2000), "Sweeping the e-commerce patent minefield: the need for a workable business method exception", *Seattle University Law Review* **24** (1): 79–105.

Labich, K. (1988), "The innovators", *Fortune* **6 June**: 27–32.

Lamberton, D.M. (1999), "Information: pieces, batches or flows?", pp. 209–24 in S.C. Dow and P.E. Earl (eds), *Economic Organization and Economic Knowledge, Essays in Honour of Brian J. Loasby, Volume 1*, Cheltenham, UK and Northampton, MA, US: Edward Elgar.

Landes, W.M. and R.A. Posner (2004), *The Political Economy of Intellectual Property Law*, Washington, D.C.: AEI-Brookings Joint Center for Regulatory Studies.

Lanjouw, J.O. and J. Lerner (1997), "The enforcement of intellectual property rights: a survey of the empirical literature", *NBER Working Paper No. 6296*, Cambridge, Mass.: National Bureau of Economic Research.

Lanteigne, H.K.C. (2003), "Korean IPR Protection: A Study of Intellectual Property Rights protection in Korea and, in particular, Patent protection for Computer-Implemented Business Method Inventions", *Journal of Korean Law* **3** (1): 39–73.

Lawson, C. (2007), "Evolution of 'inventive step'-like elements in Australian patent laws", *Australian Intellectual Property Journal* **18**: 130–48.

Lawson, C. (2008), "Quantum of obviousness in Australian patent laws", *Australian Intellectual Property Journal* **19**: 43–65.

Layne-Farrar, A. (2005), "Defining software patents: a research field guide", *Working Paper 05-14*, Washington, D.C.: AEI-Brookings Joint Center for Regulatory Studies.

Lehman, B.A. (2001), "The leadership of the USA in the field of intellectual property", *Business Perspectives* **13** (4): 16–27.

Lemley, M.A. (2001), "Rational ignorance at the Patent Office", *Northwestern University Law Review* **95** (4): 1495–532.

Lemley, M.A (2005), "Property, intellectual property, and free riding", *Texas Law Review* **83**: 1031–75 (also comment by John F. Duffy and reply by Lemley, pp. 1076–97).

Lemley, M.A. and K.A. Moore (2003), "Ending abuse of patent continuations", *George Mason Law & Economics Research Paper No. 03-52; UC Berkeley Public Law Research Paper No. 140.*

Lerner, J. (2002), "Where does State Street Lead? a first look at finance patents, 1971–2000", *Journal of Finance* **57** (2): 901–30.

Lerner, J. (2004), "The new new financial thing: the sources of innovation before and after State Street", *NBER Working Paper No. 10223*, Cambridge, Mass.: National Bureau of Economic Research.

Lesavich, S. (2001), "Are all business method patents "one-click" away from vulnerability?", *Intellectual Property & Technology Law Journal* **13** (6): 1–5.

Levin, R.C., A.K. Klevorick, R.R. Nelson and S.G. Winter (1987), "Appropriating the returns from industrial research and development", *Brookings Papers on Economic Activity, Special Issue on Microeconomics* **1987** (3): 783–831.

López, A. (2009), "Innovation and appropriability: empirical evidence and research agenda", pp. 1–32 in *WIPO, The Economics of Intellectual Property: Suggestions for Further Research in Developing Countries and Economies in Transition*, http://www.wipo.int/ip-development/en/economics/pdf/wo_1012_e.pdf#page=13 (accessed 7 October 2012).

Lunney, Jr, G.S. (2001), "E-obviousness", *Michigan Telecommunications Technology Law Review* **7**: 363–422.

Lunney, Jr, G.S. (2004), "Patent law, the Federal Circuit, and the Supreme Court: a quiet revolution", *Supreme Court Economic Review* **11**: 1–79.

Macdonald, S. (2002), "Exploring the hidden costs of patents", pp. 13–39 in P. Drahos and R. Mayne (eds), *Global Intellectual Property Rights: Knowledge, Access and Development*, Basingstoke: Macmillan.

Macdonald, S. (2004), "When means become ends: considering the impact of patent strategy on innovation", *Information Economics and Policy* **16** (1): 135–58.

Machlup, F. (1958), *An Economic Review of the Patent System*, Washington, D.C.: US Government Printing Office.

Machlup, F. and E. Penrose (1950), "The patent controversy in the nineteenth century", *The Journal of Economic History* **X** (1): 1–29.

Maddock, R. (2002), "Social costs and benefits from public investment in innovation", *Business Council of Australia Papers* **2** (2): 88–93.

Magee, G.B. (2002), "Rethinking invention: cognition and the economics of technological creativity", *Dept. Economics Research Paper No. 861*, Melbourne: University of Melbourne.

Mandeville, T.D. (1996), *Understanding Novelty: Information, Technological Change, and the Patent System*, Norwood, N.J.: Ablex.

Mandeville, T.D. (1998), "An information economics perspective on innovation", *International Journal of Social Economics* **25** (2/3/4): 357–64.

Mansfield, E. (1986), "Patents and innovation: an empirical study", *Management Science* **32** (2): 173–81.

Mansfield, E., J. Rapoport, A. Romeo, S. Wagner and G. Beardsley (1977), "Social and private rates of return from industrial innovations", *Quarterly Journal of Economics* **71**: 221–40.

Mansfield, E., M. Schwartz and S. Wagner (1981), "Imitation costs and patents: an empirical study", *The Economic Journal* **91** (364): 907–18.

Mazzoleni, R. and R.R. Nelson (1998a), "The benefits and costs of strong patent protection: a contribution to the current debate", *Research Policy* **27**: 273–84.

Mazzoleni, R. and R.R. Nelson (1998b), "Economic theories about the benefits and costs of patents", *Journal of Economic Issues* **32** (4): 1031–52.

Merges, R.P. (1997), *Patent Law and Policy*, Charlottesville, VA: Michie.

Merges, R.P. (1999), "As many as six impossible patents before breakfast: property rights for business concepts and patent system reform", *Berkeley Technology Law Journal* **14** (2): 577–615.

Merges, R.P. (2003), "The uninvited guest: patents on Wall Street", *Economic Review – Federal Reserve Bank of Atlanta* **88** (4): 1–14.

Merges, R.P. and R.R. Nelson (1990), "On the complex economics of patent scope", *Columbia Law Review* **90** (4): 839–916.

Miceli, C. (2005), "Quietly tying down Gulliver: the software patent fairy tale", http://www.groklaw.net/pdf/Swptft(final)(v2)-2.pdf (accessed 8 Jan 2012).

Moir, H.V.J. (2008), "Who benefits? An empirical analysis of Australian and US patent ownership", paper presented at *European Consortium for Political Research (ECPR), Workshop 14, The Politics of Intellectual Property*, Rennes: ANU, Centre for Governance of Knowledge and Development Working Paper.

Moir, H.V.J. (2009a), *Do Patent Systems Improve Economic Well-Being? An Exploration of the Inventiveness of Business Method Patents*, PhD dissertation, Australian National University, http://papers.ssrn.com/sol3/papers.cfm?abstract_id=1423248.

Moir, H.V.J. (2009b), "What *are* the costs and benefits of patent systems?", pp. 29–54 in W. Van Caenegem and C. Arup (eds), *Intellectual Property Policy Reform*, Cheltenham, UK and Northampton, MA, US: Edward Elgar.

Moir, H.V.J. (2009c), "Who benefits? an empirical analysis of Australian and US patent ownership", pp. 182–210 in S. Haunss and K.C. Shadlen (eds), *Contestation over the Ownership, Use, and Control of Knowledge and Information*, Cheltenham: Edward Elgar.

Moir, H.V.J. (2011), "Understanding innovative firms: an exploration of the use of USPTO data to identify innovative firms in small and medium-sized economies", paper presented at *European Policy for Intellectual Property (EPIP) Conference*, Brussels.

Mojibi, A. (2010), "An empirical study of the effect of KSR v. Teleflex on the Federal Circuit's patent validity jurisprudence", *Albany Law Journal of Science & Technology* **20** (3): 559–96.

Monk, P. (1992), "Innovation in the information economy", pp. 35–50 in C. Antonelli (ed.), *The Economics of Information Networks*, New York: Elsevier.

Mooney, B. and C. Oppenheim (1994a), "The cost of patent protection to U.K. industry", *Journal of the Chartered Institute of Patent Agents* **23** (4 April): 144–60.

Mooney, B. and C. Oppenheim (1994b), "How much does British industry pay for patents and patent information?", *World Patent Information* **16** (3): 140–9.

Moser, P. (2005), "How do patent laws influence innovation? Evidence from nineteenth century world fairs", *American Economic Review* **95** (4): 1214–36.

Murphy, F.H. (2002), "The occasional observer <www.uspto.gov> a new source for what is happening in operations research practice", *Interfaces* **32** (3): 26–9.

New Zealand Ministry of Economic Development (2002), *Review of the Patents Act 1953: Boundaries to Patentability: A Discussion Paper*, Wellington, http://www.med.govt.nz/business/intellectual-property/patents/review-of-patents-act (accessed 6 August 2012).

NOIE (2004), *Productivity Growth in Australian Manufacturing*, Canberra: National Office for the Information Economy.

Noveck, B.S. (2006), "Peer to patent: collective intelligence and intellectual property reform", *Harvard Journal of Law and Technology* **20** (1): 123–62.

Nowotarski, M. (2007), "Using KSR to Overcome an Obviousness Rejection", *Intellectual Property Today* **14** (9): 13.

Olson, M. (1971), *The Logic of Collective Action: Public Goods and the Theory of Groups*, Cambridge, Mass.: Harvard University Press.

Oppenheim, C. (2000), "Patent Information Usage in British Small and Medium Sized Enterprises", http://scientific.thomson.com/free/ipmatters/bti/8199738/ (accessed 8 March 2007).

Pakes, A., M. Simpson, K. Judd and E. Mansfield (1989), "Patent renewal data", *Brookings Papers on Economic Activity, Special Issue on Microeconomics*: 331–401.

Palombi, L. (2004), *The Patenting of Biological Materials in the Context of the Agreement on Trade-Related Aspects of Intellectual Property Rights*, PhD thesis, University of New South Wales (Law School).

Palombi, L (2009a), *Gene Cartels: Biotech Patents in the Age of Free Trade*, Cheltenham, UK; Northampton, MA, USA: Edward Elgar.

Palombi, L (2009b), "The role of patent law in regulating and restricting access to medicines", *SCRIPTed* **6** (2): 394–410.

Pascarl, I. (2002), "The implications of the changes effected by the Patents Amendment Act 2001 for successful patenting of inventions and innovations", *Australasian Biotechnology* **12** (2): 37–9.

Pavitt, K. (1984), "Sectoral patterns of technical change", *Research Policy* **13** (6): 343–73.

Penrose, E.T. (1951), *The Economics of the International Patent System*, Baltimore: The Johns Hopkins Press.

Pila, J. (2001), "The common law invention in its original form", *Intellectual Property Quarterly* **3**: 209–24.

Pila, J. (2011), "Software patents, separation of powers, and failed syllogisms: a cornucopia from the enlarged borad of appeal of the European patent Office", *Cambridge Law Journal* **70** (1): 203–28.

Pilch, H. (2003), "Why are software patents so trivial?", paper presented at *OECD Intellectual Property Rights (IPR), Innovation and Economic Performance Conference*, Paris: OECD.

Pitkethly, R. (1999), "The European patent system: implementing patent law harmonisation", presented at *International Symposium on Innovation and Patents, Institute of Innovation Research*, Hitotsubashi University, Japan.

Plant, A. (1934), "The economic theory concerning patents for inventions", *Economica, New Series* **1** (1): 30–51.

Porter, M.E. (1990), *The Competitive Advantage of Nations*, New York: Free Press.

Potts, H.E. (1944), "The definition of invention in patent law", *The Modern Law Review* **7** (3): 113–23.

Pray, C.E., S. Ribeiro, R.A.E. Mueller and P.P. Rao (1991), "Private research and public benefit: the private seed industry for sorghum and pearl millet in India", *Research Policy* **20** (4): 315–24.

Quillen Jr, C.D. (2006), "Innovation and the U.S. patent system", *Virginia Law and Business Review* **1**: 210–25.

Quillen Jr, C.D. (2008), "Commentary on Bessen and Meurer's Patent Failure: an industry perspective", *Journal of Intellectual Property Law* **16**: 57–81.

Ricketson, S. (1992), "New wine into old bottles: technological change and intellectual property rights", *Prometheus* **10** (1): 53–82.

Sampat, B.N., K.C. Shadlen and T.M. Amin (2012), "Challenges to India's pharmaceutical patent laws", *Science* **337** (27 July): 414–15.

Samuelson, P., R. Davis, M. Kapor and J.H. Reichman (1994), "A manifesto concerning the legal protection of computer programs", *Columbia Law Review* **94** (8): 2308–431.

Sarginson, C.L. and S. Langan (2001), "The patentability of business methods: a global perspective", Bereskin and Parr, http://www.bereskinparr.com/Doc/id207 (accessed 4 October 2012).

Saviotti, P.P. (1998), "On the dynamics of appropriability, of tacit and of codified knowledge", *Research Policy* **26** (7–8): 843–56.

Schankerman, M. and A. Pakes (1986), "Estimates of the value of patent rights in European countries during the post-1950 period", *Economic Journal* **96** (384, Dec): 1052–76.

Scherer, F.M. (2006), *The Political Economy of Patent Policy Reform in the United States*, Washington, D.C.: AEI-Brookings Joint Center for Regulatory Studies.

Scherer, F.M. and S. Weisburst (1995), "Economic effects of strengthening pharmaceutical patent protection in Italy", *International Review of Industrial Property and Copyright Law* **26** (6): 1009–24.

Scotchmer, S. (1991), "Standing on the shoulders of giants: cumulative research and the patent law", *Journal of Economic Perspectives* **5** (1): 29–41.

Scotchmer, S. (1996), "Protecting early innovators: should second generation products be patentable?", *RAND Journal of Economics* **27**: 322–31.

Sell, S.K. (2003), *Private Power, Public Law: The Globalization of Intellectual Property Rights*, Cambridge: Cambridge University Press.

Sena, V. (2004), "The return of the Prince of Denmark: a survey on recent developments in the economics of innovation", *The Economic Journal* **114**: 312–32.

Shadlen, K.C. (2011), "The rise and fall of 'prior consent' in Brazil", *The WIPO Journal* **3** (1): 102–12.

Smith, B.L. and S.O. Mann (2004), "Innovation and intellectual property protection in the software industry: an emerging role for patents", *The University of Chicago Law Review* **71**: 241–64.

Sorensen, J.B. and T.E. Stuart (2000), "Aging, obsolescence, and organizational innovation", *Administrative Science Quarterly* **45** (1): 81–112.

Stallman, R.M. (2001), *The Danger of Software Patents*, speech at Government Model Engineering College, India, http://www.gnu.org/philosophy/stallman-mec-india.html.

Stern, R.H. (1999), "Scope-of-protection problems with patents and copyrights on methods of doing business", *Fordham Intellectual Property, Media & Entertainment Law Journal* **10** (1): 105–58.

Stern, R.H. (2001), "Amazon's one-click patent loses its teeth", *IEEE Micro [H.W. Wilson – AST]* **21** (2): 7–10.

Stiles, H. (1961), "The association factor in information retrieval", *Journal of the Association for Computing Machinery* **8** (2) 271–9.

Stoianoff, N. (1999), "Patenting Computer Software: An Australian Perspective", *European Intellectual Property Review* **21** (10): 500–7.

Teece, D.J. (1986), "Profiting from technological innovation", *Research Policy* **15** (6): 285–305.

Thambisetty, S. (2009), "Increasing returns in the patent system: institutional sources and consequences for law", *LSE Law, Society and Economy Working Papers 7/2009*, London: LSE.

Thomas, J.R. (1999a), "The patenting of the liberal professions", *Boston College Law Review* **40** (5): 1139–85.

Thomas, P. (1999b), "The effect of technological impact upon patent renewal decisions", *Technology Analysis & Strategic Management* **11** (2): 181–97.

Tisdell, C.A. (1981), "A review of the economic principles of the patent system", pp. 45–54 in T.D. Mandeville, D.M. Lamberton and E.J. Bishop (eds), The Economic Implications of Patents in Australia, Canberra: Australian Patent Office.

Tyacke, N. and T. Webb (2007), "Business method patents in Australia and the US: the difficulties continue", *Australian Intellectual Property Law Bulletin* **19** (8): 117–22.

Ullman, J.D. (2000), "Ordinary skill in the art", Stanford (based on the 2000 Knuth-Prize Lecture), http://www-db.stanford.edu/~ullman/pub/focs00.html (6 August 2012).

van Caenegem, W. (2002), "The technicality requirement, patent scope and patentable subject matter in Australia", *Australian Intellectual Property Journal* **13** (Feb): 41–59.

van Caenegem, W. (2007), *Intellectual Property Law and Innovation*, Cambridge: Cambridge University Press.

van Pottelsberghe, B. (2011), "The quality factor in patent systems", *Industrial and Corporate Change* **20** (6): 1755–93.

Wagner, S. (2008), "Business method patents in Europe and their strategic use – evidence from franking device manufacturers", *Economics of Innovation and New Technology* **17** (3): 173–94.

Walterscheid, E.C. (1995a), "The early evolution of the United States patent law: antecedents (part 2)", *Journal of the Patent and Trademark Office Society* **76** (11): 849–80.

Walterscheid, E.C. (1995b), "The early evolution of the United States patent law: antecedents (part 3)", *Journal of the Patent and Trademark Office Society* **77** (10): 771–802.

Whitmeyer, R.M. (1991), "A plea for due process: defining the proper scope of patent protection for computer software", *Northwestern University Law Review* **85** (4): 1103–38.
Wilmot, H.R. (1954), "Some aspects of the Australian patent system", paper presented at *ANZAAS General Meeting*.
Winter, S.G. (1993), "Patents and welfare in an evolutionary model", *Industrial and Corporate Change* **2** (2): 211–31.

Index

Introductory Note

References such as '178–9' indicate (not necessarily continuous) discussion of a topic across a range of pages. Wherever possible in the case of topics with many references, these have been divided into sub-topics and/or only the most significant discussions of the topic are listed. Because the entire volume is about 'patent policy', the use of this term (and certain others which occur throughout) as entry points has been minimized. Information will be found under the corresponding detailed topics.